KARL MARX

The Arguments of
the Philosophers

EDITOR: TED HONDERICH

Reader in Philosophy, University College, London

The group of books of which this is one will include an essentially analytic and critical account of each of the considerable number of the great and the influential philosophers. The group of books taken together will comprise a contemporary assessment and history of the entire course of philosophical thought.

Already published in the series

Plato	J. C. B. Gosling
Meinong	Reinhardt Grossman
Santayana	Timothy L. S. Sprigge
Wittgenstein	R. J. Fogelin
Hume	B. Stroud
Descartes	Margaret Dauler Wilson
Berkeley	George Pitcher
Kant	Ralph Walker
The Presocratic Philosophers (2 vols)	Jonathan Barnes
Russell	Mark Sainsbury
Socrates	Gerasimos Xenophon Santas
Sartre	Peter Caws
Karl Popper	Anthony O'Hear
Gottlob Frege	Hans Sluga
Schopenhauer	David Hamlyn

KARL MARX

Allen W. Wood

Routledge & Kegan Paul
London, Boston and Henley

First published in 1981
by Routledge & Kegan Paul Ltd
39 Store Street,
London WC1E 7DD,
9 Park Street,
Boston, Mass. 02108, USA, and
Broadway House,
Newtown Road,
Henley-on-Thames,
Oxon RG9 1EN
Set in IBM Journal by Columns
and printed in the United States of America by
Vail-Ballou Press, Inc.

British Library Cataloguing in Publication Data

Wood, Allen W.

Karl Marx — (Arguments of the philosophers).
1. Marx, Karl
I. Series
193   B3305.M74   80-41119

ISBN 0 7100 0672 1

To Rega

Contents

CONTENTS

CONTENTS

Preface

The literature on Marx is so massive that no one could possibly read all of it. The quality of this literature (especially what is available in English) has been improving in recent years, but on the whole it is still depressingly low. The interest of Marx's thought is sufficiently great that no apology need be made for writing yet another book about it, if the book is a good one. But while it is quite easy to write an above average book on Marx, it is very difficult to write a good one. I wish I could be sure I had done so. In any case, I believe there is some originality (perhaps even merit) in my approach to certain topics, such as Marx's concept of alienation and his use of Hegel's dialectic. My views about Marx on morality, developed a bit more here than else-where, have been widely criticized, and I suppose that is some sort of testimony to their interest. Some of what I have to say about Marx on alienation and Marx's philosophical materialism may also draw criticism, since it is at odds with a large body of self-styled 'humanistic' interpretation of Marx's philosophy. On historical materialism, what I have to say would be more original were it not for G. A. Cohen's excellent book, which I had the good fortune to read in manuscript just after I had first drafted my chapters on this topic. I was gratified by the extent of Cohen's agreement with what I was saying, and profited greatly from his lucid exposition of Marx's theory of history.

It is impossible to discuss Marx's ideas at all without raising complex empirical questions about the accuracy of his account of capitalist society and his predictions about its future. In this book, however, I have given such questions only minimal treat-ment. Marx wrote over a century ago, and he wrote about a society which he insisted was in process of radical change. Insofar as I consider Marx's critique of capitalism at all, I will be concerned with his picture of capitalism as he knew it, and not with the appropriateness of his economic theory and social criticism to present day societies. My own conviction is that we are seriously mistaken if we suppose social and political events of the past century have 'falsified' Marx's predictions, rendered his approach to economics obsolete or his attack on capitalism irrelevant to our own time. But the issues involved in defending this conviction are complex, and many of them are not particularly philosophical.

The central focus of Marx's thought as a whole is the economic theory of *Capital*. This theory, moreover, raises some important philosophical questions about the aims and methods of economic science and about some central economic conceptions. My only thematic discussion of these matters is presented in Chapter XV, and its scope is quite limited. The book does not pretend to provide an adequate discussion of Marxian economics, even of its philosophical aspects. I have not treated even such central issues as the proper interpretation of Marx's theory of crises and law of the tendency of the rate of profit to fall, and the question whether Marx's theory predicts that capitalism will end in a general economic 'breakdown'. Much more could have been said too about the *philosophical* superiority of Marxian economics over orthodox economic theory, that is, about the superiority of its aims and the greater depth and pertinence to social reality of the questions it asks. My neglect of these matters is due partly to considerations of space, but partly also to doubts about my competence to give these topics the sophisticated and many-sided treatment they deserve. The present book will have succeeded if it is capable of serving as a sort of philosophical prolegomenon to the study of the economic theory presented in *Capital*.

Some passages in Chapters IX and X are drawn from 'The Marxian Critique of Justice' and 'Marx on Right and Justice: A Reply to Husami'. These articles originally appeared (respectively) in the Spring, 1972, and Spring, 1979, issues of *Philosophy and Public Affairs*, published quarterly by Princeton University Press.

I wish to thank my wife, Rega, for taking our son, Henry, to Nantasket Beach on August 2, 1979.

Biographical Sketch

Karl Heinrich Marx was born on May 5, 1818, in the Rhenish city of Trier. His father was a successful Jewish lawyer of conservative political sentiments who converted to Christianity in 1824. Although there was a Rabbinic background in his family, Marx was not brought up as a Jew and never thought of himself as one. Probably the deepest influence on Marx in his early youth was his neighbor, Baron Ludwig von Westphalen, a cultured nobleman, a political progressive, and Marx's future father-in-law.

In 1835 Marx left the Friedrich-Wilhelm Gymnasium in Trier and entered the University of Bonn, where he was to study law. A year later Marx transferred to the University of Berlin, where (to his father's dismay) he joined the radical young Hegelian *Doktor Klub* and abandoned the study of law for philosophy. For a time, Marx intended to follow his friend Bruno Bauer from Berlin to a position teaching philosophy at the University of Bonn. But with the accession of Friedrich Wilhelm IV to the Prussian throne in 1840, the Ministry of Culture began a systematic attack on young Hegelians. Bauer lost his chance for a professorship at Bonn and Marx lost any hope for an academic career in philosophy. He nevertheless completed his doctoral thesis (on Democritus and Epicurus), received his degree from the University of Jena in 1841, and returned to the Rhineland in 1842, where he became editor of the *Rheinische Zeitung* in Cologne. Increasing censorship of this publication prompted Marx's resignation from the editorship in March, 1843. In addition to some provocative articles, Marx's chief writing of this period was his unpublished *Critique of Hegel's Philosophy of Right* (1842-3).

In June, 1843, Karl Marx and Jenny von Westphalen were married after an engagement of over six years. A few months later,

Marx joined Arnold Ruge in another publishing effort, which brought him to Paris. Here he made contact with socialists from many countries, and renewed his acquaintance with Friedrich Engels, beginning a lifelong friendship and collaboration between the two men. It was Engels who in effect introduced Marx both to the study of political economy and to the British working class movement. The first confrontation of Marx's economic studies with his young Hegelian philosophy is exhibited in his *Excerpt Notes* on James Mill and his *Economic and Philosophic Manuscripts* (1844). The first collaboration of Marx and Engels was *The Holy Family* (published 1845), a polemic against Bruno Bauer and other young Hegelian philosophers. More important was their next (unpublished) collaboration, *The German Ideology* (1845-6), which contains the first self-conscious expression of historical materialism.

Early in 1845, Marx was expelled from France. Until the February revolution of 1848, he resided in Brussels. Marx's economic views received their first developed expression in his polemic against Pierre Proudhon, *The Poverty of Philosophy* (published 1847). In the same year, Marx and Engels played a key role in founding the Communist League (which lasted until 1850) and wrote the *Manifesto of the Communist Party* (published 1848). After the February revolution, Marx spent a short time in Paris, but soon returned to Germany, where he worked as a publicist in behalf of the insurrection which was underway there. After successfully defending himself and his associates in a Cologne court against charges of 'inciting to revolt', Marx was expelled from Prussian territory. After a brief stay in Paris, he took up lifelong residence in London. Here he soon composed two of his most brilliant historical writings, *The Class Struggles in France, 1848-1850* (published 1850) and *The Eighteenth Brumaire of Louis Bonaparte* (published 1852).

The first years in England were a time of bitter, brutal poverty for the Marx family. Three of the six children died of want before 1856, and Marx's own health suffered a decline from which it perhaps never fully recovered. Throughout most of the 1850s, Marx wrote for the *New York Tribune* at £1 per article. By the end of the decade, inheritances to Jenny Marx and financial help from Engels had relieved the family's hardships somewhat. The American Civil War brought an end to Marx's writing for the *Tribune* and also somewhat curtailed the income from Engels' textile mills. Marx sought employment as a railway clerk, but was unsuccessful owing to the (now renowned) illegibility of his handwriting.

Throughout the 1850s and 1860s Marx regularly spent ten hours of every day at the British Museum studying and writing, except when he was confined to his bed by illness. After returning home, he often wrote far into the night. In 1859 he published *Critique of Political Economy*. Perhaps even more important, however, was the long unpublished preparatory draft (*Grundrisse*, 1857-8) for a major book of which the *Critique* was to be the first part. Reworking this project, Marx sketched the whole of *Capital* between 1863 and 1865, and the first volume was published in 1867. The two remaining volumes occupied Marx for the rest of his life, and he left both uncompleted. After Marx's death, Engels edited and published them (in 1884 and 1893 respectively).

Marx was instrumental in the founding of the International Working Men's Association in 1864, and in guiding it through six congresses in the next nine years. The demise of the first International in 1876 was brought about by a combination of factors, notably the organization's support for the Paris Commune of 1870, and intrigues within the International by Michael Bakunin (expelled in 1872). The International's official position on the Commune is presented in Marx's address *The Civil War in France* (1871). Throughout his life, Marx remained active in the working class movement. From his exile, he combatted in Germany both reformist tendencies of the Social Democrats and the Lassalleans' accommodations with Prussian statism. In Britain, he fought to preserve the socialist character of the movement from the Liberal politics of the trade unionists.

After 1873 Marx's health was never good. In 1878, Jenny Marx became ill with cancer, and died in December, 1881. Early in the following year, Engels took Marx to France, Switzerland and Algiers, in the hope that an escape from the British climate might improve Marx's chronic respiratory ailments. In January, 1883, after Marx had returned to London, he learned of the death in Paris of his eldest daughter, Jenny Longuet. Marx himself died on March 4, and was buried next to his wife in Highgate cemetery, London.

Introduction

This book attempts to expound the philosophy of Karl Marx. But the first question it must address is whether Marx has a philosophy at all. Marx's principal academic training was in philosophy, but in his mature thought Marx focuses on political economy and the history of capitalism, and usually tends to neglect the philosophical side even of his own theories. Even in his early writings, Marx does not often address himself directly to philosophical questions, but treats such questions only in the course of developing his ideas about contemporary society or criticizing the ideas of others. If it is possible to describe Marx as a philosopher, it is probably more accurate to describe him as an economist, historian, political theorist or sociologist, and above all as a working class organizer and revolutionary.

Yet Marx is also a systematic thinker, who attaches great importance to the underlying methods and aims of his theory and the general outlook on the human predicament expressed in it. In his mature writings, every topic — from the most technical questions of political economy to the most specific issues of practical politics — are viewed in the context of a single comprehensive program of inquiry, vitally connected to the practical movement for working class emancipation. Further, Marx views his own thought as heir to a definite philosophical tradition, or rather as combining two traditions: that of German idealist philosophy from Kant to Hegel in which he was educated, and that of Enlightenment materialism which he greatly admired. Most of all, Marx's social theories consciously raise important philosophical questions: about human nature and human aspirations, about society and history and the proper business of those who would study them scientifically, about the right way to approach the rational assessment and alteration of social arrangements. At least in some cases, Marx supplies some original and distinctive answers to these questions. Thus the tradition of thought in which Marx's social theory consciously stands, the breadth of its scope and the questions it addresses all justify us in speaking of Marx as a philosopher.

Nevertheless, when we speak of Marx's philosophy, it is not immediately clear what we are talking about. If the scope and aims of Marx's thought are philosophical, it still remains a plain fact that Marx's concentration of elaborating a historical-economic theory of capitalism, his dedication to the workers' movement and to a lesser extent the illness and hardships he faced during his exile in England prevented him from devoting any sustained effort to the articulation of his views as a philosophical system. Consequently, anyone who desires to expound the philosophy of Marx is virtually compelled to attempt the task of reconstructing a coherent philosophy on the basis of fragments not meant for publication and *obiter dicta* written in the course of other investigations. The danger inherent in this task is that one's interpretation may turn into a fantasy, supplying tacit philosophical 'foundations' for Marx's theories and reading the things he actually says as answers to questions he never asks. There is no way to avoid these dangers altogether, but they can be minimized. One way to do this is to respect the texts, and distinguish interpretations which can be based directly on them from those which require philosophical inferences or speculation. Another way is to concentrate attention on philosophical themes which plainly do matter to Marx.

This book is organized around five themes. The first of them is alienation. Marx's earliest important writings are focused on alienation: its nature, forms, social causes, and its significance in human history. Marx draws the notion of alienation from the philosophies of Hegel and Feuerbach. From the beginning, however, Marx's use of this notion involves some distinctively Marxian views. In the early writings alienation seems to be the principal evil Marx sees in modern society. Further, the Paris manuscripts appear to identify one basic or paradigmatic form of alienation (alienated labor) as the fundamental cause of a whole system of social evils to which modern men and women are subject. In Marx's writings after 1844, alienation no longer plays a central role in Marx's social theory. But the terminology of the early writings is still employed occasionally, and the concept of alienation is still quite recognizable even where the terminology has been abandoned.

Part One of this book tries to say what 'alienation' (*Entfremdung*,

Entäusserung) means to Marx, and to describe the role of this concept in his mature thought. I will argue that the theory of alienation sketched in Marx's early writings is a first, muddled version of some of the most characteristic ideas in his later social theory. After 1845, I will contend, the concept of alienation plays a role different from the fundamental, explanatory one given it in the Paris manuscripts. Throughout his career, however, Marx continues to hold that alienation is a serious and characteristic problem of modern society and a systematic result of modern labor and its capitalistic social conditions. Marx also continues to hold views about the human essence, human labor and the conditions for a fulfilling human life on which his diagnosis of alienation rest. Part One will try to expound these views.

The most basic thesis of Marx's mature social theory is what he calls the materialist conception of history or historical materialism. Marx holds that the basis of all social institutions and social consciousness is the economic structure of society, the system of relations of production, whose character is in turn determined for each historical epoch by the stage of development of society's productive powers or productive forces. The intelligibility of history rests on the growth of people's powers of production and their continual revolutionizing of social relations in order to accommodate this growth. The institutions of a society, its political forms, its philosophical and religious ideologies, are all to be explained in terms of the function they fulfill in maintaining the existing mode of material production or contributing to its historical development.

Historical materialism is not a metaphysical theory of history, like Hegel's, which sees human history as the expression of speculative principles or the actualization of divine purposes. Marx's theory is conceived as an empirical hypothesis, and motivated by a few fairly simple postulates about human social behavior. But Marx's theory is sufficiently basic in conception and sweeping in scope to be called a philosophical theory of history. Like Hegel, Marx attempts to discover an underlying progressive pattern in history, in light of which particular events can be understood, and the significance of historical trends and movements can be appreciated. Historical materialism raises some fundamental issues about the nature of historical explanation and its relation to social theories. Many common criticisms of historical materialism are based (as I think) on errors either about these issues themselves or about what Marx's position on them is. Part Two of this book will try to understand Marx's historical materialism better.

Whenever people advocate radical social change, they presumably believe that by following their recommendations we can either achieve great social goods or alleviate great evils. Writers on Marx have often speculated about the 'moral foundations' of Marx's critique of capitalist society and his advocacy of communism. Marx, however, had little to say about the philosophical status of his reasons for condemning capitalism and advocating a communist revolution. Neither Marx's moral convictions nor his theoretical views about morality count as a theme to which he gave prominence in his writings. Yet I think careful attention to the texts at least permits us to avoid some errors into which commentators habitually fall. I believe that Marx's condemnations of capitalism are not based on moral considerations at all, but that Marx held some views about the nature of morality which are sufficiently unconventional, interesting and plausible to be worth careful exposition. In Part Three I will try to explain and defend these beliefs.

Marx sees himself as heir to two philosophical traditions, that of German idealism culminating in Hegel, and that of materialism, which reached him in the already somewhat teutonized version of Feuerbach. In many places, Marx expresses his adherence to a 'materialist' world outlook and his opposition to 'idealism' in all its forms. Yet he also distinguishes his materialism emphatically from that of earlier materialists, including Feuerbach. Part Four attempts to identify the main philosophical tenets of Marx's materialism, and discusses his materialist critique of theism and of skepticism about material things.

In the second edition of *Capital*, Marx openly avows himself a 'pupil' of Hegel, and professes to use a 'dialectical method of presentation'. Part Five attempts to understand Marx's relation to Hegel and to dialectical thinking. It also takes a look at *Capital* in light of its dialectical structure. It focuses in particular on the Marxian law of value and its relation to a Marxian theory of relative prices, in light of its rationale and function within Marx's dialectical economic theory.

PART ONE

Alienation

I

The Concept of Alienation

---

1 *The young Marx's 'theory' of alienation*

In his essays and manuscripts of 1843 and 1844, the young Marx uses the terms *Entfremdung* ('alienation' or 'estrangement') and *Entäusserung* ('externalization' or 'alienation') to refer to a great many things. Apparently, the point of this usage is to indicate a close connection in reality between the various things to which the terms are applied. The challenge is to discover what this connection is, and in what way the notion of alienation serves to represent it.

The terms *Entfremdung* and *Entäusserung* themselves evoke images: they suggest the separation of things which naturally belong together, or the establishment of some relation of indifference or hostility between things which are properly in harmony. On the most obvious level, Marx's use of them expresses the idea that the phenomena he describes are characterized by abnormalities or dysfunctions which follow these general patterns. Moreover, we can see this quite clearly in some of the things to which Marx applies the concept of alienation. Workers are said to be deprived of, and hence 'alienated' (separated) from their products; they stand in an 'alien' (hostile) relation to the environment in which they work, and they experience the labor they perform as 'alien' to them (indifferent or inimical to their natural human desires and aspirations).[1] The division of labor is 'alienating' in that it separates people into rigid categories, and sets human activities in an 'alien' relation to each other by developing the ones needed for each specialization to the detriment of each person's individuality and integral humanity.[2] The economic system, as Marx depicts it, further separates or 'alienates' people from one another, by making them indifferent to the needs of others, and

3

pitting the interests of each against those of everyone else.[3]
Further, Marx tells us, in the modern state the individual's conscious participation in society as 'citizen' is separated from everyday
life, experienced as an alien or false identity to be assumed at odd
intervals for ritual purposes. The political state itself is 'alienated'
from the realm of material production and exchange in which
people sustain their actual common life.[4] And following Feuerbach,
Marx views the prevailing Christian religion as separating everything valuable and worthwhile from man and nature, positing it
(in imagination) in an alien being outside the world.[5]

All these phenomena, and more besides, are described by Marx
as forms of 'alienation'. In his early writings, and especially in his
celebrated fragment 'Alienated Labor', Marx seems to be trying to
argue that they are all merely aspects of a single system or whole,
based on one paradigm form of alienation: alienated laboring
activity. Thus he describes his task in this manuscript as one of
'comprehending' (*begreifen*) the economic laws of modern society,
'grasping the intrinsic connection between them', by 'grasping the
whole alienation' to which they belong. Marx ostensibly proceeds
to perform this task by 'formulating the facts of political economy
in conceptual (*begrifflich*) terms as estranged, externalized labor'.
As the manuscript breaks off, Marx is in the midst of 'seeing
further how the concept (*Begriff*) of estranged, externalized labor
must express itself in actual life'.[6]

A great deal of paper and ink has been consumed in the attempt
to spell out the 'theory of alienation' hinted at in this early fragment. But I think to no avail; there are strong reasons to doubt
there could be any such theory worth explicating. Insofar as the
various phenomena to which Marx applies the concept of alienation fall under that concept, they have in common only that they
seem to involve some kind of unnatural separation or hostile
relationship. That they have this feature in common does little to
suggest that there is any real connection between them or that
they all arise from a single underlying cause. It is hard to believe
that 'alienation' (that is, unnatural separation or hostility) designates anything like a natural kind among human or social dysfunctions, and still harder to believe that it designates a 'concept' or
essence whose presence in human laboring activity explains all
the various sorts of separation or hostility which we find in the
phenomena to which Marx applies the notion of 'alienation'.

Consider some of the claims made on behalf of Marx's 'system
of alienation' by its exponents. Istvan Meszaros, perhaps the most
painstaking of them, declares that 'Marx's system of alienation and
reification is not less but more rigorous than the philosophical

4

systems of his predecessors', and that Marx's 'analysis of "alienation of labor" and its necessary corollaries' constitute 'the core of
Marx's theory: the basic idea of the Marxian system'.[7] Both these
statements, I submit, are simply preposterous. Marx's early
writings are original, provocative, profound, rich in both social and
philosophical insights. But they could only be called 'rigorous' by
someone who has little familiarity with the property that term
denotes. The theory presented two decades later in *Capital* is
undoubtedly a 'system', even one possessing a certain degree of
'rigor'. But it certainly cannot be accurately described as a 'system
of alienation'. Whatever continuity there is between Marx's early
and his later writings, there is no evidence that he ever thought of
'alienation' as 'the basic idea of the Marxian system' at any time
after 1844. Meszaros very accurately describes the ideas of the
Paris writings when he calls them a 'system *in statu nascendi*'. But
(to cite Hegel) neither a child nor a system is fully formed as soon
as it is born; the idea which may have seemed 'basic' to Marx in
his first groping sketch of this theory may very well assume a very
different, even peripheral role in more mature versions.

One prominent theme which Marx stresses is the 'alienation' of
human creations when they turn into hostile powers dominating
or enslaving their human creators. Many writers have even identified the young Marx's concept of alienation with this theme.
Marx's own emphasis (in the later as well as the early writings)
supports the contention that this theme was central to his use of
the terms *Entfremdung* and *Entäusserung*. Moreover, such a
notion of alienation is arguably less diffuse than the image or
metaphor of 'unnatural separation'. But even on this reading, the
prospects are not bright for an explanatory theory of the sort
adumbrated in the 'Alienated Labor' manuscript. The sorts of
human 'creations' which Marx speaks of as 'alienated' and
dominating their creators are extremely varied in character, including not only material products of labor, but also social institutions
and practices (such as the state and private property) and even
thoughts and ideas (such as religious ones) to which no extramental reality corresponds. These items are not all human
'creations' in the same sense (unless a rather slippery or rubbery
one). And people are 'dominated' in very diverse ways by religious
illusions, by the state, and by their product in the form of capital.
Once again, it is extravagant to suppose that 'positing something
which turns on its creators and enslaves them' designates a natural
kind among human activities, or that all activities which this
description can be made to fit are caused by some fundamental or
paradigm activity. If Marx's theory is to be taken seriously, such

suppositions must once again be defended by arguments of a sort which neither the young Marx nor his enthusiasts have produced.

Our doubts on this score are not relieved by the reasoning Marx uses when he does attempt to establish a connection between the different forms or manifestations of alienation. 'Alienation', he says,

> shows itself not only in the result but in the act of production, in the producing activity itself. How could the laborer come to stand over against the product of his activity as something alien unless in the act of production itself he was alienating himself from himself? The product is only the resumé of the activity of production. If the product of labor is externalization, then production itself must be active externalization, the externalization of activity, the activity of externalization.[8]

Here Marx seems to be relying on some principle whose import is that the properties of an effect must always somehow pre-exist in the cause.[9] But even the scholastics who endorsed this dubious idea restricted it only to the 'perfections' in an effect, and alienation (whatever it is) is arguably not a perfection. If, moreover, we ignore the metaphysics of Marx's argument and examine the particular case in light of his other statements, it is difficult to make any sense of the explanatory claim he is making. Marx seems to be saying that alienation of the worker's product must result from alienation in the activity which produces it. Now as Marx describes it, 'alienation of the product' includes both the fact that workers do not appropriate or own the product of their labor, and the fact that they find themselves in servitude or bondage to it in the form of capital. The 'alienation of productive activity', on the other hand, consists in the fact that in labor the worker 'does not affirm himself but denies himself, feels not well off but unhappy, develops no free physical and spiritual energy but mortifies his *physis* and ruins his spirit'. Thus Marx's apparent claim is that wage labor's unpleasant and unfulfilling nature is what *explains* the fact that the worker's product belongs to someone else. Likewise, the unappealing nature of labor is what causes this product to dominate the worker in the form of capital. Those who wish to defend the young Marx's theory of alienation must discover a way of reading its explanatory claims which saves them from being mere gibberish.

2 What is 'alienation'?

The 'Alienated Labor' fragment contains Marx's first recognizable attempt at a systematic theory of capitalism. The attempt fails because the philosophical concept of alienation is simply too vague and metaphorical to perform the explanatory function Marx tries to assign it. The attempt is of interest, however, because it already embodies (though in a muddled form) three ideas which are central to Marx's mature theory of capitalist society.

First, Marx perceives a complex interconnection between the various ills and irrationalities which beset people in modern society. Second, he insists that what is distinctive about modern society, and what fundamentally explains its system of inter-connected irrationalities, is something about the kind of labor or production which goes on in it. And third, he regards this peculiar kind of labor as characteristic of a determinate and historically transitory phase in the generally progressive movement of human history. ('Alienation', as the fragment puts it, 'is founded in the essence of human development.')[10] In the mature theory the interconnection does not consist in a 'system of alienation' but in the economic structure of capitalist society. The mature Marx traces this structure to a kind of labor or production because he holds that the social relations of production which make it up are determined by the degree of development of society's productive powers, and hence by the nature of its material labor. Finally, for the mature Marx the 'essence of human development' is not a process predetermined in the womb of the human species-essence but only the relentless expansion of society's productive powers, which determines the course of development taken by the social relations of production.

Marx's mature theory, then, does not assign to alienation the basic, explanatory role projected for it in the early fragment. Yet Marx does not simply abandon the concept of alienation in his mature writings. On the contrary, we still find it used in many places in the *Grundrisse*, *Capital* and elsewhere. Marx's use of it in these writings, I suggest, is no longer explanatory; rather, it is descriptive or diagnostic. Marx uses the notion of alienation to identify or characterize a certain sort of human ill or dysfunction which is especially prevalent in modern society. This ill is one to which all the various phenomena exemplifying the images or metaphors of 'unnatural separation' or 'domination by one's own creations' contribute in one way or another. These images or metaphors, however, seem insufficient to describe the ill Marx has in mind. Perhaps it is impossible to improve upon them, but I will try.

One of the meanings *Entfremdung* had in Marx's day was 'mad-ness' or 'insanity'.[11] Marx does not regard alienated individuals as insane, but he does regard them as involved in some sort of irrationality, as both producers and victims of life-circumstances which somehow do not make sense. Further, a central application of his image of 'unnatural separation' is that alienated individuals are in some sense separated from, at odds with, or hostile to themselves. These considerations motivate a provisional suggestion that alienation might be seen as the condition of a person who experiences life as empty, meaningless and absurd, or who fails to sustain a sense of self-worth. Of course, Marx regards many people as alienated who do not think of themselves or their lives in this way. (For example, religious believers, whose sense of meaning and self-worth is sustained by a faith in God's love for them.) But it seems to be Marx's view that such people possess a sense of meaning and self-worth only because they build their lives on consoling falsehoods.[12] He plainly believes that alienated people who sustain a sense of meaning and self-worth only through religious illusions would be unable to sustain such a sense if they were undeceived.

My provisional suggestion, then, is that we are 'alienated' if we either experience our lives as meaningless or ourselves as worthless, or else are capable of sustaining a sense of meaning and self-worth only with the help of illusions about ourselves or our condition.[13] Alienation, I think, is usually meant in some such sense when it serves as a vehicle of popular social criticism. So understood, of course, alienation is not an affliction only of men and women in modern capitalist society. And it is not plausible to think that in every case of it the primary cause must be found in the social arrangements which surround the victim. Yet Marx may be right in believing that alienation in this sense is more systematically prevalent and more serious in modern bourgeois society than in any other; and this fact makes it worthwhile to investigate whether there is something about bourgeois social forms which systematically produces it.

I have spoken of alienation both as a lack of sense of 'meaning' and a lack of a sense of 'self-worth'. The two things are different, but they are closely related. If I find little or nothing in myself which is worthy of value or esteem, I will have a hard time seeing any real meaning or serious purpose in my life. Conversely, if I experience my life as devoid of meaning, it will be difficult for me to place a high valuation on the self whose life it is. Of course it might be (and I might recognize) that I am not to blame for the emptiness of my life. But a blameless self may still be an impoverished, impotent and degraded self, a worthless self. (Blamelessness is no strong recommendation for a self which finds itself unable to purpose or achieve anything which it can regard as meaningful

8

or worthwhile.) A sense of meaning and a sense of self-worth, therefore, although they are different, usually go together, and a concept of alienation which refers indifferently to either will not be dangerously ambiguous.

Marx comes quite close to describing alienation explicitly as a lack of meaning or self-worth. He says that alienated workers are people 'robbed of all actual life content', and rendered 'worthless, devoid of dignity'. Under existing social relations, 'man is a degraded, enslaved, forsaken, despicable being'.[14] Moreover, the images of 'unnatural separation' and 'dominion by one's product' naturally lend themselves to the description of conditions which would give rise to alienation in the sense I have suggested. Someone lacking in self-worth may be described as 'alienated' from that person's true self or humanity, and Marx does speak of 'self-alienated' individuals in this way.[15] Alienated workers, according to Marx, spend their days in enervating drudgery, and must do so if they are to obtain the means of physical subsistence, and so sustain the whole absurd cycle of their alienated lives. 'Life itself appears as only a means of life, . . . [man's] life-activity, his *essence* is made into only a means to his *existence*.'[16]

Further, there seem to be a great many ways in which the disruption of harmonies or vital relationships either within a human self or between the self and the world, could contribute to a person's loss of a sense of self-worth or of coherence and meaning in life. Marx's early writings are full of examples (some of which I have already mentioned) of ways in which the metaphor of 'alienation' can be used to depict this vividly and compellingly.

Alienation, as the experience of one's self and life as empty, worthless and degraded, is admittedly a rather vague notion. But for our present purposes there is little point in trying to make it more precise. The vagueness is built into the notion of alienation both as it can be found in Marx's writings and as it belongs to popular social thought. It may be that the concept of alienation is too vague to serve as a useful tool of social analysis or criticism. But several generations of fruitful social thought have treated alienation as an important and a characteristically Marxian idea. This is reason enough for us not to ignore it.

Vague as the notion is, however, alienation is nevertheless a specific human and social evil, clearly distinguishable from others. It is not the sum and substance of all evils, and it is by no means the only important evil which Marx believes to be a systematic result of capitalist social relations. For capitalist relations, according to him, also produce social conflict, poverty, disease, ugliness, insecurity. And none of these evils, bad as they are, necessarily

9

involves the loss of a sense of meaning or self-worth on the part of their victims. Yet perhaps even these evils, in their characteristically bourgeois form, are in fact allied with alienation, or contribute to it. Insecurity, for example, threatens me as a wage laborer in the specific form of unemployment, which poses not just the threat of not getting what I need to live, but of not getting it because I myself am not needed, because there is nothing productive for me to do, no place in society for me. Eskimo seal hunters certainly know as much about deprivation and a precarious mode of existence as any wage laborer; but in this specific form, they do not know it at all.

3 *Alienation and false consciousness*

The concept of alienation is not original with Marx. His use of it in the early writings draws upon, and presupposes familiarity with, the philosophers through whom he acquired it, especially Hegel and Feuerbach. From the beginning, however, Marx's views about the nature and causes of alienation differ decisively from theirs.

Both of Marx's predecessors regard alienation as consisting fundamentally in a certain form of acute false consciousness, in a certain error or illusion about onself, one's humanity or one's relation to ultimate reality. For Hegel, the paradigm of alienated life is the 'unhappy consciousness'. This term refers to a form of misunderstood Christian religiosity (that is, to any Christianity which has not yet reinterpreted itself according to Hegel's rationalistic pantheism). In *The Phenomenology of Spirit*, the unhappy consciousness is described as the finite, individual self-consciousness which mistakenly conceives of its own ground or spiritual 'essence' (*Wesen*) as a being outside it and opposed to it, a divine being dwelling outside the world in a supernatural 'beyond'. Because the unhappy consciousness takes itself, and the whole changeable world, to be at odds with its own essence, it regards itself and the natural world as 'inessential' (*unwesentlich*); it feels itself, its activity and the whole sphere of its finite temporal existence to be, empty, worthless, devoid of true reality or significance. As Hegel puts it: 'The conciousness of life, existence and action is only a sorrowing over this existence and action, for it has in it the consciousness of its opposite as the essence, and of its own nothingness.'[17] The unhappy consciousness thus consumes itself in a desperate yearning after the beyond, and in a ceaseless penitential labor and desire aimed at reconciling it with its divine essence. Yet just because these acts proceed from it, they are straightway recognized as 'inessential' and hence futile. The only comfort for the unhappy consciousness lies in its faith that God has himself effected this reconciliation. Yet the unhappy consciousness is too permeated by a sense of its own poverty to be able to comprehend this reconciliation or enjoy it directly. It therefore conceives the act of atonement as wholly contingent and miraculous, performed in the remote past in a distant land, whose fruits it can hope to enjoy only in an after life. The unhappy consciousness can experience a sense of reconciliation with its own essence only in the rite of communion, which even here is mediated by the power of an external agency, the priesthood.

Hegel sees the unhappy consciousness as an important stage in human history, that is (in Hegelese), in the world spirit's coming to awareness of itself in time. In the unhappy consciousness, spirit's 'particularity', in the form of the individual human personality, feels separated or alienated from its essence or ground in the universal world spirit. Just for this reason, however, it is in the unhappy consciousness that the individual self in all its depth first becomes an object of awareness. In other words, according to Hegel, it is in Christianity that the individual human person first comes to be truly recognized as a spiritual power, and the proper vehicle of spirit's self-knowledge. This is why Hegel insists that the message of his philosophy itself is really just the Christian message of reconciliation, translated out of the 'unhappy' form of the contingent, the remote and the miraculous, and demonstrated to be a matter of metaphysical necessity.

On Hegel's diagnosis, the unhappy consciousness is unhappy only because it does not interpret the world aright. It does not recognize that the natural realm, far from being 'inessential', is the necessary expression or objectification of the divine world spirit, of which consciousness itself is only the particularization. The alienation of the unhappy consciousness is consequently just a matter of finite spirit's imperfect knowledge of its own infinite essence. The only remedy for alienation is the attainment of a higher stage of self-knowledge, where God and man, the universal essence of spirit and its particular self-consciousness, are seen to be fundamentally in harmony or identical with each other.

Feuerbach's critique of religion frees Hegel's analysis of the unhappy consciousness from its mystical trappings, and makes explicit its latent humanism. According to Feuerbach, the idea of God is really no more than our idea of our own human essence, our *Gattungswesen*, erroneously conceived as an entity distinct from and opposed to us. Religion is the 'self-alienation of man, the division (*Entzweiung*) of man from himself'.[18] Religion's

11

appeal is really the appeal of each person's own self-affirmation and love for the human species; but it involves a love and an affirmation which has been perverted, misdirected, focused on an imaginary being beyond man and nature. In order to love and praise God, men and women must despise and degrade themselves: 'What is positive, essential in the intuition or determination of the divine being can only be human, and so the intuition of man as an object of consciousness can only be negative, hostile to man. To enrich God, man must become poor; that God may be all, man must be nothing.'[19] Moreover, despite the fact that the central idea in Feuerbach's critique of religion is borrowed directly from Hegel, the Hegelian philosophy really fares no better in his judgment. For it, like the unhappy consciousness, locates what is essential in human thoughts and deeds not in real, natural, living human beings, but in an abstraction, a supernatural and superhuman world-mind. In this way, says Feuerbach, 'absolute [Hegelian] philosophy externalizes (*entäussert*) and alienates (*entfremdet*) from man his own essence and activity.'[20]

Feuerbach's account of alienation is aimed not only at prevailing religious ideas, but also at their harmful psychological and social consequences: the devaluation of our earthly well being, and the separation of men and women from one another and from their common essence as human beings. Like Hegel, however, Feuerbach thinks of alienation fundamentally as a form of false consciousness, an erroneous conception of the human essence. Hence he too conceives the overcoming of alienation as primarily a theoretical victory, a triumph of a true species consciousness over a false one. For him, the main requirement for a satisfying human life is that people should correctly understand and affirm their essence as species beings, at home in nature and destined for loving unity with other human beings. Feuerbach thus holds the view, typical of the young Hegelians, that once people renounce their religious illusions about themselves and come to be animated by the true and rational ideal of what human life should be, the unhappy social consequences of their religious illusions will fall away of themselves, and a truly human society will naturally arise in place of the old, alienated one.

4 *Alienation and practice*

Marx agrees with Hegel and Feuerbach that alienation is closely associated with a certain kind of false consciousness about one's essence, and that the paradigm case of this false consciousness is to be found in religion, especially in Christianity. But he does not agree that alienation *consists* in a condition of false consciousness, or that it is *caused* by one. The curious thing about religious illusions is that they both give expression to alienation, to a sense of the emptiness and worthlessness of human life, and also offer us comfort and consolation for his alienation, in the form of an unworldly spiritual calling and the promise of an unalienated life in the beyond. Alienated consciousness thus involves two contrasting ideas: it laments that our natural human life, considered in itself, is alienated, unsatisfying and worthless; yet it proclaims that our existence is not really alienated after all, if only we place on it the right supernatural interpretation. Hegel and Feuerbach hold that people are alienated only because they misunderstand themselves and the real nature of the human condition. Consequently, it is their view that the illusion of alienated consciousness consists only in the first idea, in its negative attitude toward earthly human life. According to both philosophers, the comforting assurances of religion (at least when these assurances themselves are given the right philosophical interpretation) contain the real truth of the matter.

To Marx, however, the whole phenomenon of alienated consciousness becomes intelligible as soon as we adopt just the reverse supposition: that the unhappy consciousness tells the truth in its laments, not in its consolations. Religion gives expression to a mode of life which really is alienated, empty, degraded, dehumanized. 'Religious misery is in part an expression of actual misery and in part the protest against actual misery. Religion is the sigh of the oppressed creature, the soul of a heartless world, the spirit of spiritless conditions.' Religious illusions have a hold on us because their false promises provide a semblance of meaning and fulfillment to our alienated lives. Religious hopes are 'the fantastic actualization of the human essence, because the human essence possesses no true actuality'.[21] Religion reconciles us to an alienated life and makes it *seem* tolerable to us; it offers us illusory meaning for a mode of life which without this illusion would be experienced directly for what it is: unredeemed meaninglessness.

An alienated society supports religious illusions because they support it. Society will obviously be more stable if alienated individuals accept some conception of themselves which encourages them to think either that their lives do affirm and fulfill their humanity, or else that their feelings of frustration and emptiness are due to the finitude of the human condition as such, and not to the transitory system of social relations in which they are entangled.

The social function of religion, then, is to cloud people's minds

13

and anaesthesize them to the sufferings of their alienated condition. This is what Marx means when (famously) he calls religion 'the opium of the people'.

Marx thus rejects the view of Hegel, Feuerbach and the young Hegelians that alienation fundamentally consists in false consciousness. In so doing, he rejects the long tradition of philosophical and religious thinking based on the pious axiom that human life is always meaningful to those who have the wisdom of spirit to lay hold of this meaning. Marx need not deny that alienation might be due to a lack of wisdom. He only holds that this is not in fact the cause of the systematic alienation in modern bourgeois society. Marx holds then, that alienation is *real*: that we feel our lives to be empty and meaningless because they really are so, because we live under conditions which make a fulfilled and worthwhile mode of life impossible for us.

This is not the view of Hegel and the young Hegelians. The explicit aim of Hegel's speculative theodicy is to reconcile us to the world as it is, to teach us that what is must be, and that it is rational. Of course Feuerbach and the young Hegelians do not recognize any theodicy of this sort. Like Marx, they believe that society must be changed, made rational, brought into harmony with the human essence. But they too place their faith fundamentally in a kind of philosophical wisdom. For in their view the alienation of man in existing society consists in the fact that men and women misconceive the human essence, and consequently have only false or perverted ideals on which to model their lives. Philosophy will be their liberator, releasing them from these illusions, supplying them with a correct conception of the essence of man, and thus pointing the way to a fulfilling way of life.

Marx is prepared to agree that alienated individuals are in the dark about what goals to pursue, about how to lead fulfilling lives, about what sort of society to build. But he does not see this as the basic problem. The basic problem is that alienated individuals lack the practical power to take meaningful action, whether individually or collectively, to realize whatever worthwhile ideals they might have. This is because there are real, extramental obstacles standing in their way. Before they can begin to decide how a truly human life ought to be constituted, they must first come to terms with these obstacles, understand their nature, and set about removing them.

It follows that the critique of false consciousness for Marx is not by itself a liberating act or a victory over alienation, as it was for Hegel and the young Hegelians. On the contrary, the only positive thing this critique can do is sharpen alienation, make

14

people more painfully aware of their condition, and motivate them to do something about it:

> The abolition of religion as the *illusory* happiness of the people is the demand for its *actual* happiness. The demand to give up illusions about its condition is the demand to give up a condition which *needs* illusions. . . . the critique of religion undeceives or disappoints (*enttäuscht*) man, so that he will think, act and form his own actuality like a man who has been undeceived, who has come to his senses.

Religious false consciousness is only a symptom of alienation. The battle against it must be seen as only one aspect of the struggle against alienated practice, a battle which cannot be wholly won until the more fundamental practical struggle is successful. 'Religion', says Marx, 'no longer counts for us as the *ground* but only as the *phenomenon*.'[22] In his view, people will continue to fall prey to illusions as long as they need them, and they will continue to need them as long as they are alienated in real life. It is primarily the struggle against alienation which Marx has in mind when he declares that 'the philosophers have only *interpreted* the world in various ways; but what matters is to *change* it.'[23]

II

The Human Essence

1 *The species being*

In Chapter I, I have tried to defend the proposal that in the context of Marx's philosophy we should understand alienation as the condition of people who either experience their lives as meaningless or themselves as worthless, or else would do so if they were not duped by consoling illusions. But Marx also holds, as we have seen, that alienation is real or practical, that it is not an illusion or state of mind, but is rooted in people's actual conditions of life. Apparently, then, if we are to understand the causes of alienation, we must both know in at least a general way what men and women require in order to lead meaningful lives, and also see what it is about existing social conditions that frustrates these requirements. It will be the business of the next three chapters to investigate Marx's views on these points.

Human beings have many needs. There are many conditions which must be met if they are to survive, and to live in health, security and comfort. These conditions (or at least some portion of them) may also be prerequisites for a meaningful life and a sense of self-worth. But meaning and self-worth still seem to be goods over and above these others, and moreover to be distinctively human goods. Animals may feel pleasure and pain, they may lead lives which are contented and happy, or full of suffering, fear and disquiet. But only a man or woman is capable of experiencing life as something full or empty, worthwhile or worthless, meaningful or meaningless. Marx thus calls an alienated life a 'dehumanized' life, and opposes such a life to a 'human' mode of life, a life led in a manner befitting human nature or corresponding to the 'human essence'. It seems evident, then, that Marx's concep-

16

tion of what is required for a meaningful human life is closely tied to his conception of a life lived in correspondence to the human essence. Marx's theory of alienation thus rests on views of some sort about human nature.

It is sometimes denied that Marx has any concept of human nature at all, on the ground that for him the nature of men and women depends on historical circumstances and alters along with them. Marx also explicitly says, in the sixth thesis on Feuerbach, that 'the human essence is no abstraction inhering in the single individual. In its actuality it is the ensemble or social relationships.'[1] But these views do not necessarily entail a rejection of the idea that there is something distinctive about human beings which marks humankind off from the rest of nature, and perhaps even helps to make intelligible the sort of variation and development which the human essence undergoes in history. The sixth thesis on Feuerbach does not deny that there is a 'human essence' shared by individuals, but only asserts that this essence is inextricably bound up with the social relationships in which those individuals stand, and must be understood in light of them. In any case, it is undeniable that Marx, in his later as well as his early writings, often speaks of the life of wage laborers as 'dehumanized', and of future communist society as a genuinely 'human' one. And Marx does have quite a bit to say about the human essence which serves, in at least a general way, to back up his judgments of this sort.

Following Feuerbach, Marx describes man as a *Gattungswesen*, a term which can be translated either as 'species being' or 'species essence'. The term itself is derived from Hegel, and it is used by Feuerbach and Marx to signify several different but related things.[2] To begin with, in virtue of the ambiguity just mentioned, *Gattungswesen* is a term which can be naturally applied both to the individual human being and to the common nature or essence which resides in every individual man and woman. Or again, very significantly for Feuerbach and Marx, it can be applied to the entire human race, referring to humanity as a single collective entity or else to the essential property which characterizes this entity and makes it a single distinctive thing in its own right. The main intention of both philosophers in using the term, in fact, seems to be to imply that there is some sort of intimate connection between each man or woman and all other human individuals, and that the source of this connection is the fact that the qualities which constitute the essence of each individual are somehow bound up with those which are essential to the whole species, considered as a single collective being. To understand the meaning

17

of *Gattungswesen*, as Feuerbach and Marx employ it, is to understand what they take these connections to be.

Certainly the most obvious thing Feuerbach and Marx mean in calling man a *Gattungswesen* is that human beings live in societies, and the mode of life of each individual is essentially dependent on interaction or intercourse with others. Especially in Feuerbach, there is sometimes a deliberate allusion to the etymological connection between *Gattung* ('genus' or 'kind') and the words *Gatte* and *Gattin* (poetic words for 'husband' and 'wife').[3] The allusion itself is derived from Hegel, but in Feuerbach its principal aim is to express the giddy idea that love-making is the archetypal expression of human interdependence. For Marx, however, and especially for Marx after 1845, the term *Gattungswesen* is often equivalent to (even replaced by) *Gemeinwesen* ('community' or 'commune') or *Gesellschaft* ('society').[4] The stress in Marx is on the idea that human beings are essentially connected to their species because man is by nature a 'herd animal' or 'social animal', an animal who dwells with others of the same kind and survives by living and working in some sort of co-operative relationship with them. (This co-operative character pertains for Marx to all societies, and is if anything stronger in capitalist society than in any previous one. Individualist ideologies may mask or falsify the social relations of capitalism, but cannot do away with them.)

In other passages where Marx speaks of man's 'species being', however, what he has in mind cannot be merely the fact that men and women are social beings. Marx says that man is a species being 'in that he makes his own species his object', and 'behaves toward, is conscious of or relates to (*verhält sich zu*) himself as to the present, living species.'[5] In these remarks, the emphasis seems to be on the *consciousness* which men and women have of their interdependence, or of conduct that is consciously oriented to this interdependence. The terminology Marx uses to describe this species-relation or species-consciousness is extremely abstract, and there are several different possible interpretations which may quite naturally be put on his words. It seems to me, in fact, that Marx probably has several different things in mind, and expresses himself as he does in order to convey the idea that these things are all bound up with one another.

In the first place, Marx is referring to the fact that any man or woman not only belongs to the human species, but is also aware of doing so, and that this awareness itself is a distinctly human characteristic. No doubt some other animals recognize members of their own kind as potential mates, helpers or rivals, but it is doubtful that any of them have a concept of their own species as

18

such, or of themselves as members of a species or kind. But in Marx's view, it is essential to being human at all that we do have some conception of the human species, that we 'make our species our object,' and have an awareness of ourselves as members of this species.

For both Feuerbach and Marx, man's species being is bound up very closely with the fact of our own self-consciousness, as well as with our characteristically human intellectual abilities. Feuerbach believes that it is our consciousness of our own species nature which makes it possible for us to be conscious of the species nature of other things, and hence that our species being is the foundation of our ability to form universal concepts. There are some passages in Marx which may be read as endorsing this thesis.[6] Neither philosopher, however, presents any real argument in favor of the thesis, and I confess that I see no way in which one could be made out. Prima facie, in fact, the truth would seem to be just the opposite, that it is the human ability to form universal concepts which makes it possible for people to know themselves as members of a species.

2 Species consciousness and alienation

More defensible and more relevant to Marx's aims, however, is the idea that there is some intimate connection between species consciousness and self-consciousness. But 'self-consciousness' here should not be understood in an austere, epistemologist's sense, as the subject of the Cartesian *cogito* or the Kantian 'unity of apperception'. We ought rather to think of the consciousness people have of themselves in having what is sometimes called a 'self-image' or 'self-conception'.[7] Every normal human being after a very early age has some sort of idea of who he or she is, some conception which represents (more or less accurately) what we call 'self' or 'identity' (in the sense in which people undergo 'identity crises'). Many different things about me may go into my self-conception, including my perception of my physical appearance and social status, my beliefs about my character traits, past deeds, present abilities and possibilities, and my awareness of my intentions, aspirations and hopes. The particular components of an individual's self-conception, and their relative importance to that individual (both actual and perceived importance) may vary greatly from person to person and culture to culture. But the fact of being self-conscious in this sense, of having some perceived identity or self, does not vary. All but the most incapacitated men and women have this consciousness of self, while it is doubtful that any nonhuman creature has it. Thus we may plausibly regard self-consciousness, in this sense, as a trait distinctive of the human species, and hence as 'species consciousness' in that sense.

But we may also regard self-consciousness as tied closely to 'species consciousness' in the sense of consciousness of the human species as a natural kind or a collective entity. For not only does a man or woman have an individual self-conception, but because each person is aware of membership in the human species, he also 'makes his own species his object', that is, has a conception of it as well. First, a human being is conscious of the species (collectively) in the form of society. Human beings are social (or species) beings not only in living with and depending on others of their kind, but also in being (in some degree) conscious of the social relationships in which they stand to these others. And second, human beings also have a conception of their humanity itself, of the human condition which they share with all other members of their species, a conception of what it means to be human. Each man and woman is conscious of engaging in a mode of life which is specifically human, however much it may differ from the lives of other human beings.

Further, an individual's self-conception is closely bound up in self-consciousness with a conception of the human species. Because I am aware of myself in the context of my society and understand my mode of life as an essentially human one, I also understand myself, my individual self-conception, both in terms of my place in society and in relation to my own conception of humanity. This has to be at least part of Marx's meaning when he says that the species being 'relates to himself as the present, living species', and 'relates to the species as his own essence'. Marx means that my conception of myself always involves my view of what the human species is and can be; it is essentially my conception of the way my life fits into the larger life of society, and the manner in which it serves to actualize the possibilities of the human species.

Of course if we say that every human being has both a self-conception and a conception of humanity or the species essence, it must not be supposed that either of these conceptions is necessarily clear or explicit, or that it can always be put into words by the individual in question. Marx says that 'man practically and theoretically makes his own species his object.' It is Marx's view, I think, that some sort of species consciousness is ingredient in each person's practical dealings with the world, even where the content of this consciousness has not been made theoretically explicit. No doubt both people's individual and their species self-

20

conceptions come to be more explicit (if not more faithful to reality) in societies where there are priests, poets and philosophers whose job it is to produce interpretations of species consciousness for public consumption. Yet in Marx's view even in the simplest and most primitive societies there is some consciousness of self, nature and the human community 'interwoven in the material activity of men'.[8]

There are some reasons for thinking that the possibility of alienation is closely related to the essentially human trait of self-consciousness. To experience oneself or one's life as worthless or worthwhile, as meaningless or meaningful, seems to presuppose some conception of what is felt to be worthwhile or worthless. For this reason, only a being who has some sort of self-conception seems to be capable of either an alienated or a fulfilled life. Further, the possibility of alienation, at least for Marx, is closely bound up with the human trait of species consciousness. Marx often speaks of alienated life as one in which human beings fail to 'affirm' (bejahen), 'confirm' (bestätigen) or 'actualize' (verwirklichen) themselves. A human life which is self-affirming, self-confirming and self-actualizing is a meaningful life; a self which affirms, confirms and actualizes itself is a self which has worth, and recognizes the worth it has. But Marx also indicates that to affirm, confirm and actualize oneself is to affirm, confirm and actualize one's essence, that is, the human species-essence. The measure of this self-actualization, of an individual's satisfaction of a 'natural vocation' (natürliche Bestimmung), is 'the extent to which man as species being, as man, has become himself and grasped himself'.[9] Alienation is thus conceived by Marx as a separation and estrangement of individuals from their human essence. Their 'being does not correspond to their essence', is not 'in harmony' with it; their lives are not lives in which 'the human essence feels itself satisfied'.[10]

Thus in the remark that 'man makes his own species his object,' the term 'object' seems to mean not only 'object of awareness' but also to bear the sense of 'goal' or 'purpose'. It is my humanity or 'species essence' which determines my 'natural vocation', which sets the goals whose pursuit and fulfillment will constitute a meaningful life for me. The extent to which I have fulfilled my vocation, moreover, depends also on the extent to which I consciously recognize and affirm my human essence, the extent to which I have 'grasped myself as man', and my actions have taken on a 'self-conscious human form'.[11]

21

3 Self-actualization

But what is it to 'grasp' and 'affirm', to 'confirm' and 'actualize' the human essence? What sort of life does this involve?

Part of Marx's purpose in speaking of my self-affirmation, self-actualization and so forth as the affirmation and actualization of my 'human species essence' is to emphasize the human value of community, and the other-directed character which any fulfilling human life must have. To 'produce as a human being,' Marx says is 'immediately in the expression of my life to have created your expression of your life, and therefore to have immediately *confirmed* and *actualized* in my individual activity my true essence, my *human*, my communal essence (*Gemeinwesen*)'.[12] Since my self-actualization is the actualization of my human essence, and since my human essence is a species essence or a community (*Gemeinwesen*), I cannot truly actualize myself or my individuality without also actualizing the self or individuality of others. My own good, the worth of myself and the meaningfulness of my life, thus requires (because it partly consists in) my achievement of the same good for others.

But my actualization of their good must also be 'immediate'. This means, I think, that it must be something done consciously and for its own sake and not unintentionally or as a mere means to some other end. Part of the alienation of capitalist society for Marx consists in the fact (so celebrated by Adam Smith) that in this society people serve the interests of others while consciously pursuing only their own.[13] For Adam Smith, as commodity producers we serve others' interests because we must do so as a means to obtaining our own good; for Marx, we can achieve our own good only by pursuing (among other things) the good of others for its own (or their own) sake. Commodity production, however, according to Marx, frustrates the human good by imposing an indirect, egoistic form on our pursuit of the good of others:

> I have produced for myself and not for you, just as you have produced for yourself and not for me. . . . That is, our production is not production by man for man, i.e. not *social* production. Thus neither of us as man has a relation of enjoyment to the product of the other. We are not present as human beings for our reciprocal production.[14]

But the social or communal nature of man is only part of what Marx means when he insists that my self-actualization is the actualization of my human essence. He means also that a genuinely human mode of life is one which manifests or exemplifies certain things, and that what these things are is determined by my essence. Marx's language at this point is the Aristotelian language of potency and act. A 'human' mode of life is one which involves the 'development' (*Entwicklung*), the 'exercise' (*Betätigung*), and thereby the 'actualization' (*Verwirklichung*) of the 'human essential powers' (*menschliche Wesenskräfte*). According to *The German Ideology*, communists maintain that 'the calling, vocation and task of human beings is to develop themselves and all their capacities in a manifold way.'[15]

Not only Marx's language, but also this thought is at this point profoundly Aristotelian. For both philosophers a fulfilling human life consists in the development and exercise of our essentially human capacities in a life of activity suited to our nature. Of course, as Aristotle himself pointed out, to conceive of the human good as 'activity in accordance with excellence' is only to provide a sketch or outline of the good, which needs to be filled in if it is to be informative.[16] As we shall see in the next chapter, however, Marx quite consciously abstains from filling in his notion of self-actualization beyond a very minimal point, and even insists that he is unable to say much more than he does about the sort of life and the sort of society in which the human essence can be actualized. Pages 26-43 below will investigate what Marx does say about the essential capacities of human beings, and will attempt to identify what is distinctively Marxian in his conception of their content.

We are now in a position to replace our provisional conception of alienation as a lack of a sense of meaning and self-worth with a more fundamental and characteristically Marxian one. Alienation in our provisional sense might conceivably have any of a wide variety of causes, and be symptomatic of any of a number of ills. But as Marx sees it, the systematic cause of the fact that people in bourgeois society cannot sustain a sense of meaning or self-worth (or can do so only with the aid of illusions) is that they find themselves in conditions where their need for self-actualization is frustrated, where they are unable to develop and exercise their essential human capacities. The alienation Marx finds in capitalist society, then, is the condition of being unable to actualize oneself, unable to develop and exercise the powers belonging to one's human essence. More basic than consciousness of alienation (the lack of a *sense* of meaning and self-worth) is real alienation: the failure (or inability) to actualize one's human essential powers. This means that for Marx whether I lead a fulfilling and meaningful life or a wretched and alienated one is not ultimately a matter of whether my conscious desires are satisfied, or of how I think about myself or my life. Rather, it is a matter of whether my life in fact actualizes the potentialities which are objectively present in my human essence, whether I fulfill my 'natural vocation' as the human being I am. If we take the liberty of identifying a meaningful and self-actualized life for Marx (as for Aristotle) with *happiness*, then we must say that Marx holds what Richard Kraut has called an 'objective' conception of human happiness.[17] (This is of course not to deny that for Marx people do naturally tend to desire consciously what objectively fulfills their essence.)

Marx's diagnosis of capitalist alienation identifies human fulfillment with self-actualization, and identifying an alienated, unfulfilled life with one in which the need to develop and exercise our essential powers is frustrated. Marx's diagnosis of alienation is thus vulnerable to any objections which might successfully challenge these identifications. For this reason, it may be worthwhile to consider briefly some objections of this sort which have been put forward by John Plamenatz in his thoughtful book, *Karl Marx's Philosophy of Man*. Plamenatz ascribes to Marx an ideal of self-realization similar to that held by John Stuart Mill: 'the striving to excel, the setting up for oneself of aims difficult to achieve because they make large demands on the self, the proving of one's worth to oneself and others by conspicuous achievement'.[18] Plamenatz is wary of Marx's apparent presumption that a good and satisfying life consists in the unhindered pursuit of self-realization so conceived:

> We must not take it for granted that the more there is of
> this self-realization the more likely it is that people will find
> ways of life that satisfy them. Striving for excellence and
> happiness, though they are not incompatible, do not run
> easily in harness together. If happiness is what we want, there
> are perhaps better ways of getting it than by living strenuously
> and making large demands of ourselves.[19]

> It can happen that the type of society in which this ideal comes
> to be widely accepted frustrates people in their pursuit of it.
> Social conditions may encourage them to believe that they
> ought to aim high and yet make if difficult for them to form
> firm and realistic aims, and so produce in them the sense that
> they are aimless and lost. . . . . Or though able to form clear
> and firm ambitions, they may lack the means, material and
> cultural, to pursue them with much hope of success.[20]

These two passages contain different ideas. The first passage says that self-realization cannot be identified with happiness because a life of striving for excellence may be a dissatisfied life, even when the striving meets with considerable success. The second says that pursuing the ideal of self-realization may lead to aimlessness or frustration because social conditions may make it difficult for people to define and realize concrete aims which accord with this ideal. The second passage seems to agree with Marx that people may be alienated because social conditions prevent them from realizing themselves. But Plamenatz's point seems to be that people's lostness and hopelessness may sometimes be due partly to the very fact that they espouse the goal of self-realization. And this he takes to be a defect in the goal itself.

To take the second criticism first: there is an important difference between holding that human fulfillment *consists* in self-realization and recommending to people that they pursue 'self-realization' as a goal. I think there is good evidence that Marx holds the former view, but little or no evidence that he holds the latter. It is a truism among moralists that we seldom achieve happiness when we make it our goal. Likewise, it may be that we seldom succeed in actualizing ourselves when we pursue the 'ideal of self-actualization', but rather achieve self-actualization by developing and exercising our powers in the course of pursuing other meaningful aims. Marx believes that capitalist social conditions inhibit the formation of such aims and hinder their pursuit. Hence, Plamenatz's perceptive observation is no criticism of Marx. It fits very well with his diagnosis of capitalist alienation that in capitalist society the 'ideal of self-actualization' should be widely accepted but that people should have no clear idea how self-actualization is to be achieved.

The first of the two passages from Plamenatz does appear directly to challenge the claim that happiness or fulfillment consists in self-actualization, since it holds that people may achieve a good measure of self-actualization and still be dissatisfied with themselves and their lives. But Plamenatz's criticism depends on the assumption that self-actualization for Marx involves a 'striving for excellence' which makes great demands on the self and pins one's sense of self-worth to high (perhaps unrealistic) hopes for individual achievement. This assumption is without basis in Marx's texts. Of course, a highly individualistic and competitive society may encourage excessive aspirations of this sort in its members, and thus contribute to their alienation. But once again, this confirms Marx's diagnosis and does not contradict it.

Plamenatz's objection is faulty at a deeper level. For Marx, alienation consists in a kind of frustration or self-dissatisfaction. But it does not follow that every form of self-dissatisfaction is alienation. Probably some degree of discontent and dissatisfaction with oneself is part of any serious striving after worthwhile goals. But we may be dissatisfied with ourselves and our achievements, in the sense of having a strong desire to improve upon them, without failing to recognize their worth or to take satisfaction in it. I fear that Plamenatz has confused (as J.S. Mill would say) the notion of happiness (or human fulfillment) with the very different notion of mere contentment. Perhaps there can be no fulfillment or happiness without some discontent, and wretches who are contented simply because they have no desire to develop their essential human powers are the more and not the less wretched for their contentment. (This is the element of truth in Nietzsche's contemptuous portrayal of the 'last men' who boast that they have 'discovered happiness' because they are 'no longer able to despise themselves'.)[21]

According to some of Marx's cruder critics (Plamenatz is not one of these) Marx depicts communist society as one in which all sources of conflict, tension and discontent have melted away. And these critics suggest (quite properly) that such a picture is not only fantastic but also unattractive. Marx does hold that communism will do away with alienation, with the systematic social causes of unfulfilled, wasted human lives. And he does think that change and development in post-capitalist society will occur through conscious, collective human decisions rather than through destructive class struggles. But it is a caricature both of Marx's conception of humanity and his vision of communist society to suppose that he either predicts or desires a static society in which all sources of human discontent have been done away with.

4 Human essential powers

According to Marx, men and women are natural beings, part of the system of nature. Because of this, a human being is also what Marx calls an 'objective being'. This means, to begin with, that a human being is 'a conditioned and limited being like animals and plants', that men and women are confronted by real, corporeal objects outside and alongside them, and their very survival depends on their relation to these objects. But it is not only the natural conditions of subsistence which make human beings 'objective beings'. By describing human beings in this way, Marx means also to be saying something about the sort of attitude it is healthy and proper for people to take toward their lives, and about the relative importance for human life of the various powers men and women have and the corresponding activities in which they engage. Because a human being is for Marx wholly a natural being, a healthy human life is not one which turns 'inward' after the manner of the religious ascetic or the philosophical contemplative; it is rather one which adopts an outward, worldly orientation, and affirms both material nature and the relation of men and women to the natural world of which they are a part. The human essential powers, therefore, are chiefly man's 'objective essential powers', which 'exist in him as tendencies and faculties, as drives (*Triebe*)'. 'The objects of man's drives', says Marx, 'exist outside him, as objects independent of him. But these objects are objects of his need, objects which are indispensable and essential to the exercise and confirmation of his essential powers.'[22] The exercise of the human essential powers is thus at the same time their 'objectification', the establishment of an essential relation between human beings and the external objects of their need.

Perhaps we are disposed to think of this relation of men and women to the objects of their drives or needs chiefly as consumption: as the using up of natural objects, or at least the expenditure of their useful properties, in order to stay alive and to satisfy people's various wants. Marx, however, does not think of it only in this way, but also, and more inclusively, as the relation of laborers to the objects they create, the process of production. In the *Grundrisse*, he argues that production and consumption are two essential aspects or 'moments' of a single process or act.

To begin with, Marx claims (in good dialectical fashion) that each of these two categories is 'immediately its opposite', which in this instance seems to mean that each can, from a certain point of view, be regarded as a special case of the other. Production is a case of consumption because the process of production always uses up raw materials and tools as well as the powers, energies and lifetime of the laborer. Consumption is a case of production because through it 'man produces his own body', and by satisfying his various wants reproduces his own powers as a laborer.

Consumption and production are also 'identical' in that they 'mediate' or reciprocally condition and determine each other. People produce in order to consume, and consume in order that they may be able to produce. The manner and content of their production and consumption, moreover, mutually influence each other. What people produce depends on their needs, and the sort of consumables that satisfy them. But needs are also directly created by production, both because people's needs are just the requirements for sustaining the mode of productive life in which they engage, and because human needs and wants themselves are influenced by what is there for them to consume. Consumption, as Marx puts it, 'is itself mediated as a drive by its object'.[23]

Production and consumption, therefore, are 'moments of one process'. The concept of consumption, however, distinguishes those aspects of it which involve the satisfaction of needs, adjoined to the human life process, the fulfillment of the indispensable requirements for it to continue and to be the sort of life process it is. Production, however, indicates not just the external means by which consumption is made possible, but even more the activities which constitute the human life process itself, the actual exercise of the human essential powers. Production, as *The German Ideology* says, involves 'a determinate activity of individuals, a determinate way of expressing their life, a determinate *mode* of life for them. As individuals express their life, so they are. What they are coincides with *what* they produce and *how* they produce.' Consequently, Marx insists that production includes consumption, is the 'encompassing moment' of the whole human life process.[24]

Human beings are essentially productive beings, then, because they are essentially objective beings and because productive activity is the encompassing moment of their essential objectivity. But this argument may very well leave us unpersuaded that production is the most essential human function. For surely there are other 'objective' powers besides productive ones. Our powers (for example) of rational deliberation, or scientific inquiry, or aesthetic expression and enjoyment all possess an 'objective orientation' and all seem to be at least as distinctively human as our powers of production are. Why not identify the function of man with their exercise rather than with production, or at least include them along with production in our conception of the essential human powers? As we shall see presently, however, Marx's notion of production is not intended to exclude these other powers. On the contrary, rational self-determination is an essential ingredient of the 'free human production' he looks toward in post-capitalist society; and science and art seem to serve as his chief models for the forms which production will take in the post-capitalist 'realm of freedom', where 'labor has become not merely a means of life but life's first need', and where men and women for the first time 'truly produce' because they 'produce in freedom from physical need'.[25]

But then why does Marx insist on calling fulfilling human activity by the name 'production' and treating these various human functions all as forms of 'labor'? At certain points, the suggestion seems to be that labor is 'fundamental' to all human activity because people could not survive without engaging in it.[26] But this provides no very good reason for regarding labor as

28

the 'encompassing moment' of human activity (for there are other human functions, such as eating and sleeping, which are also 'fundamental' in the sense that they are required for human survival). And it provides no reason at all for applying the terms 'labor' or 'production' to 'true production' which goes on precisely in 'freedom from physical need'.

Marx gives no real argument for identifying labor or production as the most basic or essential human function. But I think he may have been persuaded of this identification by considerations drawn from his materialist conception of history. According to this conception, the basic determinant of social life and historical development is the relentless tendency of human beings to develop and exercise their capacities to dominate nature and creatively shape it to satisfy human wants and express human aspirations. Marx proposes to render intelligible the structure of human societies, the nature of their institutions, the forms of their art and culture, ideas and values, by tracing all these things back to the character of the productive powers human beings possess and the basic historical tendency of these powers to expand. Marx takes production to be the fundamental and encompassing human function because human beings, in practice, acknowledge it to be of fundamental importance to the character of their lives. And he believes the development and exercise of productive powers is man's most basic aspiration because it shows itself in human history to be such. His justification for this belief consists in whatever empirical evidence there is that the materialist conception of history is a correct conception.

But even supposing that Marx's theory of history is correct, is this any reason for him to hold that production is man's basic function in the sense that what makes human life fulfilling and worthwhile is the development and exercise of human productive powers? The fact (if it is a fact) that people do something does not entail that they should do it, or that it is good for them to do it. If Marx reasons as I have suggested, does this not amount to Mill's infamous fallacy of equating the desirable with the desired? And does it not in addition commit the cruder fallacy of equating what people desire with whatever they in fact do?

Yet I do not think it is so obvious that Marx reasons badly if he reasons as I have described. For then, with Mill, he does not equate the desirable with the desired, but rather holds that the best evidence we can produce that something is desirable is that people do naturally and normally tend to desire it. And, with Aristotle, he holds that the desires which it is correct to ascribe to an agent are not only (or necessarily) those which the agent

29

may consciously avow, but those which best make its behavior intelligible.[27] But human history (on Marx's theory) is best made intelligible in terms of the fundamental human aspiration to develop and exercise the productive powers of society. Consequently, we have good evidence for regarding this as the fundamental or chief human good.

Of course, there is still room for doubting whether the materialist conception of history by itself provides ample justification for this conclusion. Marx's theory of history might show that the development and exercise of productive powers is *one* thing people pursue, but it does not show that this is their only important goal, nor does it imply anything definite about the priorities among their different goals. (For instance, it does not preclude the possibility that people have other goals which are always preferred to productive development whenever they conflict with it, but which conflict with this goal so infrequently that they never endanger a materialist account of history.) Or again, it can be objected that the argument moves too quickly from supposed facts about collective human behavior on the broad canvas of history to conclusions about the goals and welfare of individuals. It is one thing to discover a certain historical tendency or (if such a notion can be tolerated) a collective human aspiration, and quite another thing to ascribe this aspiration to individuals and to say that their good consists in fulfilling it. If the argument I have suggested is to work, these difficulties (and perhaps more besides) will have to be met. But my defense of Marx's identification of production as the essential human function was somewhat speculative to begin with, and there is no space here to develop it further.

III

Human Production

1 *Conscious life activity*

So far we have seen that Marx holds production to be both the most fundamental and the most encompassing of human activities. But we have not yet seen that there is anything distinctively human about it. Other living things also have powers whose exercise is characteristic of their species, and enables them to survive by relating them to the objects they need within their natural environment. Some animals even 'produce' in the sense that they generate useful substances from their bodies, or gather or form objects in their environment so as to make these objects more serviceable to themselves: they store up food, secrete honey, spin webs, dig burrows, build nests, dams or hives. The productive powers of men and women may be different from those of other living things, more varied and more extensive; but it is not yet clear that they are powers so wholly different that man can be called a 'laboring' or 'productive' being in a sense that other things cannot.

Marx attempts to identify the distinctive feature of human labor or production in *Capital*:

A spider conducts operations which resemble those of a weaver, and a bee through the construction of its wax cells puts many a human architect to shame. But what above all distinguishes the worst architect from the best of bees is that he has already built the cell in his head before he builds it in wax. At the end of the labor process a result comes about which was already present ideally in the representation of the laborer at its beginning. He not only works a change in form on something natural; he at the same time actualizes in something natural his own

31

purpose, and he knows this purpose as determining the kind and mode of his action, and as something to which he must subject his will.[1]

Marx's view is that human labor or production is to be distinguished from the life activities of other animals because it involves a certain kind of consciousness and purposiveness which animal behavior does not. In the remarks just quoted, however, this view is not well expressed. It may be true that the labor of weavers and architects involves conscious desires, plans and purposes in a way that the activities of spiders and bees do not. But man is not the only animal who acts from conscious purposes and intentions. Surely Engels is correct when he says that the behavior of many non-human animals exhibits not only conscious purposiveness, but even adherence to a conscious plan.[2]

Marx expresses himself better in the Paris writings. There he makes the distinctive feature of human activity not the human being's consciousness of his purpose, but his consciousness of his activity itself. 'The animal is immediately one with its life activity. It does not distinguish itself from this activity.' A human being's activity, on the other hand, 'is not a determination with which he immediately fuses'. Unlike the animal, 'man makes his life activity an object of his will and consciousness.' Thus for Marx 'conscious life activity is the human species character'; it is 'what distinguishes man from animal life activity'.[3]

Obviously 'conscious life activity' is very closely connected with the human attributes of self-consciousness and species consciousness which we examined earlier. Just as each man and woman has in practice some sort of individual and species self-conception, so people also have some conception of their own activity or practice itself. They see themselves, as no animal can, in relation to their mode of life, and they are capable of judging this mode of life as a human or inhuman one, as a life which suits them or not. In a way, therefore, 'consciousness' is after all what distinguishes human beings from other animals on the Marxian theory. The important thing to Marx, however, is that this consciousness is always a feature of *practice*, or an ingredient in it. 'Consciousness', as *The German Ideology* puts it, 'can never be anything other than conscious being, and the being of men is their actual life process.'[4] This is for Marx an important qualification, as we will see in Chapter VIII, for it amounts to a rejection of what Marx calls 'ideology' or 'idealism', the view that the course of human history is determined by people's ideas. For Marx, on the contrary, socially prevalent ideas are always prevalent because of the function they fulfill relative to social practice.

Another distinctive feature of human labor or production according to Marx and Engels is the use of tools or 'means of labor', 'a thing or complex of things which the laborer sneaks in between himself and the object of labor, and which serves him as the conductor of his activity to his object'.[5] In part, the use of tools is a distinctive feature of human activity simply because human beings have proven themselves cleverer than other animals at exploiting their environment, and have, unlike any other animal, come to make use of things in varied and historically changing ways. For Marx, in fact, the historical development of the means of labor are in a sense the clue to human history as a whole. For in his view 'the history of industry is the open book of the human essential powers.' The means of labor 'are not only the measure of the development of the human powers of labor, but also the indicator of the social relations within which labor goes on'.[6]

More precisely, however, what characterizes the human labor process for Marx is not just the use of tools but also their creation or fabrication, and for this reason he endorses Benjamin Franklin's definition of man as 'a tool-making animal'.[7] There is a connection between the deliberate or conscious creation and use of tools and the fact that human labor alone is a conscious life activity. Only human beings, it seems, can properly have the concept of a tool, and thus make or use tools with an explicit consciousness of so doing, because only people have a concept of their own laboring activity, through which they can distinguish it from other natural processes, and consciously set it over against them. The tool, according to Engels, implies specifically human activity because it implies a reciprocity or 'reaction' (*Rückwirkung*) of man on nature.[8] It is only because people have a concept of their own activity as distinct from other natural processes that they can come to regard objects outside their bodies as complicit in their labor, standing on the human rather than the natural side of the interaction between man and nature. Through the use of tools, says Marx, 'something natural itself becomes an organ of [man's] activity, which he adds on to the organs of his own body, adding to his natural stature in spite of the Bible.'[9]

The development or 'self-genesis' of man in history is for Marx fundamentally an expansion of man's productive powers. And it is laboring activity itself which in his view brings about this development. 'While [man] works on nature and changes it, he simultaneously changes his own nature. He develops the potencies slumbering in it, and subjects the play of its powers to his own sway.'[10] Because human labor is the conscious exercise of man's power over nature, people can and do make a conscious effort to transmit, acquire and expand their powers. Not only do individual men and women develop their laboring skills by exercising or practicing them, but society as a whole, as the powers of labor develop, devotes an increasing share of its collective labor time to the development of technology, of new powers of humanity over nature.

These developments also bring about other changes in the human essence. By changing both the way in which people spend their productive lives and by accustoming them to new kinds of useful goods, the expansion of laboring capacities also expands and humanizes people's needs and wants. 'The first need satisfied,' say Marx and Engels, 'the action of satisfying it and the acquisition of the instrument of its satisfaction leads to new needs — and this generation of new needs is the first historical act.' The creation of new needs in people spurs them on to find new ways of satisfying their needs, to expand their productive capacities and even to change their social relations in order to facilitate the co-operative exercise of these new powers.[11]

2 *Labor as self-affirmation*

When Marx says that human beings make their life activity 'an object of volition', it is evident that here again 'object' means (in part) 'goal' or 'purpose'. When men and women labor or produce, they not only aim at the result to be achieved by their labor, but — unlike any other animal — they also regard their life-activity itself as worthwhile, at least whenever they understand it as harmonizing with their human essence. In Marx's words, man 'relates to his species powers as objects';[12] human beings do this in two senses: they treat their own exercise of these powers as an end in itself, in addition to the external ends achieved by it; and they consciously develop their productive or laboring capacities, regarding this expansion of themselves as something desirable over and above the new goods and conveniences it procures them.

I think this is what Marx has in mind when he speaks of people not only as 'actualizing', but also as 'affirming' themselves, their individuality or their species essence through labor or production. Because the human essential powers can be developed, exercised and actualized consciously, and with a conscious awareness that this activity is meaningful and worthwhile, the actualization of these powers can also be an act of self-expression of self-assertion on the part of men and women. It is an act which has meaning for them, in fact, partly because through it they affirm both to themselves and to others their dignity as individuals and the worth of their lives and their humanity.[13]

Marx is very critical of Adam Smith's view that labor must always be a 'sacrifice' on the part of the worker, that equal amounts of labor time confer equal values on commodities because 'in his ordinary state of health, strength and spirits; in the ordinary degree of his skill and dexterity the laborer must always lay down the same portion of his ease, his liberty and his happiness.'[14] Marx readily admits that 'the measure of labor must appear to be given externally, by the purpose to be achieved and the obstacles to their achievement which labor must overcome.' But it does not follow from this that labor must be experienced as unpleasant and confining. For, Marx says, 'the individual "in his normal state of health, power, activity, skill and dexterity" also has a need for a normal portion of labor and the suspension of ease.'[15] The overcoming of obstacles itself, he insists, is not in itself a loss of liberty but rather a *Betätigung der Freiheit*, a manifestation or exercise of freedom.[16]

Marx is perfectly willing to concede, of course, that labor under dehumanizing conditions is experienced as Smith describes it. What Marx is not prepared to admit is that the essential life activity of human beings must necessarily be experienced by them as alienating and oppressive, that the time and energy a person spends working must be experienced as time wasted. It is one of the chief absurdities of alienated labor in Marx's view that wage laborers feel at home with themselves only when they are not working, that they work only when compelled to, that laboring activity 'is not the satisfaction of a need, but merely the means to satisfy needs external to it'. The depth of the workers' alienation, the meaninglessness of their lives, is above all attested by the fact that they spend most of their waking lives engaged in enervating drudgery, merely in order to satisfy the basic requirements for physical survival. Alienated labor, says Marx, 'degrades spontaneous, free activity to a means'; the worker's 'life itself appears only as a means to life', and contains nothing in it which makes sense of the exertion necessary to acquire these means. A life of such labor is therefore a life lost to the man or woman who leads it, essentially a life (like that of Hegel's unhappy Christian) of 'self-sacrifice' or 'mortification'.[17]

Alienated life activity is for Marx a feature of any condition of servitude or class oppression. But Marx does not think that labor has been equally alienated in all past societies, and it is certainly not his view that the alienation of labor automatically decreases as productivity increases. On the contrary, he appears to regard alienation as something which has if anything tended to increase over most of human history, and which is especially characteristic of modern industrial capitalism.[18]

To understand this, we must keep in mind that human needs and wants vary with circumstances, and expand along with the productive capacities of society. Alienated activity is activity which fails to satisfy the need people have to exercise the human essential powers, to actualize and affirm themselves and their humanity. The degree to which people are alienated is a function of the extent to which their lives fall short of actualizing the human essence, of exercising their essential human powers. These powers, however, are not fixed but historically varying and on the whole expanding. Oppressed people will therefore become more and more alienated the greater the gap becomes between the essential powers belonging to the human species and the degree to which their own lives participate in the development and exercise of these powers. In productively undeveloped societies, alienation may not exist simply because the powers possessed by human beings are so rudimentary as not to permit it. When all members of society must work to full capacity just in order to insure the physical survival of the community, there will be no room for the division between oppressor and oppressed, and no way in which people can survive at all without in effect actualizing all the essential human powers which are available to them. The very poverty of such people can therefore give their lives that sense of contentment and fulfillment which Rousseau and others have favorably contrasted with the alienated lives of more 'civilized' human beings. Alienation reaches its peak when, as in modern capitalist society, an awesome expansion of the productive powers of society is accompanied by a life of poverty and the brutalizing toil of factory labor for the great mass of those who produce.

Alienation, in Marx's view, can be overcome only when the productive powers of society expand to such an extent that the labor time necessary to satisfy people's basic needs can be reduced to an amount small enough that their activities can be made more flexible, and the less fulfilling kinds of labor can be more evenly distributed throughout society without condemning the great mass of workers to lives of dehumanizing toil. According to Marx, 'man truly produces only in freedom from physical need', so that people can engage in the most genuinely human and self-affirming kinds of labor only in the 'realm of freedom' which lies beyond, but is founded upon, the 'realm of necessity', the labor required to satisfy their basic needs. In this higher kind of labor, says Marx,

> the external purposes [of labor] are stripped of the appearance
> of mere natural necessity and come to be posited as purposes
> which the individual himself posits — and so as self-
> actualization, the objectification of the subject, hence as real
> freedom, whose action is just — labor.[19]

Marx plainly envisions a society where the life of each individual involves some degree of necessary labor, consisting of relatively simple and mechanical activities which make use of only rather low level capacities, but where each individual's portion of this kind of labor is small enough to leave quite a bit of time for other pursuits, and no individual is condemned to it to the complete exclusion of more fulfilling kinds of activity. Marx makes no real attempt to say just what this free activity will consists in, since he supposes that it will depend on the direction in which emancipated individuals will choose to develop their powers. (His own paradigms for it are drawn from science, art and scholarship.)

What Marx does insist on is that human self-realization is to be found in labor, in production, and by no means 'in mere fun, in amusement, the way Fourier, naive as a *grisette*, conceives it. Really free working, e.g., composing, is at the very same time the most damned serious, intensive exertion.'[20] Marx's view at this point, it seems to me, is once again essentially the same as Aristotle's. Play or amusement, according to Aristotle, is a form of rest or recreation, which is rightly viewed not as an end in itself but a means to further activity. The good life, for both Marx and Aristotle, consists chiefly in the actualization of one's powers, and includes amusement only as a temporary relaxation needed to keep our powers in good condition.[21] The alienation of capitalist society, as Marx sees it, consists almost as much in its waste of human leisure time in the idle, degenerate and unproductive life of the coupon clipper, as it does in the enervated and degraded life of the overworked producers.

3 Objectification and appropriation

Human beings are, as we saw earlier, 'objective beings', beings which stand in an essential relation to natural objects. They need these objects both for their physical subsistence and in order to maintain a healthy human life style. The human essential powers, therefore, must be, or at least must prominently include, 'objective essential powers', whose exercise consists in or involves the 'positing' of these powers in the form of external objects. The actualization or exercise of the human essential powers thus involves their 'objectification', the creation of humanly useful objects which Marx describes as 'the objectified essential powers of man'. 'The product of labor', he says, 'is labor which has been fixed in an object, which has been made real or material (*sachlich*), it is the objectification of labor. The actualization of labor is its objectification.'[22]

Remarks like these are intriguing but largely metaphorical. They need some clarification and qualification if Marx's real doctrine is to be extracted from them. The central metaphor of labor power or activity as 'fixed', 'posited' or 'objectified' in its product is not an especially difficult one. Because human beings are conscious of their activity and value the exercise of their essential powers for its own sake, they are capable of looking upon the changes they work on nature as expressions of themselves. They view the objects they create as a sort of evidence or testimony to the self-actualization of their capacities and the meaningfulness of their lives. This, it seems to me, is what Marx has in mind when he says that the object of labor 'confirms' the worker's individuality or humanity. It is only through contemplating the finished product of my activity that I become truly conscious of the successful exercise of my powers, and thus consciously verify the fact of my own self-actualization. Thus it is only in the object or product of labor that the worker can 'confirm' the meaningfulness of a life which is 'affirmed' in activity itself. Human products, unlike those of animals, are not only means and adjuncts to the life process, but things which, in both their creation and their use, involve the conscious self-expression of human beings, and serve as essential vehicles of their human self-consciousness. Our products, in Marx's words, are 'so many mirrors from which our essence shines forth'.[23]

It is all these ideas which lie behind the metaphor of 'objectified' human power or activity. In their products, laborers consciously confront external things in which the exercise of their essential human powers have become visible and evident. These things confirm and express both the laborers and their human essence. Hence it is as if the laborer's capacities, activities and individuality themselves had been 'objectified', turned into an object, made material or actual, given a shape in which their full worth can at last be verified and appreciated.

More problematic than the metaphor itself is Marx's apparent belief that it can be applied universally to all human labor. For it is plain that not all labor can be described as 'objectification' in the sense that it directly creates or forms material objects. No doubt this is true of the labor which builds houses, raises food-stuffs, weaves clothing, or manufactures goods of other kinds. But the labor of the transporter, for instance, does not in any but a rather far-fetched sense shape or create the objects with which it deals, and the labor of the physician or the teacher consists rather in services rendered to people than in any effect it has on objects in man's natural environment.

Marx, however, is well aware of all this. He says explicitly that the objectification of labor is not to be conceived of only in the form of labor which 'fixes itself in a tangible (*handgreiflich*) object'.[24] All labor does, however, display or embody itself in an 'object' if that term is understood broadly as any result or state of affairs in the external world which labor has brought about. Worthwhile labor for Marx is always 'objective' in that it involves an 'outward' orientation toward external goals or objects, and especially toward our fellow human beings whose needs and wants labor can satisfy. There is, moreover, a good reason why Marx emphasizes labor which is 'objective' in the narrower sense that it forms or shapes objects in the natural world. For he is especially impressed by the way in which social labor as a whole, especially in modern industrial society, succeeds in transforming or reshaping man's whole environment, so that 'he sees (*anschaut*) himself in a world he has created.' Any labor which makes a genuine contri-bution to society does, directly or indirectly, contribute to this 'world creating' function of social labor, and does in that sense participate in the 'objectification of man's species life'.[25]

Marx says that the objects in which men and women objectify themselves become *their* objects, and that human 'behavior or relation (*Verhalten*) to an object is the appropriation of it', the making of it into human 'property'.[26] Terms like 'property' and 'appropriation' naturally make us think of social systems appor-tioning the possession, control and use of things to individuals and groups, and especially of the moral and legal rights which people may have over things. Some philosophers have held that 'property' and 'appropriation' in the most basic sense refer to some direct, natural relationship between human agents and the things which are the objects of their will or activity. Locke, for instance, says in a famous passage that a man makes something his 'property' whenever he 'removes [it] out of the state that nature hath provided and left it in', and 'mixes his labor with it'. Hegel says that I take possession of a thing or make it my property by 'putting my will into it'. Kant uses very similar language in the *Rechtslehre*.[27] Probably it is most natural to take Marx's statements about 'objectification' and 'appropriation' as expressing some kind of agreement with these philosophers. But to identify the exact points of agreement is no easy task.

Because he treats labor or production as the essential life-activity of human beings, Marx usually regards 'objectification', and hence 'appropriation', as closely bound up with labor. In the Paris manuscripts, however, he sometimes treats the scope of both notions as much broader:

> Man appropriates his all-sided essence in an all-sided way,
> as a total man. Every one of his human relations to the world,
> seeing, hearing, smelling, tasting, feeling, observing, sensing,
> willing, acting, loving, in short, all the organs of his individ-
> uality . . . are, in their objective relation (*Verhalten*), or in
> their *relation to the object*, the appropriation of it. The appro-
> priation of *human* actuality, its relation to the object is the
> *exercise of human actuality*, human activity and passivity or
> suffering (*Leiden*), for suffering, humanly grasped, is a self-
> enjoyment of man.[28]

In this passage, Marx seems to be saying that objectification and appropriation take place not only (or even chiefly) in labor or production, but in any relation toward it which is sufficiently 'human' to count as an 'exercise of human actuality' or a 'self-enjoyment of man'. The implication of the passage is that in present society we do not genuinely objectify ourselves or appropriate objects because alienation has cut us off from a 'human' form of seeing, hearing, smelling, and so forth. This implication is confirmed by the critique of private property which immediately follows:

> Private property has made us so stupid and one-sided that an
> object is only *ours* when we have it, when it exists for us
> as capital or is immediately possessed, eaten, drunk, worn on
> our body, dwelt in, etc., in short, used. . . . Thus in place of
> all physical and spiritual senses there steps the simple alienation
> of all these senses, the sense of *having*. . . . The abolition of
> private property is therefore the complete *emancipation* of all
> human senses and properties.[29]

Marx's idea here seems to be that the institution of private property somehow renders me (psychologically?) incapable of any self-actualizing or self-enjoying relation to objects except when I directly possess or use these objects, when I experience them (through the alienated 'sense of having') as 'my private property'. Perhaps this idea is related to Marx's belief that all the 'organs of our individuality' are (directly or indirectly) social, so that these organs are stunted and warped when people adopt a form of appropriation according to which one individual's appropriation of an object excludes others from appropriating it. But the idea is difficult to accept. Does Marx really think that the institution of private property renders me incapable of enjoying the sight of a sunset because the sun is not my private property, or the sound of an orchestra because its members are not my employees? Of course, Marx holds that capitalism is responsible for depriving most people of the opportunity for such enjoyments, but his claim in the above passages seems to amount to a good deal more than this. The additional idea is what it is hard to accept. What Marx says also apparently implies that Rockefeller's factories are not truly his 'property', because (as a victim of private property) he sustains no 'human' relation to them, while a person who smells a flower or hears the first cuckoo in spring in a truly 'human' way would genuinely 'appropriate' them. Surely this notion of 'property' is too poetic to be useful to social theory.

Fortunately, Marx's use of 'property' and related terms in later writings is not so broad, and is more closely related to the social and economic institutions with which we usually associate it. But even there, Marx treats 'appropriation' as a basic human act, closely associated with labor, and more fundamental in character than any of the social institutions within which productive labor takes place. 'All production', he tells us in the *Grundrisse*, 'is appropriation of nature on the part of the individual within and mediated by a determinate form of society.'[30] But not only does appropriation occur through labor, it is even presupposed by labor. Appropriation through labor is possible only because human society already stands in a natural relation of 'ownership' to the earth and other conditions of labor as the 'inorganic body' of man. 'Property therefore originally means nothing but the relation of man to the natural conditions of production as belonging to him.'[31] Thus the fact that in slavery and serfdom some people are the property of others means for Marx that 'one part of society is treated by another as a mere inorganic and natural condition of its own reproduction.'[32] And the *Grundrisse* represents part of the 'alienation' of wage-labor as consisting in the fact that this form of labor is founded on a 'dissolution' of the laborers' natural relation to the earth and to the instruments of production as their own property, on the fact that the natural conditions of labor are 'the property of another' or 'alien property' (*fremdes Eigentum*).[33] Quite evidently, the failure of wage-laborers to 'appropriate' both the conditions and products of their labor is

41

seen by Marx as an important factor in their alienation. He even treats 'appropriation' and 'alienation' as direct opposites.[34]

In wage labor, however, these opposites seem to be united. Since all labor involves the appropriation by the laborer of the conditions and products of labor, it follows that wage labor must also appropriate them. Yet wage laborers are alienated from, that is, they do not own, the materials, instruments or products of their labor. How is this possible? I think Marx's view is that wage labor does appropriate its conditions and products, but owing to its social form it appropriates them for the non-laborer (the capitalist) and not for the laborers themselves. Wage laborers do objectify their labor, they shape nature to human purposes and bring it under the dominion of human society. But it is the capitalists and not the laborers who have the effective control, the use and disposal, the moral and legal title to what wage labor appropriates. And this is due to the social fact that the laborer's activity is something the capitalist has bought for a wage, which therefore is 'alienated' from the laborers and no longer belongs to them. As Marx puts it in *Capital*: 'Since before [the laborer's] entrance into the process his own labor is alienated from him appropriated by the capitalist and incorporated in capital, this labor objectifies itself during the process in an alien product.'[35] Owing to its social form, wage labor objectifies itself in a way which does not actualize and confirm the laborer's humanity but sacrifices and alienates it. By contrast, in meaningful and fulfilling (truly 'human') labor, the laborer would have, or at least participate in, the effective control, use or disposal of the activity, conditions and products of labor. 'Labor would thus be true, active property.'[36]

If we keep in mind the resemblance between Marx's idea of appropriation and the philosophical theories of property in Locke, Kant and Hegel, it is tempting to interpret Marx's view here in terms of the property rights of laborers and the violation of these rights by capital. For these three bourgeois philosophers, labor or the volitional act of appropriation is conceived of fundamentally as an act which makes an object into the agent's private property, which creates a moral right on the agent's part to use or dispose of the object. It is tempting to read Marx in a similar way: laborers, through their natural relation to the conditions and products of their labor, acquire a right to these products. Capital, by appropriating the product for itself, violates this right and does the workers an injustice.

Tempting as this interpretation may be, it is one which Marx will not permit us. To begin with, Marx denies that the basic human act of appropriation implies (as the bourgeois philosophers assume) the institution of private property, or indeed any specific social form of property:

> All production is appropriation of nature on the side of the
> individual, within and mediated by a determinate form of
> society. In this sense it is a tautology to say that property
> (appropriation) is a condition of production. But it is ridiculous
> to leap from this to a determinate form of property, e.g.,
> private property. [37]

All labor appropriates, but the extent to which it appropriates for the laborer as opposed to others depends on the social forms, the economic relations through which the appropriation is mediated. Further, Marx holds that 'juridical relations' (*Rechtsverhältnisse*), matters involving rights or justice, all 'arise out of economic relations', and constitute no sort of Archimedean point outside, or foundation beneath these relations on the basis of which they might be criticized. Speaking of the exchange process, Marx says: 'The juridical relation of individuals as owners of private property whether developed into the form of law or not, is a relation of wills which mirrors the economic relation. The content of this relation of rights or wills is given through the economic relation.' [38]

It follows from these considerations that although capitalist exploitation alienates, dehumanizes and degrades wage laborers, it does not violate any of their rights, and there is nothing about it which is wrongful or unjust. In Chapter IX, we will examine Marx's reasons for holding this surprising view.

IV

Alienation and Capitalism

1 *The capitalist division of labor*

In Chapter I, I suggested that we should look on alienation in Marx's mature thought not as an explanatory concept but as a descriptive or diagnostic one. More specifically, I suggested provisionally that we view it as describing the condition of a person who lacks a sense of self-worth or of meaning in life, or else preserves such a sense only by being the victim of illusions or false consciousness. Chapters II and III have expounded Marx's concept of humanity or the human essence, with a view to extracting his ideas about what people require to lead meaningful or fulfilled lives, and thus about the circumstances which might cause them to be alienated in practical life. The present chapter attempts to say something about Marx's views concerning the social causes of alienation under capitalism.

Marx's thinking on this topic is rich and resists neat systematization. The account we have been developing in previous chapters, however, provides us with one route of access to it. According to Marx, what is vital for the self-worth of human beings and the meaningfulness of their lives is the development and exercise of their essential human powers, whose focus is labor or production. Because these powers are historical in character, varying from society to society and (on the whole) expanding in the course of history, the degree to which alienation is a systematic social phenomenon also varies, as a function both of what society's productive capacities are and of the extent to which the human potentialities they represent have been incorporated into the lives of actual men and women. Generally speaking, the degree of systematic, socially caused alienation in a society will be proportional to the gap which exists in that society between the human potentialities contained virtually in society's productive powers and the actualization of these potentialities by the society's members. Thus the possibilities for alienation increase along with the productive powers of society. For as these powers expand, there is more and more room for a discrepancy between what human life is and what it might be. There is more and more pressure on social arrangements to allow for the lives of individual human beings to share in the wealth of human capacities which belong to social labor.

Marx's criticisms of capitalism make it clear that he regards it as a social system in which social arrangements have failed utterly to accommodate the potentialities for self-actualization which the social powers of production have put within people's reach. According to the *Communist Manifesto*:

> The bourgeoisie during scarcely a hundred years of its rule
> has created productive powers more massive and colossal than
> all past generations together. The subjection of nature's powers,
> machinery, application of chemistry to industry and agriculture,
> steam navigation, railways, . . . — what earlier century dreamed
> that such productive powers slumbered in the womb of social
> labor? [1]

In contrast to this unprecedented progress at the level of social production, capitalism has utterly failed to translate its expanded powers into expanded opportunities for individual self-actualization. It has diminished rather than increased the extent to which individual laborers, their intelligence, skills and powers, participate in the potentialities of social production, as well as sharply limiting the extent to which the laboring masses share in its fruits. As Marx puts it in *Capital*:

> Within the capitalist system all methods of raising the produc-
> tive power of labor are effected at the cost of the individual
> laborer; . . . they mutilate the laborer into a fragment of a man,
> degrade him to an appendage of a machine, annihilate the
> content of this labor by turning it into torture; they alienate
> from him the mental and spiritual potentialities of the labor
> process in the same measure as science is incorporated into it
> as an independent power. [2]

How do capitalist social relations frustrate the human need for self-actualization? In the present chapter, I intend to identify two related themes in Marx's account of the way capitalism leads to alienation. But there is some risk at this point of putting too

45

much emphasis on the philosophically interesting evils, and not enough on the drabber ones. Self-actualization and spiritual fulfillment usually do not mean much to people whose more basic physical needs are still unsatisfied. And it is an important tenet of Marx's theory that capitalism cannot exist without imposing a brutalizing poverty on a sizeable proportion of the human race. There are a number of passages in which Marx appears to be saying that the downfall of capitalism is inevitable not because under capitalism people are alienated or spiritually unfulfilled, but simply because beyond a certain point capitalism will prove incapable of supplying the working population with the basic conditions for physical survival. The bourgeoisie, he says, becomes 'incapable of ruling because it is incapable of securing its slaves even their existence within their slavery'. The proletariat will overthrow capitalism (and with it alienation) not in order to lead more fulfilling lives but merely in order to be certain of survival: 'Things have now come so far that individuals must appropriate the present totality of productive powers not only in order to achieve self-activity, but even to make their existence itself secure.'[3]

Marx does, however, identify some features of capitalist social relations which lead specifically to the crippling of people's powers and the frustration of their needs for self-actualization. One principal theme in Marx's account of the way capitalism 'robs workers of all life content' is the special manner in which it accentuates the division of labor. Modern capitalist manufacture, says Marx, is carried on increasingly by a 'collective laborer', whose actions are the carefully engineered result of the activities of many men, women and children. The labor process is carefully analyzed, its various operations are 'separated', 'isolated', 'rendered independent', and then 'laborers are classified and grouped according to their predominant properties. If their natural specificities are the basis for grafting them onto the division of labor, manufacture, once it is introduced, develops labor powers which are by nature fitted only to a one-sided special functioning.' In this way, 'the individual laborers are appropriated by a one-sided function and annexed to it for life... The habit of a one-sided function transforms them into its unfailing organ, while their connection with the collective mechanism compels them to operate with the regularity of the parts of a machine.' Yet 'the one-sidedness and even the imperfection of the detail laborer comes to be his perfection as a member of his collective laborer.'[4]

But the process of capitalist manufacture not only deprives

people of the well-rounded variety of powers and activities which they need to be full human beings; it also tends to render their specialities themselves more and more mechanical, dehumanizing in nature, less and less a matter of developed skills or powers: 'Every process of production is conditioned by certain simple manipulations of which every human being who stands and walks is capable. They too are cut off from their fluid connection with the content-possessing moments of activity and ossified into exclusive functions.'[5] Consequently, capitalist manufacture creates a positive need for mechanical, 'unskilled' labor, a need unknown to pre-capitalist handicraft manufacture: 'If it develops a one-sided specialty into a virtuosity at the cost of the whole laboring faculty, [capitalist manufacture] also makes the absence of development into a specialty. . . . In [capitalist] manufacture the enrichment of the collective laborer, and hence of capital, is conditioned by the impoverishment of the laborer in his individual productive powers.'[6]

It is plain that Marx blames capitalist social relations, and not the technical requirements of modern industry, for the fragmentation of human beings and the impoverishment of their individual powers. Why? Capitalist society is characterized fundamentally by the fact that the means of production are privately owned by a minority of the members of society who, acting largely independently of one another, tend to employ these means in such a way as to maximize the profit each earns on the investment. The nature of the means of production, moreover, is to a considerable extent at the discretion of this capitalist class, since their investment choices ultimately determine the selection of these means from the range of possibilities afforded by the technical capabilities of society, and even exercise a certain influence on the rate and direction of technical developments. These choices, moreover, are in the long run not arbitrary or at the mercy of individual capitalists, but are tightly constrained through competition with other capitalists by the requirement of profit maximization. Those capitalists who choose methods of production which maximize profits will survive and flourish; those who make different choices will lose their capital and the social power it represents. But the division of labor and the nature of individual laboring activity are largely determined by the means and techniques labor must employ. Hence under capitalism the factors which determine the life activities of the laboring majority are not in its hands but in the hands of a minority whose interests are opposed to its own; and the choices made by this minority are constrained by a principle (profit maximization) which is indifferent to the question

47

whether the lives of wage laborers are rich and fulfilled or degraded and alienated. Of course it might be that self-actualizing
labor and maximal profits are facilitated by the same set of
productive forces and techniques; but in Volume 1, Part Four,
of *Capital*, Marx argues in detail that there is no such happy
coincidence, that it is just the kind of production dictated by
profit maximization which has led to the alienating division of
labor he describes.

Marx believes that far from being incompatible with the technical requirements of modern industry, the potentiality for varied,
well-rounded human activity is inherent in modern scientific
manufacture itself, and will begin to appear naturally as soon as
production comes to be regulated consciously by the workers
instead of being driven blindly by dead capital's vampire-like
thirst for profit at the expense of human life. 'The nature of large
industry', he says, 'conditions change of labor, fluidity of
function, all-sided mobility of the laborer.' Every step in technical
progress demonstrates this fact, by changing the laboring function required for manufacture, thus rendering whole categories
of detail laborers (who have been trained only for one function)
productively superfluous, and (under capitalist conditions) doing
away with their only marketable skill. 'Change of labor' and
'fluidity of function' are not, however, inherently destructive
or crippling. On the contrary, they represent precisely the potentiality for all-sided human development whose suppression under
capitalism is a chief cause of alienation:

> But if change of labor now imposes itself as an overpowering
> natural law, . . . large industry through its catastrophes makes
> it a question of life or death to recognize the change of labor
> and hence the greatest possible many-sidedness of the laborer
> as a universal law of social production, and adapt its relation
> to the normal actuality of this law; . . . to replace the partial
> individual, the mere carrier of a detail function, with the totally
> developed individual, fit for the changing demands of labor,
> for whom different social functions are only so many modes
> of activity relieving one another. [7]

2 *Capitalism and freedom*

One cause of alienation cited by Marx is the frustration or abor-
tion of human potentialities by the capitalist division of labor.
Another, perhaps even more prominent and fundamental in Marx's
account, is the way in which people under capitalism are placed

in a condition of degrading servitude, not merely to other human beings, but even more basically to impersonal and inhuman forces of their own creation. *The German Ideology* describes 'alienation' as 'the positing of social activity, the consolidation of our product as a real power over us, growing out of our control'. [8] *Capital* speaks of the conditions of wage labor as 'alienated from labor and confronting it independently', and of capital as 'an alienated, independent social might, which stands over against society as a thing (*Sache*)'. [9]

This use of 'alienation' is clearly an extension of Feuerbach's notion of religious alienation. In religion, according to Feuerbach, the human essence has come to be thought of by people as an alien (divine) being, which dominates them and makes them worthless (sinful) in their own eyes. The difference is that for Marx the human essence is not merely species consciousness but social labor; the alien being, the dominion and the state of worthlessness are thus not unhappy illusions but monstrous realities. In *Capital*, Marx makes the parallel with Feuerbach quite explicit: 'As in religion man is ruled by a botched work (*Machwerk*) of his own head, so in capitalist production he is ruled by a botched work of his own hand.' [10]

Under capitalism, production and distribution are not regulated collectively but determined by the interaction of independent individuals as private owners of commodities. This system, its apologists tell us, insures the maximum freedom of individuals to dispose of themselves and their property as they choose. Yet in capitalism, the large scale consequences of all this 'free' behavior, the market mechanism and economic system resulting from it, will fall outside anyone's control, and may react catastrophically on each or all of us in a manner which we are powerless, both individually and collectively, to prevent. This powerlessness is most noticeable in a trade crisis, when many capitalists are suddenly ruined, workers thrown out of employment, not through any natural disaster or any failure on the part of society's productive capacities, but simply by the social disaster inherent in the capitalist trade cycle. The alienating feature, however, is not just that the market system leads periodically to disastrous results. What is alienating is more basically that under capitalism human beings cannot be masters, whether individually or collectively, of their own fate, even within the sphere where that fate is a product solely of human action. As *The German Ideology* puts it: 'Their own conditions of life, their labor and with it all the conditions of existence of modern society, have become something accidental for them, over which individual proletarians have no control and over which no *social* organization can give them control.'[11]

The two themes I have identified (alienation as frustration of human self-actualization by the division of labor and alienation as the domination of social conditions over their creators) are closely related in Marx's thinking. For one thing, Marx counts the division of labor as one of the inhuman conditions over which people lack control: 'As long as there exists a cleavage between the particular and the common interest, as long, therefore, as activity is divided not freely but naturally (*nicht freiwillig, sondern naturwüchsig*), man's own deed becomes an alien might standing over against him, subjugating him instead of being dominated by him.'[12] People are forced into stunting and degrading forms of activity only because they lack control over the social conditions which determine the way labor is divided. From this point of view alienation as frustrated self-actualization through the capitalist division of labor can be regarded as a special case of alienation as the degradation of human beings through subjection to their own creations. But from another point of view, this subjection can also be regarded as a special case of frustrated human self-actualization. The Paris manuscripts complain that under capitalism the worker's life activity is not 'his own activity', not 'self-activity' (*Selbsttätigkeit*) but is rather the 'loss of his self' (*Verlust seiner selbst*).[13] *The German Ideology*, using a slightly different terminology, declares that the proletarian revolution will 'transform labor into self-exercise' (*Selbstbetätigung*), by 'producing the form of intercourse', 'the conditions of [people's] self-exercise will be produced by this self-exercise'.[14]

What does Marx mean by 'self-activity' or 'self-exercise'? I think at least part of what Marx intends to designate by them is a kind of activity or a mode of life which is consciously determined by the agent's own understanding and choice rather than being forced on him or her by alien external factors. I 'activate' or 'exercise' my 'self' when I exercise my essentially human capacity to be practically conscious of my humanity in my activity, giving the form of self-understanding and rational choice to the life I live, and making my plans and deliberations effective in shaping my life. When I do this, I 'make my life activity its own object', in that I bring that activity under my conscious control. At the same time, I 'appropriate' my own life, it comes to belong to me instead of belonging to alien forces which master me instead of being mastered by me. By subjecting human beings to the socially produced conditions of their labor, capitalism frustrates the exercise of these powers of self-understanding and self-determination, and this is part of the way in which it frustrates their self-actualization.

If this interpretation is correct, then Marx's emphasis on 'self-activity' or 'self-exercise' involves an affirmation of the value of human freedom, and belongs to a definite tradition of thinking about what this value consists in. Freedom for Marx is self-determination, the subjection of one's self and its essential functions to one's own conscious, rational choice. This concept of freedom, in such philosophers as Spinoza, Rousseau, Kant and Hegel, is given such names as 'spontaneity', 'moral liberty', 'autonomy' and 'self-possession' (*Beisichsein*). For these thinkers, as for Marx, freedom in the 'negative' sense, the absence of constraint or coercion on individuals, has value mainly because it provides the opportunity for the exercise of freedom in this deeper, 'positive' sense. Marx's adherence to this notion of freedom is explicit: to be free 'in the materialistic sense' is to be 'free not through the negative power of avoiding this and that, but through the positive might of making one's true individuality count'. [15]

In most modern thinkers before Marx, however, the conception of positive freedom is given a predominantly individualistic and moralistic interpretation. To be sure, they note that the exercise of this freedom requires the satisfaction of certain social (especially political) conditions. But they conceive self-determination itself chiefly as the inner volitional disposition of individual human agents, their mastery over their impulses and passions through rational self-knowledge and moral fortitude. Given Marx's materialist conception of human beings as socially productive beings, he cannot be content with an introverted, spiritualistic sort of self-determination. For Marx, true self-determination must rather consist in the imposition of human control on the social conditions of human production.

Marx often insists that social institutions and relations of production are not facts of nature but historically transient social forms which are the products of human activity every bit as much as wheat, cloth or machinery. [16] He does so in part to give the lie to those who would defend existing institutions by declaring them unalterable; but his purpose is also to make clear how much is required if human beings are to have genuine freedom or self-determination. If social relations are human products, then people cannot be accounted free until they create these relations with full consciousness of what they are doing. Human freedom requires not only that people should not be (as Locke says) subject to the arbitrary will of others; it requires also that the social relations in which they stand should be products of their own will. To recognize this fully is already to see through the sophistry which represents capitalist society as free because its relationships result not from coercive laws or the will of rulers but (apparently) by accident, from unregulated economic decisions made by individuals. As Marx puts it: 'In imagination (*Vorstellung*), individuals under the dominion of the bourgeoisie are freer than before, because their conditions of life are accidental to them; but in reality they are more unfree, because they are more subsumed under a reified social power (*sachliche Gewalt*).'[17]

Because freedom for Marx requires the conscious production of people's social relations, it is something which can be achieved only in community with others, and cannot be attained by retreating into oneself or by the exercise of one's self-determination within the confines of a jealously guarded 'private domain' in which society does not interfere. Yet Marx does not neglect to emphasize the complementary point that no society can be free unless it 'gives to each the social room for his essential life expression'.[18] There can be no genuine freedom unless men and women have the opportunity to exercise choice over their own lives and develop their individuality fully and freely. Marx is the consistent foe of political repression, press censorship, and other such measures which curb the free development and expression of individuals. He has only contempt for any brand of communism which would turn the state or community into 'the universal capitalist' by imposing a uniform, impoverished mode of life on all members of society alike.[19] There can be no doubt that for Marx individual liberty is necessary to a free society. But it is equally evident, to Marx at least, that the liberty proclaimed by bourgeois liberalism is not sufficient for genuine (that is, positive) freedom.

Human freedom can be attained only when people's social relations are subject to conscious human control. Therefore, it is only in communist society that people can be truly free, because human control over social relations can only be collective control, and only in communist society can this control be exercised by and for all members of society: Communism, says Marx, 'consciously treats all natural (*naturwüchsig*) presuppositions as creations of earlier human beings, divesting them of their natural character (*Naturwüchsigkeit*) and subjecting them to the might of the united individuals'. Only communist society can do this, because communist society will be a classless society, in it people will 'participate in society just as individuals. For it is the unity of individuals (of course within the presupposition of developed productive powers) which gives individuals control over the conditions for their free development and movement.'[20] Up to now, the class character of society has precluded the possibility of this unity, and hence of the freedom which can be attained only through it: 'The apparent community in which individuals have united themselves up to now always made itself into something independent over against them, and since it was always a unity of one class standing over against others, it was at the same time for the dominated class not only an illusory community, but a new fetter as well.' Further, because individual self-expression and self-actualization are possible only through the capitalist division of labor, even individual freedom will become possible only with the collective human control over people's conditions of life:

> The transformation of personal power (relations) into reified
> (*sachliche*) ones, . . . can only be abolished by individuals
> subsuming these reified powers again under themselves and
> abolishing the division of labor. This is not possible without
> the community. Only within the community has each individual
> the means of cultivating his abilities on all sides; hence personal
> freedom becomes possible only within the community. [21]

Marx does not conceive of social control over the means of production as the exclusion of individuals from ownership of what they produce and use. On the contrary, it is capitalism which involves such an exclusion, since it delivers the means and objects of production over to a class of nonworkers. Communism, as Marx sees it, will be a system of 'individual property for the producer', based on 'cooperation and the possession in common of land and the means of production'. [22] The means of production must be owned collectively, because in modern industry labor is directly social, and the disposition of the means of production is always an act affecting society as a whole. Such acts, in Marx's communism, will be performed consciously. Decisions about them will be made democratically, by society as a whole, and not by a privileged class, acting contrary to the interests of the laboring majority and subject to the alien constraint of profit-maximization.

Marx's critique of capitalism is based on some familiar philosophical value conceptions, such as self-actualization and positive freedom. But it is wrong to conclude from this, as some writers on Marx appear to do, that his denunciations of capitalist alienation invoke or presuppose a conception of a future communist lifestyle or future social arrangements, and 'ideal' of what human beings could, would and should be. Marx never describes future social arrangements in detail, and the main point he makes about them is that they are bound to change in ways we cannot now foresee. Further, Marx often explicitly repudiates the intention of formulating 'ideals' of future society. As early as 1843 Marx writes to Ruge that any honest social reformer 'must admit to himself that he has no exact view about what ought to be. But again this is just the advantage of the new trend, that we do not dogmatically anticipate the world but only want to find the new world through a critique of the old one.' *The German Ideology* denies that 'communism' is an 'ideal' or 'state of affairs which ought to be brought about'. Communism rather is 'an actual movement which is abolishing the present state of affairs'. 'The workers', says *The Civil War in France*, 'have no fixed and finished utopias to introduce by popular decree, . . . no ideals to realize.' The task of the working class is 'only to posit freely the elements of the new society which has already developed in the womb of the collapsing bourgeois society'. [23]

The plain import of these passages (and others like them) is that Marx does not pretend to know what the lifestyle or social arrangements of future society will be like. He evidently believes that these matters are dependent largely on the further growth of our knowledge, and hence beyond our power to forecast. Marx's desire to overthrow capitalist society is not motivated by any ideal picture of communist society, but by the real alienation and deprivation of people in capitalist society, together with the conviction that these conditions result from capitalist social arrangements. Marx views his task not as one of concocting 'recipes for the cookshops of the future', but rather one of identifying the historical tendencies and social movements which promise to bring down the outmoded society and point the way to a future in which people will enjoy more of such goods as self-actualization and freedom. [24] It is wrong to think that Marx's judgment that the victory of the proletarian movement will bring about a world which is richer in these goods commits him to having some more definite conception of what this world will be like.

3 *Assessing Marx on capitalist alienation*

The issues involved in assessing Marx's thoughts about alienation under capitalism are difficult and complex. I think in the end most of these issues are empirical ones, but this does not mean that they are clear cut or easily resolved. Any adequate assessment of Marx's views at this point would certainly take up far more space than I have already used in expounding them. Even then, I suspect, any assessment seasoned with the proper scholarly caution would probably be inconclusive. It is unlikely that anyone, in

Marx's time or today, knows enough to be entitled to a strong opinion for or against what Marx says about alienation and its social causes. If many people (the present writer included) do hold strong opinions, this is largely because the only alternative to committing oneself in practice for or against Marx would be to take no effective stand whatever on the social reality around us. In the present section I will try to identify (but not to resolve), some of the main issues raised by Marx's account of alienation as it has been expounded here.

Marx's account of alienation in capitalist society aims at substantiating three principal theses:

(1) The vast majority of people living under capitalism are alienated.

(2) The chief causes of this alienation cannot be removed so long as the capitalist mode of production prevails.

(3) Alienation as a pervasive social phenomenon can and will be abolished in a postcapitalist (socialist or communist) mode of production.

These three theses are obviously interrelated. (1) is more or less presupposed by both (2) and (3). But (1) itself, as Marx understands it, is also dependent on (2) and (3), and on his grounds for holding them. In support of (1), a Marxist might cite widespread feelings of disorientation and dissatisfaction among people living in capitalist societies, or he might point to the preoccupation of philosophers, artists, social thinkers and popular consciousness with the problem of alienation, whether in an overtly Marxian or in various non-Marxian forms. But these considerations, however well substantiated, would not strictly show that alienation, as Marx understands it, exists in capitalist society. By the same token, a critic of Marx cannot successfully rebut (1) merely by arguing that people in capitalist societies are on the whole satisfied with their lives, even if a convincing case for this could be made out. Alienation, as Marx conceives of it, is not fundamentally a matter of consciousness or of how people in fact feel about themselves or their lives. Alienation is rather a state of objective unfulfillment, of the frustration of really existing human needs and potentialities. The consciousness people have of this unfulfillment is merely a reflection of alienation, at most a symptom or evidence of it. Marx's real grounds for believing that people in capitalist society are alienated is not that they are conscious of being alienated, but rather the objective existence of potentialities for human fulfillment that must be frustrated as long as the

55

capitalist mode of production prevails.

As we saw in section 2, Marx has no very definite conception of postcapitalist society or of the possibilities for fulfillment which he believes will be actualized in it. Hence Marx does not believe (3) because he has some clear idea of the ways in which socialism or communism will provide people with opportunities for self-actualization. Rather, he seems to believe (3) because he is confident that people can achieve a fulfilling life when the main obstacles to it are removed, and because he thinks he has identified these obstacles: they are the outmoded social relations of bourgeois society.

The most direct way of attacking Marx's theory would be to deny that people really are alienated under capitalism, that people in capitalist society really do fall far short of actualizing their human potentialities. We could do this and still admit that many people in capitalist society are dissatisfied with their lives, so long as we hold that this dissatisfaction is due to causes other than the actual frustration of genuine potentialities of the sort Marx believes in. We could even go so far as to admit that people's dissatisfaction is due to their belief that they are being prevented by capitalism from actualizing their essential powers, so long as we hold that this belief is mistaken, perhaps that it is a tantalizing illusion disseminated by dangerous social malcontents.

It is often said that Marx is too optimistic about the inevitability of historical progress, and that the twentieth century's bitter experiences have taught us that the potentialities for human fulfillment in mass society under industrial technology are not nearly as great as nineteenth century thinkers (including Marx) believed them to be. These common opinions can easily be pressed into service against Marx's account of capitalist alienation. For if they are correct, then Marx's belief that most people in capitalist society are alienated is based on an exaggerated estimate of the human potentialities of modern society.

Marx certainly does not defend his nineteenth century optimism against twentieth century objections. Nothing he says (perhaps nothing he could say) rules out the possibility that he is wrong to believe that the colossal and unprecedented expansion of society's productive powers during the capitalist era has created comparably colossal and unprecedented potentialities for human self-actualization. But it is not so obvious as many of Marx's critics might like to suppose that his belief is unrealistic or excessively optimistic. Modern technology increases people's ability to exercise control over nature, over themselves and over their relations with each other. It shortens the time required for people to produce the necessaries of life, and thus gives people at least potential mastery over time, over the hours, days and years which are the substance of human life. If technology also adds to people's needs, it is evident (at least to Marx) that some of these needs expand and enrich human life, and that freed from the influences of an alienating social order, people could exercise rational control even over the creation of new needs.

Further, modern science has increased our knowledge both of ourselves and of nature outside us, providing us with what we apparently need most to make wise use of our increased powers. Modern society has become mass society just because science and industry have increased people's powers of communication with each other, and intensified the web of human interdependence. Marx's confidence in the human potential of modern science and technology is initially plausible. To reject it is to embrace the paradox that increasing people's powers, their self-understanding and their interdependence has no tendency to enrich their lives, their freedom and their community. The burden of proof seems to be on anyone who would defend such paradoxes. It is not obvious that events in our century have rendered them more defensible than they were in Marx's time.

Especially important for Marx's conception of our potentialities for freedom is his belief that the values of individuality and community are reconcilable, that postcapitalist society can simultaneously achieve greater individual autonomy and greater social unity than people's productive powers and social relations have hitherto permitted. Marx's critics have been particularly suspicious of his silence concerning the social decision procedures through which free individuals are to achieve the rational collective regulation of their associated labor. At least since Rousseau, philosophers and political theorists have set themselves the problem of finding a form of human association which could unite individuals, putting the common might of society at the disposal of each while at the same time leaving all completely free to follow a self-chosen plan of life. To many it has seemed highly questionable whether such an association is possible even in theory, let alone in practice. They are bound to be skeptical of Marx's apparent presumption that modern technology puts the goal within reach, and the abolition of capitalism is all we require to attain it.

Marx does say very little about the political or administrative structure of postcapitalist society, beyond insisting that it will be democratic, and will involve control by 'society itself' rather than by a separate political mechanism or state bureaucracy.

57

Fundamentally, however, he does not see the problem as a procedural one at all. For Marx, the chief obstacle both to individual
freedom and social unity is the division of society into oppressing
and oppressed classes. Of course as long as we tacitly assume a
class society, the goals of freedom and community will look
both separately unattainable and diametrically opposed. In a
society where one individual's freedom is not necessarily another's
servitude, and where people have no motives to use community
as a pretext for advancing some people's interests at the expense
of others, questions of social decision making will not appear to
people in the form of theoretical paradoxes or insoluble technical
problems.

Marx also refuses to address himself to procedural questions
because he regards them as premature. Such questions presuppose
that we who ask them are all people of good will, pursuing a
disinterested search for the right way to live together. They
presuppose also that the object of such a search is, at least in its
fundamentals, something which can be determined independently
of detailed information about the technical resources available to
society as regards its material production. Both presuppositions,
in Marx's view, are false. As long as class society persists, the
viability of any political mechanism will necessarily be a function
not of its suitability for promoting genuine liberty or community,
but only of the class interests it serves. Only after the abolition of
class society can people begin to decide, on the basis of the
productive capacities then at their disposal, how they will live
together as free individuals.

We have been considering challenges to Marx's account of
capitalist alienation based on the denial that people in capitalist
society are really alienated. But many of Marx's critics might be
prepared to admit that alienation is a serious problem of modern
society. The question remains whether it is capitalist social relations as such which are responsible for it. Most political moderates
and reformists live on the hope that the evils of modern society
can be abolished, or at least greatly mitigated, without abandoning
the framework of commodity production and private ownership
of the means of production. These hopes are often matched with
the fear that a socialist revolution would do little or nothing to
abolish alienation, and might even undermine such freedom and
productivity as capitalism has.

Other critics, even more pessimistic, sometimes wonder whether
alienation can be abolished at all, at least within the framework of a
modern, sophisticated and technologically developed society. Exis-
tentialists have in effect interpreted alienation as an ineradicable

58

fact of the human condition, built into the ontology of our existence or the transcendental structure of consciousness. Their views are sometimes continuous with older religious ones which treat alienation as a consequence of our sinful nature, remediable only by supernatural means. Social pessimists (such as Freud) have seen alienation as the inevitable result of subjecting man's animal nature to the confinement of a social order. Others (in a manner reminiscent of Rousseau) have viewed alienation as the price we must pay for living in a society which is too far from nature: a society too large and sophisticated, too developed scientifically and technologically, too dependent on complex forms of human cooperation.

Marx does believe that alienation can be overcome in a modern, complex and industrialized society. But he is not necessarily committed to denying that there might be causes of alienation other than those specifically identified by his theory. The main burden of Marx's message is that capitalist social relations are the most pervasive and obvious cause of alienation, which must be abolished first, before lesser or more hidden causes can be dealt with. But there is no reason why Marx might not grant that such traditional social ills as religious fanaticism, racism and sexual oppression also contribute to alienation, and would have to be fought against even under socialism.

Marx's explanation of alienation might also be challenged in some of its details. It is arguable, for instance, that Marx's views about the capitalist division of labor, whatever truth they might have had in his own century, are now obsolete. Certainly it would be difficult to maintain that capitalism still exhibits a tendency to turn all labor into the unskilled mechanical sort, to 'make the absence of development into a specialty'. But even if this point is no longer defensible, Marx's explanation of alienation in terms of the capitalist division of labor may still be tenable. For the constraint of profit-maximization may still exercise a powerful (and harmful) effect on the nature of laboring activity, and inhibit the development of a well-rounded humanity on the part of workers. If this is so, then Marx's explanation of alienation in terms of the capitalist division of labor may still be essentially correct, even if the specific details of his account are not. Marx is always the first to insist that capitalism is not an immutable system, but one which is undergoing constant change. It would not be inconsistent with his views to recognize that his account of alienation in nineteenth century capitalist society might not be applicable in detail to its twentieth century descendant.

PART TWO

Historical Materialism

V

Production and Society

1 'Economic determinism'

Marx and Engels regard the materialist conception of history as one of the most fundamental and distinctive tenets of Marxism. Engels ranks it, along with the theory of surplus value, as one of Marx's two great original contributions as a social scientist. [1] The central claim of historical materialism is that people's economic behavior, their 'mode of production in material life', is the 'basis' of their social life generally, that this 'economic basis' generally 'conditions' or 'determines' both the society's remaining institutions, and the prevalent ideas or forms of social consciousness.

Marx's historical materialism has often been described as 'economic determinism' — a term he never uses himself. [2] The label would be innocuous enough, except that it encourages the notion that Marx's historical materialism is a version of the 'determinism' which holds that all human actions are causally determined by factors wholly outside the agent's control — in Marx's case, by 'economic' factors. On this interpretation, Marx's thesis is that people's thoughts and actions, their political behavior as well as their moral, religious and philosophical convictions, are all causally determined by economic facts, while these actions and convictions themselves exercise no influence whatever on the economic situation.

It is not at all clear, on this interpretation, just what sorts of facts are supposed to count as 'economic' (many critics charge Marx with unclarity or inconsistency on this point). But however the term 'economic' is understood, it is fairly clear that 'economic determinism' is a false view. It contradicts not only common sense and everyday experience, but also countless things which

63

Marx himself says or takes for granted in his writings on politics and history. No matter how much people's ideas, social behavior and political decisions may be influenced by economic factors, it is also obvious that these things in turn have some impact on the economic realm. If Marx had denied that they do have any such impact, then it is hard to understand how he could have seen any point in writing books and pamphlets or engaging in political agitation, apparently with the aim of bringing about changes in the economic structure of society by changing people's ideas about it and bringing political influences to bear on it. [3]

In Chapter VIII, we will consider whether Marx is committed to the view that human actions are causally determined. For the present, the point to be made is that Marx's historical materialism does not involve 'economic determinism' in the sense just described. As a matter of fact, nothing said by either Marx or Engels commits them to any such view. Marx does say that the 'economic basis' of society 'conditions' and even 'determines' its political and intellectual life-processes. But this is not incompatible with saying that the 'conditioned' and 'determined' aspects of social life cannot also have some influence on the economic sphere. The geography and climate of a certain region certainly 'condition' and even 'determine' the kinds of living things which can survive in that region. But this does not preclude the life processes of the organisms in that region from having some influence on these 'determining' factors.

Engels in fact explicitly denies that 'the economic moment is the sole determining one'; 'It is not the case that the economic situation is the cause, alone active, and everything else is only a passive effect.' On the contrary, he asserts that while 'the material mode of life is the *primum agens*, this does not preclude that the ideal regions may react on it in turn and exercise a secondary influence'. Engels describes the interaction of economic factors with political ones as 'a reciprocal action of two unequal forces', and insists repeatedly that while ideal or political factors may 'preponderate in determining the *form*' of historical events, their 'content' is always 'determined in the last instance' by the underlying economic factors. [4] It has sometimes been suggested that such remarks by Engels represent a revision of historical materialism as earlier expounded in his own and Marx's writings. But this suggestion cannot be correct. For essentially the same thoughts can already be found in *The German Ideology*, co-authored by Marx and Engels, and containing the first self-conscious exposition of historical materialism:

This conception of history thus rests on developing the
actual process of production, and even on proceeding from
the material production of immediate life, grasping the form
of intercourse connected with this mode of production and
generated by it, hence presenting civil society in its various
stages as foundation of the whole of history and also in its
action as state, explaining from it the different theoretical
products and forms of consciousness, religion, philosophy,
morals, etc., etc. . . . ; the whole matter can naturally be
presented in its totality (and hence also the reciprocal action
of these different sides upon one another). [5]

The 'economic determinist' interpretation of Marx has been
adopted, I think, not so much because Marx uses the word 'determine' (*bestimmen*) to describe the relation of the 'economic basis'
to the social 'superstructure' as because Marx's readers have been
unable to see how he could ascribe systematic explanatory
primacy to the economic realm without ruling out the possibility
of any significant 'reciprocal action' of the 'determined' spheres
on the 'determining' one. If politics and religion can 'react' on the
economic situation and exert some 'force' on it, why does Marx
want to rule out altogether the possibility that they might 'condition' and even 'determine' the economic structure of society?
Engels' comments make it plain that historical materialism wants
to deny such a possibility (at least 'in the last instance'), but these
comments leave us in the dark about the motivation behind such
denials. They strongly imply that what makes the economic factor
the 'determining' one is its high degree of influence relative to the
other social factors with which it is supposed to interact. But they
do not explain why Marx and Engels ascribe this dominant influence to the economic sphere.
    I do not think it is misguided to see the truth of historical
materialism as turning on the question of the relative degree of
influence exercised by the facts of material production as compared with other factors in social life. But before we can appreciate what is involved in this question, we must be clearer about
the way in which the economic structure of society is supposed to
explain the constitution of society and social change. To this end,
let us first take a closer look at the elements of Marx's materialist
analysis of society, and the relations which are supposed to obtain
between them.

2 *Productive powers, production relations*

In his 1846 letter to P.V. Annenkov, Marx writes:

> What is society, whatever its form may be? The product of
> men's reciprocal action. Are men free to choose this or that
> form of society? Not at all. Posit a certain state of development
> of the productive faculties of men and you will get such and
> such form of intercourse and consumption. Posit certain degrees
> of development of production, intercourse and consumption
> and you will get such and such form of social constitution,
> such and such organization of the family, of orders or classes,
> in a word, such and such civil society. Posit such and such
> civil society, and you will get such and such a political state,
> which is nothing but the official expression of civil society. [6]

In this passage, Marx sets forth a series or hierarchy of social
factors or structures, starting with what he takes to be the most
basic and proceeding toward those which he believes can be
explained in terms of what occupies a more fundamental place
in the hierarchy. Specifically, the passage indicates three relationships of dependence:

A The 'form of intercourse and consumption' depends on the
'state of development of men's productive faculties'.
B The 'form of social constitution' or 'civil society' depends
on the 'degree of development of production, intercourse
and consumption'.
C The 'political state' depends on 'civil society'.

Marx's terminology here does not correspond exactly to that used
in some of his more familiar statements of historical materialism,
partly because this letter represents a relatively early statement of
his theory, and partly because he is writing in French. But the elements distinguished in this passage, and the relationships posited
between them, do belong to his theory in all his expositions of it.
Let us consider each of these elements in turn.

The most fundamental factor in the materialist account is what
Marx here calls society's 'productive faculties'. Marx's German
term *Produktivkräfte* was originally a translation of Smith's and
Ricardo's 'productive powers', but has more often been rendered
into English as 'productive forces'. There is some significance in
this difference. 'Productive powers' and 'productive faculties'
both suggest the capacities or abilities of human beings, whether
individual or collective, which they manifest and exercise in their
productive activity. 'Productive forces', on the other hand,

suggests the physical concomitants, the arsenal of materials and instruments used in the process of production, or facilitating that process.[7] Of course these two possible referents of *Produktivkräfte* are in fact very closely related. As soon as production makes use of tools at all, the proper instruments of production are necessary prerequisites for the exercise of people's productive capacities; conversely, a tool is productively meaningless apart from the power of the human laborer who wields it. People's capacities to produce come into being along with the tools they employ, and the tradition of laboring techniques runs parallel to the handing down of the material means for their exercise.

According to Marx, a society's production depends on and is determined by its productive powers. Taken in the abstract, however, this principle is a truism. Any human activity depends on and is determined by the powers of which that activity is an exercise. But when we consider the social character of production, the principle has a significance which is less obvious. All social production beyond a very primitive level involves a definite division of social labor, an apportionment of different activities to individuals: 'In production', says Marx,

> men do not relate to nature alone. They produce only insofar
> as they co-operate in a determinate way and exchange their
> activities with one another. In order to produce they must
> address each other in determinate relationships, and it is only
> within these relations that their relation to nature, their pro-
> duction, takes place. [8]

Historical materialism holds that productive powers determine material production in the sense that they determine the division of labor in society. 'Labor', says Marx, 'is organized, is divided differently according to the instruments it has at its disposal. The hand mill presupposes a different division of labor from the steam mill.'[9] The efficient use of a particular set of instruments and productive capacities requires a mode of social co-operation in labor which is specifically adjusted to or harmonized with them: a society which produces using hand mills and suchlike instruments will need distinct groups of laborers, in definite proportions, trained to the requisite degree in specific skills and engaged in modes of life suited to the respective types of labor they must perform. A society which employs steam machinery, if it is to produce with any degree of efficiency, must likewise accommodate its division of labor and modes of life to the productive forces. But the accommodation required may be a very different one.

Thus when Marx says that a certain stage of development in people's productive faculties gives us a certain form of intercourse and consumption, at least part of what he means is that a given set of productive powers requires, and consequently explains, a given division of labor. But this can be only part of what he means. For he tells Annenkov that by 'forms of intercourse' he means 'economic forms' or 'social relations': 'for example, the privileges, the institution of guilds and corporations, the regulatory regime of the Middle Ages', and the relationship of capital to wage labor which replaced all these relations in the modern period.[10] These economic forms and relations, however, do not belong immediately to 'material production', to the division of labor or the direct work relations of individuals with each other. The fact that two people do two different but complementary productive tasks does not directly tell us anything about their *social* relation to each other, or about the *economic* forms within which their labor is carried on. It does not tell us whether they are slaves, corvées, wage laborers or workers in a socialist state. If one person supervises the work of another, this does not tell us whether the supervisor is an overseer of slaves, a guild master supervising the labor of journeymen or a manager of wage laborers for capital.

If Marx means social or economic relations when he speaks of a 'form of intercourse', then he holds not merely that a certain set of productive faculties gives us a certain division of labor, but also that they give us a certain set of social and economic institutions, relationships of power, authority and ownership within which productive labor is carried on.

In Marx's writing after *The German Ideology*, he usually speaks not of the 'form of intercourse', but of 'relations of production', which in any society form an organic whole Marx calls the society's 'economic structure'.[11] Some critics of Marx maintain that this notion of production relations confounds work relations with social or economic relations, with relations between people which 'arise because production creates a need for them' or which 'help production go smoothly'.[12] Marx, however, is certainly aware of the difference between what he calls the 'natural' or 'material' side of production and the 'social' or 'economic' side, and he attaches considerable importance to the distinction.[13] He often criticizes bourgeois economists for confusing the two, and treating as a natural feature of production what is in fact a feature only of its specifically bourgeois social or economic form.[14] But it is true that Marx seldom draws this distinction while expounding his materialist conception of history, and probably never draws it in such contexts with the clarity we might wish. 'The production of life', we read in *The German Ideology*,

> now appears as a double relation: on the one side as a natural, on the other side a social relation. . . . From this it follows that a determinate mode of production or industrial stage is always united with a determinate mode of co-operation or social stage.[15]

Here the distinction between 'natural' and 'social' is drawn explicitly enough, but it is not clear that it separates social relations, such as guild privileges and forms of property from purely material relations, such as the apportionment of productive tasks to different people. The term 'mode of co-operation' could easily mean either, or both.

I think it must be conceded that in his accounts of historical materialism Marx does not deal with this matter as often or as clearly as he should have. But there is no reason to suppose that he was unaware of the distinction between direct work relations and the economic relations within which work goes on. The important question is: What is Marx's conception of the relationship between the division of labor, the material work relations of a given society, and its form of intercourse, in the sense of its social relations of production, or economic structure? Another passage from *The German Ideology* may help us to supply the answer:

> Through the division of labor there develop different divisions among individuals co-operating in determinate kinds of labor. The relative position [*Stellung*] , of these individual divisions is conditioned through the mode of organizing agricultural, industrial and commercial labor. . . . The different stages of development in the division of labor are just so many different forms of property, i.e. the existing stage of the division of labor also determines the relations of individuals to one another with reference to the materials, instruments and products of labor.[16]

Here Marx and Engels first appear to *identify* each 'stage in the development of the division of labor' with its corresponding 'form of property'. But their further explanation of what they mean makes clear both the distinction and the relationship: the existing division of labor 'determines' the 'relations of individuals to one another' regarding the means of production, just as the 'relative position' of the different social divisions is 'conditioned through' the way labor is organized. Material work relations, therefore,

69

along with the productive powers on which they depend, are more basic than social and economic forms, and can be used to explain these forms. As Marx tells Annenkov: '[People's] material relations are the basis of all their relations. . . . The whole inner organization of nations [is nothing else than] an expression of a certain division of labor.' 'The different forms of the division of labor [become] so many bases of social organization.'[17]

Marx's thinking here is not difficult to follow. Just as the efficient exercise of a certain set of productive faculties requires a certain social division of labor, so either or both of these material factors may also demand, or at least favor, certain patterns of ownership and relations of economic domination and dependence. One method of farming, for instance, might require the working of larger fields than another, and hence favor a system of bigger landowners over a system of small-holding peasants. Factory production requires not only a greater division of labor but also a greater concentration of means of production than manufacture by skilled manual labor: the latter may well be suited to a guild system, where the former becomes possible only through the accumulation of capital and the hiring of wage labor.

The degree to which productive powers determine the prevailing form of intercourse or social relations depends on the degree to which their efficient employment and further development places constraints on social forms. Obviously we cannot explain absolutely every detail of people's social relations in terms of material production, and Marx never claims we can. He clearly thinks that the extent to which production determines social relations is a matter for careful empirical inquiry. But Marx's theory is based on the idea that the productive powers of society impose significant constraints on such things as forms of property and economic relations of domination and subjection.[18]

3 A 'technological' theory of history?

Marx speaks of the 'determination of the organization of labor by the means of production', but he most often says of social or economic relations only that they 'correspond' to the productive forces, that they are 'connected' with them or 'intimately bound up' with them.[19] What, if anything, is the significance of this more guarded language? Some scholars believe that there is no real significance in it, that Marx's theory does hold in effect that social production relations are determined by the productive forces. Others take it to be evidence that Marx does not subscribe to a merely 'technological' theory of history, that is, to a theory which makes productive forces the basic explanatory feature. According to these writers, social relations 'correspond' to productive forces not in the sense that they are caused or explained by them, but only in the sense that the technology of a society is one of its most important characteristics, serving as an *indicator* of the social relations prevailing in it.[20]

I think people say things like this not because it is a natural way of reading Marx, but because of an excessively charitable desire to rescue Marx from what seems to them a simplistic and untenable view. Haunted by the specter of 'economic determinism', they of course want to point out that Marx often recognizes the influence of social structure on technological change, and think that this is incompatible with treating productive forces as basic to all materialist explanations. But just as Marx holds that the economic basis of society determines the superstructure without denying that the superstructure may react on or reciprocally influence the basis, so he may recognize within the economic basis itself that social relations may exert influence on social technology even if they are determined by society's productive forces. Here again, it is possible for Marx to hold that one of several interdependent factors is more powerful historically and more basic explanatorily than the others.

It is more than merely possible that Marx holds such views. Whatever the variations in his language, the clear import of the passage quoted earlier from the letter to Annenkov (and of many similar passages in Marx's writings) is that the nature of a society's economic relations depends on the faculties of production it has at its disposal. Besides, it is just not true that Marx never explicitly subscribes to this stronger thesis. *The German Ideology* tells us that 'the aggregate of productive powers accessible to men conditions the state of society'; in *The Poverty of Philosophy*, Marx says that 'a change in men's productive forces necessarily brings about (*amène, herbeiführt*) a change in their relations of production.'[21] It is clear that productive forces for Marx are not merely indicators of social relations, but the fundamental explanation of the forms they take, and of historical changes in those forms.

But there still may be some significance in Marx's typically guarded language about forces and relations of production. For one thing, economic relations are less immediately influenced by productive forces than work relations are. Even more important, productive forces for Marx are only the most prominent factor determining production relations, and not the sole factor. The economic structure of a society depends on the productive forces it possesses, but only against a background which includes the historical circumstances and social forms in which these powers happened to be acquired: 'the conditions in which men find themselves, . . . the social form which exists before them', or, as Engels puts it, 'the remains of earlier economic stages of development which have in fact been handed down and survived, often only through tradition or *vis inertiae*'.[22]

Perhaps, then, there is some truth in the idea that Marx does not hold an exclusively 'technological' theory of history, if the point is that for him productive forces explain social relations only if they are considered in connection with the social and historical circumstances in which they originated. On Marx's theory, given the material and social circumstances of Western Europe at the end of the middle ages, the productive forces of an industrial society could only be acquired and employed through the adoption of capitalist social forms: commodity production, private property in the means of production, the relation of capital to wage labor. In this sense, Marx holds that capitalist production relations in modern Europe were necessitated by these productive forces. But it is *not* Marx's view that these same productive forces inevitably require capitalist institutions for their growth and employment, whatever the historical circumstances. The fact that in the twentieth century a number of countries outside Western Europe have (through the impact of Marx's own ideas) industrialize themselves within socialist economic systems does not constitute any sort of counterexample to Marx's theory. In particular, Marx himself conjectured that a socialist revolution in Russia might well permit it to industrialize its productive forces without having to 'pass through all the disastrous ups and downs of the capitalist system'.[23]

Another reason many have hesitated to call Marx's theory of history 'technological' is the wide range of things Marx includes among society's *Produktivkräfte*. The term embraces, as we have seen, not only tools, raw materials and other physical concomitants of production, but also the knowledge and skills of the men and women who produce. In some passages the catalog of 'productive powers' even seems to include social factors which, on any 'technological' interpretation of Marx, one would have expected him to include among the things to be explained by productive forces. *The Poverty of Philosophy* speaks of 'the revolutionary class itself' as a productive power. *The German Ideology* says: 'A determinate mode of production or industrial stage is always united with a determinate mode of co-operation or social stage, and this mode of co-operation is itself a "productive power" '.[24] On the first of these passages, I agree with Cohen and Shaw that,

72

considered in context, it will not bear the weight which critics of the 'technological' interpretation of Marx want to place on it.[25] The *German Ideology* passage, however, is discussed by neither Cohen nor Shaw, and it seems to me to raise more serious problems for a 'technological' reading of Marx's theory. The inclusion of modes of social co-operation among 'productive powers' is found not only in *The German Ideology*, but also in the *Grundrisse* and even in *Capital*.[26]

On the face of it, these passages seem to threaten Marx's entire project of explaining social forms in terms of productive powers, since they appear simply to identify what is to be explained with part of what is to do the explaining. (The charge that Marx's theory involves at this point a basic confusion, incoherence or explanatory circularity is a common one.) It is understandable, then, that so clear-headed an exegete as Cohen should want to insist that production relations or social forms are under no circumstances to be treated as productive powers. I wonder, however, whether it is really necessary for him to be so stubborn. Marx is presumably tempted to include 'modes of co-operation' among productive powers because they can be seen (in Cohen's words) to 'contribute materially within and to the process of production'.[27] But it might be possible to distinguish between those features of co-operative relationships which are productive powers in this sense and other (logically separable) features which are not, and which could be explained by productive powers (including certain features of the way people co-operate). If Marx's theory is construed along these lines, then we should not expect to be able to draw his crucial distinction between productive powers and production relations apart from a careful consideration of the social and historical context. The resulting theory would be less simple and tidy even than the quite sophisticated versions of the 'technological' interpretation, such as those presented by Cohen and Shaw. In such a theory, care would have to be taken to distinguishing explanatory features of social relations from features which are to be explained by them.

Admittedly, Marx does not devote much explicit attention to these distinctions. But critics who charge him with confusing *explanans* and *explanandum* base their criticisms solely on his programmatic pronouncements, and do not show him guilty of such confusions in the course of his work as an economic historian. If we read Marx in the way I have suggested, his theory could still be called 'technological' in the weak (though possibly also misleading) sense that its aim is to explain production relations or social forms in terms of productive powers.

Marx believes that productive forces determine production relations. His ground for this belief is that a given state of society's productive forces will place constraints on the production relations, demanding or favoring some at the expense of others. But by itself this is not an adequate ground. For it is equally true to say, as Marx himself often does, that production relations also place constraints on productive forces. Large scale machinery and factory labor cannot exist in a society dominated by feudal or guild relations, but can only develop and find employment within the social relation of capital to labor. Societies tend toward a harmony between their productive forces and production relations. But the constraint of productive forces and production relations is mutual, and so by itself cannot be a sufficient ground for Marx's belief that from a broad historical perspective it is always the productive forces which represent the explanation or independent variable, and society's relations of production which must be seen as adapting themselves to its productive faculties. Can this belief be justified?

According to the letter to Annenkov, people are not free to choose the form of society in which they live because that form depends on their productive faculties, and 'it is not necessary to add that men are not free choosers of their productive forces.' People might be able to choose their political institutions, or even their economic ones, to change and adapt these institutions to their will. But it makes no sense to suppose that people might just choose which powers they have over the natural world, or bring about changes in these powers merely by willing it. 'Every productive force is an acquired force, . . . the result of men's practical energy; but this energy itself is circumscribed by the conditions in which they find themselves . . . which they did not create, which is the product of the previous generation.'[28] Production relations too, of course, are 'independent of their will', but only because they are bound up in a relation of mutual constraint with people's productive powers, which by nature lie outside their choice.

Of course people might choose to limit the exercise of their productive powers, to let these powers lie fallow and even to divest themselves of some of their productive faculties. If they did this, they might succeed in preserving or restoring social relations incompatible with more developed production. This Luddite course has even been advocated by Rousseau and others who correctly observe that the productive powers of modern capitalist society are hostile to the ideals of liberty, equality and fraternity, just as they are hostile to the noble ways of life of the simple godfearing peasant and the honest independent artisan. But Marx is convinced that the protests of such moralists have always been ignored by history. 'What matters above all else', he declares, 'is not to be deprived of the fruits of civilization, the acquired forces of production.' Historical progress consists fundamentally in the growth of people's abilities to shape and control the world about them. This is the most basic way in which they develop and express their human essence. It is the definite means by which they may in time gain a measure of freedom, of mastery over their social creations. Social forms, in Marx's view, serve the needs of human history insofar as they are conducive to the consolidation and further expansion of productive powers. But no social form is an end in itself, and none is humanly indispensable. The basic thing in history is the relentless promethean expansion of humanity's creative powers.[29] This is why even communism for Marx is not a 'state of affairs', and 'ideal' social form, but merely a historical 'movement' effecting a transition between the era of class society and the era beyond class society.

4 Productive powers and historical development

Marx's thesis that the production relations of a society are determined by its productive powers admits of two related applications: First, it can explain the economic structure of a given society at a given time. Second, it can explain the changes which economic structures undergo in the course of history. Thus far it has been the first sort of explanation which has absorbed most of our attention. The theory behind such explanations, as it has been expounded here, is based on three main considerations: (1) The efficient employment of a given set of productive powers and forces not only requires a certain material division of labor, but also — under a given set of historical circumstances — places significant constraints on the social and economic relations of individuals both to each other and to the material means of production. (2) The productive forces at the disposal of a given society at a given time tend by and large to be employed efficiently. And (3) since the productive forces of a society represent a relatively stable whole whose nature is not subject to people's voluntary control, they can be treated as the independent variable or determining factor in the essential harmony which obtains between themselves and the social relations with which they are bound up.

By far the most important application of historical materialism for Marx, however, lies not in the first but in the second sort of explanation, the explanation of changes between historical epochs. Marx's classic statement on this point comes from his *Critique of Political Economy*:

> At a certain stage of their development the material productive powers of society come into contradiction with the existing production relations, or, what is just a juristic expression for the same thing, with the property relations within which their movement up to this time has taken place. From forms of development of the productive powers, these relations turn into their fetters. Then enters an epoch of social revolution. . . No social formation ever perishes before all the productive powers which it can hold have developed; and new, higher relations of production never come on the scene until the material conditions for their existence have matured in the womb of the old society itself.[30]

Marx's theory of social change as it is presented in this passage appears to be based on the three considerations mentioned above, together with two further theses: (4) There is a basic tendency for the human productive powers to expand, whether or not this expansion is encouraged by the existing production relations. And (5) no set of production relations (at least in class or pre-class society) is capable of accommodating an indefinite expansion in the powers of production. Given these two further theses, there will thus be an inevitable tendency for any society (at least any class or pre-class society) to expand its powers of production within the prevailing production relations until the latter can accommodate no more, and eventually to expand them even beyond that point. This latter expansion must take place either through a change which has already occurred in society's production relations or else it must tend to undermine outmoded relations, and bring about a change in them. In the latter case, there is no longer that harmony or mutual adaptation between forces and relations of production which efficient material production and social stability require. The two reciprocally dependent factors come into conflict or 'contradiction'. Prevailing social forms, from 'forms of economic development', turn into 'fetters' on human progress.

In the struggle of productive powers with production relations, Marx believes it is always the former which must eventually win out. And this, in addition to consideration (3), is a powerful reason why Marx holds that productive forces determine production relations, and with them the whole structure of social life and consciousness. It is the confining production relations, not the expanding productive forces, which in his view are most likely to receive the backing of the society's 'superstructure', its political institutions, its customary morality, its established ideologies. To win out over the production relations and accommodate these relations to themselves, the expanding productive powers must wage a victorious struggle against these other social forces. The whole of society's devices for insuring peace and stability, law and order, complacency of mind and tranquility of spirit, must be too weak to withstand the power of humanity to rise above itself and attain to new forms of mastery over its world. Marx's philosophy of history is based on the conviction that the human spirit is so indomitable that these social constraints do in fact always prove too weak to withstand its growth.

Marx's theory of social development through the growth of society's productive powers is very well illustrated by his account of the rise of capitalism, presented near the end of volume 1 of *Capital*. By the end of the fifteenth century, feudal production, in its proper medieval form, has largely broken down. It has given way to what Marx calls 'petty industry' (*Kleinbetrieb*), farming and manufacture by individual laborers who privately own the land and means of production they employ. This particular form of social labor, the labor of independent individuals and family units, he says, 'only blooms, only quickens its whole energy and reaches its adequate classical form, where the laborer is the free private owner of the conditions of labor used by his own hands, the peasant of the field he tills, the manual worker of the instrument on which he plays like a virtuoso'.

But once it has developed its potentialities to the full, this system of petty industry (so beloved of petty bourgeois moralists) runs up against certain inherent limitations:

> This mode of production rests on the splitting up of the soil
> and a dispersion of the other means of production. Hence it
> excludes not only the concentration of the means of production
> but also co-operation, the division of labor within a single
> process of production, and thus the social dominion over and
> regulation of nature, along with the free development of the
> social powers of production. It is compatible only with a
> production and a society which are narrowly confined within
> natural limits. To want to eternalize it would be, as Pecqueur
> rightly says, 'to decree universal mediocrity'.[31]

The system of petty industry is not destined for immortality. 'At a certain level it brings into the world the material means of its own annihilation. From that moment new powers and passions arise in the womb of society which feel fettered by it. It must be annihilated; it is annihilated.'

Marx describes in vivid (even lurid) detail how these fetters were broken in England, by the enclosures and the 'forcible driving of the agricultural population from the land into the cities'; by the Protestant 'spoliation of church property' and destruction of the monastic way of life; by the acquisition of new agricultural techniques which permitted greater co-operation and concentration of agricultural labor and a larger ratio of wool-producing pasture to arable land; by advances in manufacturing technology, and by the shameless brigandage of colonialism, through which Europeans achieved the concentration of wealth necessary to put this technology into practice; until 'individualized and dissipated means of production [were transformed] into socially concentrated ones, the dwarf property of the many into the massive property of a few, the great mass of the people [expropriated] from the ground and the soil, from the means of life and the instruments of labor'.[32] The transformation, as Marx depicts it, is not pretty; but on his theory, it is necessary. And although terrible, it is also (to Marx at least) inspiring. For it is the victory of new and higher human powers of production over limited social relations which can no longer contain them.

It is noteworthy that in Marx's account the social changes constituting the transition from feudalism and petty industry to capitalism precede in time most of the changes in productive technique characteristic of mature capitalism. This, however, cannot be used as evidence that Marx does not explain changes in social relations by changes in productive forces. For Marx is quite explicit that it is the development of the 'material means of production' and the accompanying 'powers and passions in the womb of society' which determines the 'annihilation' of petty industry and the rise of capitalism. What it means, rather, is that in the rise of capitalism, the changes which are determined or explained largely precede in time the emergence of the productive forces which determine or explain them. This suggests either that Marx believes effects can temporally precede their causes or else that the explanations Marx employs in accounting for the rise of capitalist social relations from the growth of society's productive powers are not *causal* explanations. In Chapter VII I will argue that the latter suggestion is the correct one.[33]

Marx never says explicitly why he thinks the struggle of material progress with social tradition must always end with the victory of the former. No doubt he thinks so in part because the rise of capitalism has been one long, grisly fable acting out that argument. But we may also guess at some more general reasons which may have influenced him. As we saw earlier, Marx holds that human fulfillment consists principally in the development and exercise of people's characteristically human capacities or 'human essential powers'. Accordingly, Marx is convinced that the basic function of any set of social relations is to make possible the efficient employment of the productive forces at the disposal of society, that is, to facilitate the development and exercise of humanity's essential powers. He regards all attempts to justify social institutions in other ways, by religious, moral or philosophical considerations, as mere ideological superstition. But Marx is also persuaded that human beings are, fundamentally and for the most part, rational. Given time and opportunity, the human race collectively will tend to do what it has most reason to do, even where people consciously act from other motives. Hence there is a tendency for people to exercise and expand their faculties, and to adjust their social relations accordingly. It is this tendency, the Marxian version of Hegel's *List der Vernunft*, which makes human history fundamentally intelligible:

> Because of the simple fact that every later generation finds
> the productive forces acquired by the previous generation,
> which serve it as the prime matter for new production, there
> forms a coherence in the history of men, there forms a history
> of humanity which is all the more a history of humanity insofar
> as the productive forces of men, and in consequence their
> social relations have grown. The necessary conclusion of this
> is that the social history of men is never anything but the
> history of their individual development, whether they are
> conscious of it or not.[34]

But why does Marx believe that social forms must always eventually offer resistance to human progress? Why couldn't capitalism, for instance, open-minded as it is, ever restless and eager for what is new, always ready to submit any dispute to the frank and free arbitration of the market place, serve as a social receptacle for endless material progress? In *Capital*, Marx tries to show in some detail how capitalist relations will inevitably constrain the development of productive forces, how they are already beginning to do so. More generally, however, Marx regards the *class* character of capitalist society as setting determinate limits on the extent to which expanded productive powers can be turned into expanded opportunities for the free development or self-actualization of human beings. In any class society, material progress is monopolized by the ruling classes, while material progress creates an objective need for emancipation on the part of the oppressed classes. Such tendencies, if carried far enough, must lead to fundamental changes in class relations or else to the complete abolition of class society itself.

Marx often writes as if he believes that the scenario he describes in the *Critique* — inevitable growth of productive forces to the maximum compatible with existing social forms, conflict between productive forces and production relations, victory of productive forces and social revolution — must be the chief explanatory pattern of historical development in any society, whatever its circumstances or its level of material culture. But it would be implausible as well as uncharitable to ascribe such a belief to him.[35] The general considerations behind Marx's theory of social change point only to an inevitable tendency for social relations to adjust themselves continually to this expansion. But they say nothing about the rate at which the productive powers of society must grow: it is quite compatible with Marx's theory — and indeed a point often insisted upon by him — that the growth of productive forces may under certain social forms be imperceptible, almost non-existent, over long centuries, because these social forms are particularly effective at retarding this growth; while other social forms (such as capitalist ones) promote a very rapid rate of growth in society's productive powers, and consequently render themselves obsolete in a much shorter time.[36] Such irregular patterns of economic growth, to which Marx gives particular emphasis, have sometimes been cited by his critics as contradicting his thesis that production relations are determined by productive forces. The contradiction is illusory. To say that production relations may affect the rate at which productive forces expand is in no way to deny either that this expansion itself is the basic tendency in human history or that any given set of production relations itself exists only because, and for as long as, it can accommodate the growth of productive forces which is taking place within it.

A second point: inevitable tendencies do not inevitably prevail. They may be counteracted by other tendencies or even by extraneous accidental circumstances. Thus to say that the expansion of productive powers is a basic, inevitable tendency in human history is not incompatible with recognizing that in some cases societies have lost ground in regard to their productive capabilities, owing (say) to natural catastrophes, foreign invasions or to a particularly disastrous turn in their internal class struggles (what Marx and Engels presumably have in mind when they speak of 'the common downfall of the contending classes').[37]

Marx does believe that his scenario describes accurately both the victory of capitalist social relations over feudal ones and the eventual defeat of capitalist society by socialism. He does regard both victories as historically inevitable. This is because in these cases he sees no contrary tendencies or disruptive circumstances standing in the way of the basic historical tendencies from which his scenario naturally follows. Marx's belief in the historical inevitability of certain social changes, whether or not it is correct, is based on his assessment of the whole range of empirical circumstances which he views as affecting the outcome in the particular case. It is never, as many of his critics would have us believe, simply a matter of dogmatic guesswork inspired by a priori speculative doctrines.

VI

Classes

---

1 *Social relations, property relations*

A famous passage from Marx's *Critique of Political Economy* tells us:

> In the social production of their life, men enter into determinate relations, necessary and independent of their will, production relations which correspond to a determinate stage of development of their productive powers. The totality of these production relations forms the economic structure of society, the real basis on which a juristic and political super-structure arises, and to which determinate forms of social consciousness correspond.[1]

We have seen that Marx distinguishes between the social division of labor or system of work relations, and the 'form of inter-course', the system of social or economic relations (such as those between capitalist and laborer, landlord and tenant, guild master and journeyman). In the above passage, it is evident that it is social or economic relations, constituting the 'economic structure of society' which he considers to be the 'real basis' of society, and which play the primary role in determining society's legal, political and ideological 'superstructure'. Thus although Marx holds that the productive forces and the system of direct work relations constitute the 'basis of social organization', it is the system of social relations which count in his theory as the *'economic* basis' from which other social phenomena are to be understood.[2]

But what does Marx mean by 'production relations' in this connection? How does he conceive of the general sort of relationship of which lord/serf, and capitalist/wage-laborer are examples?

It is obvious that for Marx production relations are bound up with the relationship of human beings to land, tools and other conditions of production. Marx often suggests that production relations are closely associated with ownership or property. *The German Ideology*, for instance, says that 'the different stages of development of the division of labor are only so many different forms of property, i.e. each stage of the division of labor also determines the relations of individuals to one another in reference to the materials, instruments and products of labor.'[3] Here the point seems to be that work relations ('the division of labor') are the foundation of society's economic structure, and this structure is to be identified with the prevailing 'form of property'. Yet in the *Critique* Marx describes 'property relations' as 'the legal expression' of production relations, implying that property relations belong to the 'superstructure' erected on the 'real basis' of production relations.[4] Marxists usually follow the *Critique* at this point, distinguishing production relations from the property relations which 'express' them. But some critics either do not think Marx's analyses involve such a distinction, or else deny that the distinction is a tenable one. Ralf Dahrendorf insists that Marx's 'analyses are essentially based on the narrow, legal concept of property', and regards them as faulty for this reason. John Plamenatz, on the other hand, argues that it is futile to distinguish property relations from production relations in the way the *Critique* tries to do, since

> it is quite impossible to define production relations except in terms of the claims which men make on one another and recognize — except in terms of admitted rights and obligations. Where there are such rights and obligations, there are accepted rules of conduct, rules which require and forbid and are supported by sanctions, there are, in the broad sense of the word, laws.[5]

First, let us be clear that Dahrendorf is dead wrong. We saw in Chapter III that 'appropriation' for Marx is more basic than any system of property rights, which are only the 'juristic form' which may be assumed by social production relations. Marx distinguishes often enough between 'legal property' (or 'property *de jure*') and 'actual property' (or 'property *de facto*') to make it evident to anyone familiar with his writings that he does not hold the position Dahrendorf attributes to him. The distinction is especially clear in the following passage from *Capital*:

> Landed property presupposes the monopoly of certain persons over determinate portions of the earth, as exclusive spheres

83

of their private will to the exclusion of all others. . . . [But] nothing is settled by the juristic power of these persons to use and misuse portions of the terrestrial globe. For the use of this power depends wholly on economic conditions, which are independent of their will.[6]

Here it is evident that Marx treats landed property as amounting to the effective control over land held by some persons to the exclusion of others. He regards this control as a function of 'economic conditions', of the social relations in which the owners stand to other people and to the land as a factor in production. Legal ownership, with its attendant 'juristic powers' is distinct from property, and derives its content from the social relations it expresses. For Marx, social relations are not to be understood in terms of property relations (much less in terms of legal ownership, or property rights). On the contrary (legal or moral) property relations are to be understood in terms of social ones: 'To define bourgeois property is only to provide an exposition all the social relations of bourgeois production.' Conversely, 'every social relation can be presented as an example of the property relation.'[7]

But Plamenatz's worry remains. *Can* Marx conceive social relations independently of the legal or juridical ones which are supposed to express them? Or must Marx define social relations in terms of 'rights and obligations', in terms of 'laws, in the broad sense of the word'?

Marx does not spell out clearly his key notion of 'social production relations'. Nor does he 'define' bourgeois property (or any other sort) in the manner suggested by the remarks just quoted. But I think the general nature of his theory indicates how Marx would respond to Plamenatz's criticism. 'Society', Marx says, 'consists not of individuals but expresses the sum of relations in which these individuals stand to one another.'[8] Society is a structure, made up of roles or positions which differ determinately in the kind and degree of control their occupants have over the process of social production, the kinds of claims they have on social labor or its fruits, and the kinds of claims other members of society have on them.[9] We can illustrate this by Engels's description of the difference between serfs and proletarians:

The serf has the use of a piece of land, that is, of an instrument of production, in return for handing over a greater or lesser portion of the yield. The proletarian works with instruments of production which belong to someone else who, in return for his labor, hands over to him a portion, determined by competition, of the products. In the case of the serf, the share of the laborer is determined by his own labor, that is, by himself. In the case of the proletarian it is determined by competition.[10]

Serfs and proletarians have similar roles in production, in that both use means of production which are owned by (that is, under the effective social control of) someone else, someone who occupies a different role in the social system. For this reason, both serf and proletarian are in a position to appropriate only a certain portion of what they produce. The two roles are distinguished by the *form* taken by their occupants' shares of the product, and the *manner* in which the amount of that share is determined.

Marx obviously thinks that a given system of social roles or positions is relatively stable over time, and definable independently of the particular individuals who happen to occupy them, or the accidental manner in which these individuals may choose to exercise the powers pertaining to their roles. But he also seems to believe that the system of social relations is definable in abstraction from the kinds of motives and sanctions which insure that the occupants of social roles will meet the requirements imposed on them by the system. We might think, for instance, that a landlord can charge his tenant rent *because* he owns the land the tenant is using. His ownership of the land and the rights and moral or legal sanctions by which we might define this ownership *explains* why he has the claim on the tenant he does, and why the tenant is required to comply with this claim. Probably it is this picture which motivates Plamenatz's idea that Marx cannot define social or economic relations without referring to rights, obligations and (in the broad sense) laws.

According to Marx, however, the truth is just the reverse. 'Ground rent is only the form in which property in land is economically realized, turned into value.'[11] Landed property *consists* (at least partly) in the fact that one person (the proprietor or landlord) can charge another for using it. If we ask why the landlord or tenant stand in such a relation, Marx's answer will be an account of how the landlord/tenant relation fits into the economic structure of society, and how that structure serves to facilitate the employment of society's productive powers. Marx regards the explanation of rent in terms of property rights and sanctions as superficial, since it does not make intelligible why the sanctions should exist, why anyone should be in a position to claim the rights they enforce. Even naked force, if it is to play any determinate role in the social system, must conform itself to the economic conditions under which it is exercised: 'The form of community assumed by settling conquerors must correspond to the stage of development of the productive powers they find, or else . . . alter in accordance with the productive powers.'[12]

On the other hand, if we treat social relations as distinct from moral, legal or other sanctions, and regard the latter as 'created in the first place by production relations', we can explain such things as property rights and the moral ideologies and legal mechanisms which sanction them.[13] For we can view these rights and sanctions as ways in which a society makes efficient use of its productive powers. It does not matter to the *definition* of the social relation between landlord and tenant whether the tenant's compliance with the landlord's claim on rent is elicited by appealing to the motive of duty or must be compelled at the point of a gun. Of course, it is a fact that some conceivable ways of securing the tenant's compliance will not be employed because they are ineffective, unreliable or unnecessarily costly. Such facts help us to explain the special nature of the legal and moral institutions which belong to a society, by showing their relative effectiveness as sanctions for the particular system of social relations. Recall Marx's theory holds that a society will tend to adopt the system of social relations which best facilitates the employment and development of its productive powers. By the same token, the theory holds that a society will tend to adopt the political institutions, legal forms and moral or religious ideologies which most effectively sanction its system of social relations. This is just what Marx means when he calls (legal) property relations the 'legal expression' of social relations of production, and when he speaks of the system of production relations as the 'economic basis' of a juridical, political and ideological 'superstructure'.

The Marxian reply to Plamenatz should now be plain. The definitions of social relations cannot dispense with 'obligations, rights and laws in the broad sense' if these terms refer to the actual requirements and claims which distinguish and relate the roles constituting a given society. But Marx would consider 'obligations' and 'rights' in this sense as part of the 'economic basis' of society, and not as part of its 'superstructure'. On the other hand, the definitions of social roles and relations must not mention rights, obligations and laws insofar as the latter imply specific motives or sanctions through which the claims and requirements of social roles become effective. They *can* avoid mentioning them, because the system of claims and requirements which define social relations is logically independent of the particular sanctions which give these claims and requirements their force. And they *must* avoid mentioning them if the legal forms are to be explained on the basis of the social relations they sanction.

Although the criticisms of Marx advanced by Dahrendorf and Plamenatz are mistaken, they do point to some serious unclarities in Marx's exposition of historical materialism. Just as Marx does not always distinguish clearly between social production relations and material work relations, so he does not always distinguish clearly between social relations and property relations, understood in terms of moral or legal rights. Plamenatz is correct when he says that 'except when they are defining them, Marx and Engels nearly always speak of relations of production as if they were the same as property relations.'[14] And Dahrendorf's misinterpretation of Marx is rendered plausible by the fact that Marx never actually defines bourgeois property relations in terms of social relations of bourgeois production. Instead, Marx nearly always relies for his notion of bourgeois social relations on a common conception of bourgeois property relations which he could take for granted. This does not show that his theory itself is confused or untenable, but it does indicate how much more would need to be done to state it in a really rigorous manner.

2 History and social classes

Marx's theory holds that social relations are revolutionized when they no longer correspond to society's productive forces, or when they become fetters on the development of these forces. Yet it also holds that history is made by human beings themselves. Productive forces do not make revolutions; people make revolutions when historical circumstances provide them with the motives and opportunities for doing so.

Marx's theory holds that history is made by human individuals, acting from a wide variety of different conscious motives. But it also holds that history is not to be understood in terms of the motives and acts of particular individuals. Perhaps the best way to get at the Marxian view here is to look at a passage from Engels' *Ludwig Feuerbach*.

> Men make their history, however it may turn out, in that each
> pursues his own consciously willed ends, and history is just
> the resultant of these many wills acting in various directions
> and their manifold influence on the external world. Thus it
> all depends on what the many individuals will.

The Marxian theory does not deny that history is the cumulative result of actions of human individuals. Nor does it deny that these actions are usually performed from the motives the agents might cite to explain their own behavior: 'The will', says Engels, 'is determined by passion or deliberation', which is in turn determined by motives of various kinds, by 'external objects', 'ideal motives, ambition, "enthusiasm for truth and justice"', personal hatred or even purely individual crotchets of all kinds'. Marx, unlike Freud, does not hold that our actions are often motivated by subterranean psychic compulsions of which we are ignorant, or which we systematically hide from ourselves. In particular, Marx's theory does *not* say that when I think I am being moved by 'enthusiasm for truth and justice' I am really moved instead by my own economic interests.

Although history is the cumulative result of the actions of individuals, the conscious motives of these actions do not provide us with good explanations of historical change. Engels gives two reasons for this: First, individuals often fail to achieve what they will; their motives explain only what they will, while history is the cumulative result of what they actually accomplish: 'Most of the individual wills active in history produce results different from what they willed — often exactly the opposite. Hence for the total outcome their motives are only of secondary significance.' Second, individual motives are too multifarious and accidental to explain historical change, which results from the sustained action of great masses of people over long periods of time. Consequently, Engels argues, our theory must seek out what he calls (I think misleadingly) the 'driving powers' or 'driving forces' of history which, while perhaps not prominent in the conscious motivation of very many individuals, do account for the systematic results of their actions:

> When it is a matter of investigating the driving powers which —
> consciously or unconsciously, but very frequently un-
> consciously — stand behind the motives of men acting in
> history, . . . it cannot be so much a question of the motives
> of individuals, however prominent, as of motives which set in
> motion great masses . . . ; and this too not momentarily for the
> transient flaring up of a strawfire which quickly dies out, but
> for lasting action which flows into a great historical alteration.[15]

When Engels says that people are largely unconscious of the 'driving forces' of history, he does not mean that they are unaware of (or have false beliefs about) what motivates them individually. (This is why it is so easy to be misled by his talk of 'levers' or 'driving forces' which 'stand behind' people's conscious motives.) What he means is that people usually do not understand the social and historical significance of their motives and actions: they do not understand the way their motives and action function in the social system or contribute to large scale historical trends. They do not understand, for instance, that the religious enthusiasm in which they participate is socially available to them chiefly because it sanctions the secular status quo; they do not see how their highminded defense of individual freedom serves the social purpose of keeping most of society in chains. Of course, if they did come to understand, there would probably be changes in both their motives and their actions. Marx's theory aims at effecting such changes in anyone who is sufficiently free of class prejudice to be open to them. To acquire knowledge about the social meaning of one's motives is not to learn anything new about one's psychological makeup. But it is in an important sense to acquire self-knowledge. For it is to learn something important about oneself as a social and historical creature.

Individual motives are of secondary importance in understanding the movement of history because large scale social changes result only from the systematic and (consciously or unconsciously) co-ordinated behavior of large groups of people, of 'peoples', 'masses', above all of social *classes*.

What are classes? Unfortunately, Marx never completed the chapter of *Capital* devoted to this question. He is clearer in rejecting certain answers to it than he is about his positive account. Marx rejects the theory that classes are distinguished merely by wealth and poverty or property and propertylessness. 'The size of one's purse', he says, is 'a merely quantitative distinction', while the 'antithesis of property and propertylessness' is by itself merely an 'indifferent antithesis' not grasped in its 'active connection' or 'internal relation'.[16] Marx also rejects a definition of classes in terms of their sources of revenue:

> At first glance, the sameness of revenue and sources of revenue.
> There are three great social groups . . . who live respectively
> on the value from their labor, capital and landed property.
> But from this standpoint, physicians and officials, for instance,
> would also form two classes, for they belong to two social
> groups, with the revenues of each one's members flowing from
> the same source. The same would hold for the infinite frag-
> mentation of interests and positions into which the division of
> social labor splits laborers, capitalists and landowners — the
> latter, for example, into owners of vineyards, farms, forests,
> mines, fisheries. . . .[17]

The problem here seems to be that 'source of revenue' is too loose a notion. What Marx wants to do is to classify revenue sources in such a way that they identify the 'great social groups' on whose interaction the course of history depends. But such a classification must be based on something more than the notion 'source of revenue'.

Eric Hobsbawm suggests that 'classes are merely special cases of social relations of production'.[18] I think this is true, if it means that Marx conceives of production relations as dividing people into the economic roles out of which social classes emerge. But production relations, as defined by the various kinds of claims people may have on others and which others may have on them, might in principle be used to categorize people in all sorts of ways. The problem is to discover which ways of categorizing them enable us to identify the groups which are crucial for the understanding of large scale social change.

Marx says that classes 'arise out of' production relations because the latter create 'masses with a common situation, common interests'.[19] He conceives of the dynamics of social change in terms of the struggle of opposed class interests. It is these interests which are (to use Engels' misleading language) the 'levers' or 'driving forces' behind large scale social changes. Hence in looking for the social relations from which classes arise, we should attend especially to those relations which systematically set people's interests in opposition. Marx was well aware, however, of systematic divergences of interest between segments of the same class (between skilled and unskilled laborers or between industrial and finance capitalists). His analyses of actual historical events (such as those in France between 1848 and 1851) often turn as much on the struggle between parts of the same class as on struggles between different classes. Marx's reason for distinguishing wage laborers, capitalists and landowners as the three basic and most prominent classes in modern society seems to be that he regards the conflicts of interest between these social groupings as fundamentally more historically important than conflicts within them, or conflicts between them and less potent classes (such as the peasantry and the petty bourgeoisie).

Once we grant to Marx the very substantial thesis that the constitution of a society's noneconomic institutions and the course of its history are determined by the struggle of social groups with opposed economic interests, there is a certain triviality in the further claim that politics, ideology and historical change are the result of a struggle between *classes*. For Marx gives us no way of identifying these classes independently of judgments about which production relations and social groupings will prove socially and historically decisive.

We might think that Marx's identification of the basic social classes could be derived from another source: from the fact that in any given society there are certain dominant social forms or production relations, certain characteristic patterns of effective control over the means of production and characteristic ways of bringing human labor together with these means.[20] *Classes* would be the groups specified by the terms of these dominant relations. But this suggestion will not work. To begin with, it does not account for classes not involved in the dominant relations (classes defined by relations pertaining to relations left over from a previous era, for instance). Besides, what is meant here by 'dominant'? We might suppose that it is merely a quantitative matter: certain production relations 'dominate' in the sense that they account for the greater part of society's total product or involve the majority of social laborers. But this is clearly not Marx's view. He recognizes the parcel peasants as the most numerous class in French society, but sees this class as having real historical significance only insofar as it is content to follow the lead of the (less numerous but historically more potent) proletariat.

Further, Marx says:

> In all forms of society there is one determinate kind of production which assigns ranks and influence to all the others, and whose relations assign rank and influence to all other relations. It is the general light which dyes all the other colors and modifies their particularity. It is the particular aether which determines the specific gravity of every existence which emerges from it.[21]

Whatever this means, it does not treat the 'dominance' of a production relation merely as a matter of the proportion of laborers or social product involved in it. I suggest that Marx regards a relation as dominant when the social dynamics engendered by it are decisive in explaining the superstructural institutions of the society and its basic tendencies for historical development. Marx treats the relation of capital and wage labor as dominant in bourgeois society because he believes that by focusing on this relation he can 'unveil the economic law of motion of modern society'.[22] I conclude that his analysis of the class structure of a society cannot be separated from his judgment about its underlying dynamics. We can justify such an analysis only in terms of its usefulness in explaining the society's superstructural institutions and historical movement.

3 *Class interests*

Individuals form a class because they have 'common interests'. They have common interests because they share a 'common situation'. In view of this, it may be natural to suppose that 'class interests' for Marx are simply the interests of a class's individual members, which happen to coincide because of the similarity of their life-situations. But this is an oversimplification. For one thing, the interests of the members of a given class do not coincide in every respect. Members of the same class are often in economic competition with one another. And a turn of events which affects the interests of most members of a class in one way may accidentally have just the opposite effect on the interests of some of its members. Further, Marx would probably not want to say that some state of affairs is in the class interests of a certain class just because it happened accidentally to benefit only (or even all) members of that class. He would only want to say this if the state of affairs involved some mechanism (whether open or hidden) which systematically preferred the interests of the members of that class to the interests of others.

But there is a still deeper problem with any attempt to understand Marxian class interests simply as a function of the interests of the class's individual members. It is that so long as people are united only by shared interests based on a common situation, they do not yet properly constitute a 'class' in Marx's sense. Individuals who share a common situation and common interests are at most a class potentially, unconsciously or 'in itself'; they are not yet a class actually, consciously or 'for itself'. Of the French parcel peasants, Marx says:

> Insofar as millions of families live under economic conditions
> of existence which separate their mode of life, their interests
> and their culture (*Bildung*) from those of other classes and
> put them over against these others in hostile relation, they
> form a class. But insofar as there subsists only a local connec-
> tion between the parcel peasants, so that the sameness of their
> interests begets no community of interests, no natural combina-
> tion and no political organization among them, they do not
> form a class. They are thus incapable of making their class
> interests valid in their own name, whether through a parliament
> or convention.[23]

Marx's point here is not only that the peasants are unable to promote their shared interests politically, but also that since there is no 'combination or political organization' among the peasants, there is no 'community of interests' among them, and hence no genuine *class* interests in the fullest sense.

Classes, as Marx conceives of them, are not simply *given* along with a system of production relations. Classes 'arise' or 'develop' out of such a system when the shared interests of people in a common situation engender characteristic political movements and class ideologies promoting these interests. 'Only then do the interests they defend become class interests.'[24] 'Separate individuals form a class only insofar as they have to carry on a common struggle against another class.'[25] This 'carrying on of a common struggle' implies some sort of organized movement with goals over and above the individual interests which gave rise to the movement. These goals then 'develop in spite of the persons into common interests, standing independently over against the individual persons, and in this independence assuming the form of *general* interests'.[26] One of the functions of class ideologies, as Marx conceives of them, is to instill in its individual members a commitment to these 'general' interests:

> On the different forms of property, on the social conditions
> of existence, here arises a whole superstructure of different
> and characteristic feelings, illusions, modes of thinking and
> views of life. The whole class creates and shapes them from
> its material foundations and out of the corresponding social
> relations. The single individual, to whom they flow through
> tradition and education, can imagine that they are the real
> motives and starting point for his action.[27]

Marx of course does not think that in order to be a class 'for itself' a social group must recognize its general interests and organization as those of a 'class'. Until the work of historians such as Saint-Simon, Thierry and Guizot, the notion of social classes did not even belong to people's conceptual vocabulary. And (as the above quotation makes clear) Marx believes that people usually fail to see class movements and ideologies for what they are even when the ideologies constitute (from a social point of view) the real explanation (or 'starting point') for their own actions. This means that the connection between a class and the organized movement which makes it a class may often not be self-evident. It may need to be established by a sophisticated theoretical analysis of the long-term historical interests of the group, and what the movement actually does in relation to these interests.

Marx has a great deal to say about the class affiliation of particular movements and ideologies, and especially about those which pretend to represent the proletariat without really doing so. But he has very little to say in general about the conditions under which a social movement can be said to represent a given class. He is quite explicit, however, that the movement need not be composed chiefly of people belonging to the class. Speaking of petty bourgeois democracy, Marx says:

> One must not make the narrow minded assumption that the petty bourgeoisie wills to promote in principle an egoistic class interest. Rather, it believes that the *particular* conditions of its emancipation are *universal* conditions within which alone modern society can be saved and the class struggle denied.
> Just as little must one assume that its democratic representatives are all shopkeepers or their enthusiasts. According to their education and individual situation they may be heavens apart. What makes them representatives of the petty bourgeoisie is that in their heads they have not gotten beyond the limits which the latter haven't gotten beyond in life, that they are driven theoretically to the same tasks and solutions that the latter are driven to practically by their material interests and social situation. This is in general the relation of the *political* and *literary* representatives to the class they represent.[28]

A movement counts as the representative of the class not because of who belongs to it, or because of its professed goals, but because in its actual behavior it systematically promotes the historical interests of the class. On the other hand, the political movement has a life of its own, and pursues goals which cannot be directly identified with the interests or conscious aims of particular individuals. As Marx puts it:

> It is not a question of what this or that proletarian or even the whole proletariat *represents* to itself as its goal at a given time. It is a question of *what* the proletariat *is*, and what it is compelled to do historically by this *being*. Its goal and historical action are sensibly, irrevocably prescribed (*vorgezeichnet*) by its own life-situation.[29]

As we shall see in the next section, the basic goal or 'historic mission' of a given class is to establish and defend a certain set of production relations. It is goals of this sort which count for Marx as 'general class interests' and it is only by having an organization which promotes such interests that a class can be said to be actual or 'for itself'.

Marx thinks there is a tendency for certain social groups with a common situation and shared interests to develop into actual classes, with representative social movements and general interests. He also believes that class interests, and especially the general interests, tend to get themselves satisfied as far as historical conditions permit. He regards these tendencies as fundamentally important for the understanding of the historical dynamics of society. General class interests, however, can often oppose the individual interests of particular members of the class, and call for self-sacrifice on the part of individuals. The historical potency Marx ascribes to general class interests thus presupposes not only that people tend to organize to promote the individual interests they share, but also that they sometimes tend to sacrifice these interests for the sake of the organizations they create and for the sake of the ideal values which serve to unify and strengthen these organizations. This means that Marx's historical materialism is *incompatible* with any simple form of psychological egoism. Instead, it presupposes that people act from a combination of egoistic, altruistic and ideal motives whose nature depends largely on the kind of society in which they live and the kinds of social ties they have. Marx makes this quite explicit: 'Communists know very well that under determinate relations egoism as well as self-sacrifice is a necessary form of the successful interaction of individuals. . . . [Both egoism and unselfishness] are sides of the personal development of individuals, equally generated by the empirical conditions of life.'[30] Marx's recognition that people's actions are motivated by ideal and altruistic considerations as well as egoistic ones makes his theory in this respect much more a reflection of ordinary common sense than is often supposed. Where Marx departs from the humdrum is in his belief that the historically efficacious motives are those which serve to promote general class interests.

Marx's attitude toward individual self-sacrifice for the sake of general class interests is not a simple one. Unsurprisingly, he views it as noble and morally praiseworthy. Marx lauds the 'self-sacrificing heroism' of the Paris communards of 1871 and scorns the decadence of the French bourgeoisie of 1848, 'which every moment sacrificed its general class interests, that is, its political interests, to the narrowest and filthiest private interests'.[31] But Marx also regards the sacrifice of individual interests to general class interests as an aspect of alienation: 'As personal interests come to be independent as class interests, the personal conduct of the individual comes to be reified, alienated, thus becomes a power independent of him and without him, produced by intercourse.'[32] He does so, I think, because he views class ideologies generally as living on the illusion that they represent universal human interests.[33] This illusion is alienating in that it amounts to the rule over human beings of social relations which they have created but do not understand or control. Thus it stands in the way of free, fully self-conscious human activity.

There is no contradiction between Marx's admiration for self-sacrifice and his belief that the sacrifice of individual interests to general class interests involves ideological illusions. Once we realize that human history has unavoidably been characterized by systematic illusions of various kinds, there ceases to be any good grounds to think badly of any particular social phenomenon because it has been caught up in them. We need think no less of loyalty, devotion and self-sacrifice merely because they have often been practiced under the influence of class illusions. (If we do think less of them on this account, that is probably because we suppose they might have been put in the service of worthier goals than the promotion of class interests. But as Marx sees it, this supposition is just a symptom of our own subjection to some such illusion.) But Marx does not believe that illusions are necessary for self-sacrifice, since he does not fear that exposing them will undermine the revolutionary heroism of the proletariat.

Some people question the propriety of ascribing interests to anything but individual human beings, and in particular the propriety of ascribing them to groups (unless this is an indirect or shorthand way of referring to the interests of individuals). I must say that I do not see the difficulty. The concept of something's interests, it seems to me, is closely connected to several other concepts: what benefits it, what is good for it, what makes it well off. Something can be said to have interests if these other things can be said of it. And these things can, I submit, be said of classes quite directly and without metaphor. They may be said of classes not only because they may be said of the individual members of classes, but even more because they may be said of the political movements which (on Marx's theory) make classes actual. Roughly speaking, what is good for such a movement is the strength to achieve its ends; something benefits a movement when it contributes to this strength or aids it in the pursuit of its goals. The goals of a class movement, as we have already seen, are not to be identified with what any particular members of the class, or even the class as a whole, visualizes as its goals at any given point in history. They are instead to be identified with the class's 'historical mission', the historical potentialities which the class movement over time brings to actuality. We can speak of general class interests, therefore, simply because there is in fact a powerful tendency for definite class movements to produce definite historical results. Perhaps the real objection to the notion of general interests is that rugged individualists think people ought not to lend their strength to movements with such autonomous ends. But for Marx it is a significant fact that history never heeds the advice of these individualists.

4 *Class struggles*

The history of all previous society is the history of class struggles. Free man and slave, patrician and plebeian, lord and serf, guild master and journeyman, in short, oppressor and oppressed, stood in constant opposition to each other, and carried on an uninterrupted, now hidden and now open struggle.[34]

Why must society be torn by class antagonisms? In some passages, Marx and Engels appear to argue that class struggles are an inevitable feature of any society whose productive powers fall within a given range.[35] Very primitive societies are classless because their labor tends to be undifferentiated and because all members of society must work full time just to procure their basic subsistence. Classes at this stage do not exist because there does not exist the productive surplus which makes possible the existence of a non-laboring (oppressing) class. Society will once again be classless when its productive powers have grown far enough that everyone can enjoy a substantial degree of free, self-actualizing activity. In between, the scarcity of the fruits of human progress requires that their enjoyment should be the privilege of certain classes, while others (the majority) must remain slaves to society's limited powers of production.

But these considerations do not adequately explain the historical prevalence ascribed by Marx's theory to class antagonisms. For there is still no reason why some set of productive forces in the long intermediate phase of history might not yield a set of production relations which determines people to share equally in the limited achievements of economic progress. Engels attempts to supplement this basic account with the idea that at an early stage the administrative needs of society required a distinct, non-laboring class to attend to them.[36] But this does not explain why the administrators must always oppress and subjugate the productive majority. It also fails to explain the fact that oppressing classes often do not consist wholly (or even chiefly) of people who in fact fulfill an administrative function relative to production.

G.A. Cohen claims to find in Marx an argument to the effect

97

that class oppression is necessary to coerce laborers to raise production to the level where its collective, democratic control (socialism or communism) is possible.[37] I think he is correct as far as Marx's account of the history of modern Western Europe is concerned. But Marx does not hold in general that class oppression is always necessary for the acquisition of the productive forces of modern industrial society. He asserts (as we saw earlier) that Russia might well be able to industrialize under socialism.[38] Marx's own most general account of the historical necessity of classes explains this necessity in terms of the recognizably Hegelian postulate that dialectical progress can come about only through struggle and contradiction: 'Without antagonism, no progress: that is the law which civilization has followed until today. Until now the productive forces have developed on the basis of this dominance of class antagonism.'[39] But Marx does not say anything to justify either this metaphysical postulate or his application of it to history.

I think Marx's belief in the universality of class antagonism is motivated chiefly by his conviction that class conflict is vital to explaining the dynamics of modern European society, and his hope (built on this alleged theoretical success) that it may provide a similar explanatory key in a wide range of other cases. 'The class struggle', says Marx, 'is the proximate driving power of history, and especially the class struggle between bourgeoisie and proletariat as the great lever of modern social revolution.'[40]

In Chapter V, we saw that the materialist conception of history explains alterations in production relations through the tendency of productive powers to grow and the tendency of production relations to adjust to these powers. Class struggles are the chief mechanism through which these adjustments are effected. The social relations in a class society serve the interests of some people at the expense of others. The privileged seek ways of maintaining the relations which favor them, while the disadvantaged, who feel chafed, confined and oppressed by these relations, look for ways to modify or overthrow them.

The relation of oppressor and oppressed is, of course, not the only form class antagonisms can take. But Marx focuses on relations involving oppression because he regards them as especially important for understanding social dynamics. It is the nature of oppression that the life style of oppressors can be sustained only through a virtually total sacrifice of the interests of the oppressed. The existence of an oppressed class, especially when it becomes politically organized, compels the prevailing production relations constantly to prove their suitability as vehicles for the exercise and development of society's production. The advantage of the oppressing class, in Marx's view, derives ultimately from the fact that the production relations through which it dominates correspond to the existing stage of society's productive powers: The oppression of labor by capital, according to Marx, 'by no means arises from the political rule of the bourgeois class, but vice versa, the political rule of the bourgeois class arises from the modern relations of production'. As long as production relations correspond to these powers, class movements in behalf of the oppressed will not be victorious. Or if they are, their attempt to create a new set of production relations will be premature and their triumph will be short-lived. 'If the proletariat overthrows the political rule of the bourgeoisie, its victory will only be temporary, . . . as long as the material conditions have not yet been created which make necessary the abolition of the bourgeois mode of production.'[41] When society's productive powers have developed to the point where the existing production relations have become 'fetters' on them, then the basic tendencies of history will be on the side of the revolutionary class, whose interests demand a set of relations suited to further productive development.

This picture is plain in the *Communist Manifesto*'s account of the rise of the modern bourgeoisie:

> The means of production and intercourse on whose foundation the bourgeoisie built itself was generated by feudal society. At a certain stage in the development of these means of production, . . . the feudal property relations no longer corresponded to the already developed productive powers. They restricted production instead of furthering it. They changed into so many fetters. They had to be burst asunder; they were burst asunder.
>
> In their place stepped free competition, with a social and political constitution adapted to it, with the economic and political dominion of the bourgeois class.[42]

It is even plainer in the *Manifesto*'s account of the anticipated fall of capitalism:

> A similar movement is going on before our eyes. . . . Modern bourgeois society . . . is like the sorcerer who is no longer able to dominate the infernal powers he has conjured up. For decades the history of industry and trade has been a history of the revolt of modern productive powers against modern production relations. . . .

99

The weapons with which the bourgeoisie struck down feudalism have turned against the bourgeoisie itself.

But not only has the bourgeoisie forged the weapons which will
bring death to it. It has also generated the men who will wield
those weapons — the modern workers; the *proletarians*. . . .

What [the bourgeoisie] produces above all is its own grave-
diggers. Its fall and the victory of the proletariat are equally
inevitable.[43]

VII

Materialist Explanations

---

1 Historical materialism as an empirical hypothesis

Marx's materialist conception of history identifies the dominant factors in explaining social structures and their historical changes, and sketches a scenario of historical change based on the dominance of these factors. Marx postulates certain basic tendencies in human social behavior: the tendency of society's productive powers to increase; the tendency of social relations to adjust themselves to the efficient employment of these powers, and to change in response to changes in them; the tendency of social groups with shared economic interests to organize into social movements struggling to establish and defend the set of social relations most favorable to the group. Marx believes these tendencies are sufficiently potent and persistent to give human history a certain basic intelligibility, the broadest and deepest sort of intelligibility it is possible to give it.

Marx's postulates cohere with two of his other beliefs: that human fulfillment consists in developing and exercising people's powers of social production; and that the human race eventually tends to do (if often in a bumbling and unconscious way) what its deepest and most long-term interests demand. Marx's postulates taken together suggest a determinate pattern in history. There is some reason to see how far this pattern can be discerned in the empirical facts, and how far it might be used to explain these facts. The scientific value of a hypothesis often turns less on how true it eventually proves to be than on the discoveries which we can make in the course of testing it. From this standpoint, historical materialism might deservedly revolutionize and advance the study of history even if it turns out to be largely false.

101

Marx, of course, is firmly persuaded that historical materialism is true. But both Marx and Engels nevertheless insist that historical materialism is not as a dogma to be defended at all cost, but a 'guiding thread' for empirical research, a 'proposal for study' in a field which is 'still in its swaddling clothes'. They sternly castigate would-be 'Marxists' who 'make "historical materialism" into a mere phrase' by using it 'as a pretext for *not* studying history'.[1] It may be objected that Marx's anxiety to vindicate the materialist hypothesis sometimes leads him to do violence to the facts, to exaggerate some, ignore others, and generally to over-simplify his historical material to fit his preconceived theory. But insofar as Marx is guilty of such things, he stands condemned by his own conception of the role historical materialism ought to play in the study of history.

The postulates of Marx's historical materialism are, I think, plausible: but not self-evident. (If they were, it is unlikely that they could provide any but trivial explanations of social facts and historical changes.) Apart from detailed empirical investigation, we cannot hope to know the extent to which the efficient employment of this or that society's productive powers places significant constraints on its work relations and ownership relations. Nor can we know how far the social divisions engendered by these relations play a role in shaping its politics, art, religion or morality. Even if the tendencies historical materialism postulates are all real and effective, there is no guarantee a priori that they will be more potent than other tendencies which might be postulated with similar prima facie plausibility.

It is commonly charged, for instance, that Marx overestimates the influence of social movements based on economic class, and underestimates the power of ties based on race, religion, nationality and cultural heritage. The issues raised by such charges are complex, and not easily settled. Such issues are difficult in part because they cannot be easily divorced from questions which are philosophical, in the murkiest sense of the term. To anyone who shares Marx's belief that there is some basic tendency for people to pursue their real, objective interests (whether they are conscious of them or not) the question which social factors will have significant and independent historical potency cannot be separated from the question of what people's basic needs and interests are.[2] Some people believe that the preservation of cultural symbols, religious feelings and ties of blood and soil have genuine value for human life which is independent of their capacity to express class interests and lend support to certain economic forms. If they share Marx's view about the historical potency of objective interests, these people will also see these values as having an irreducible and enduring place in historical explanation. On the other hand, someone (like Marx) who believes that religious, racial or national ties are in themselves humanly worthless superstitions, will naturally view them as having no role to play in history once people have 'finally come to regard their life situation and mutual relations with sober eyes'.[3] The facts of history are relevant to such disagreements, but are unlikely to put an end to them.

Of course Marx and Engels never deny that extra-economic factors play a significant role in determining the course of historical events. Engels agrees it would be 'ridiculous' to try to explain every social fact ('the existence of every little German state', or 'the origin of High German consonant permutations') in economic terms. The 'form' of historical events, he says, is determined by factors of all sorts, and in fact largely by what is purely 'accidental': it is only the 'content' of history which historical materialism pretends to explain.[4] But the distinction between 'form' and 'content' here has to be a loose and relative one. To say that economic tendencies determine the 'content' of historical events is just to say that these tendencies so predominate over all other tendencies that 'in the last instance' a basic 'movement' of history can be read off from them as it cannot be read off from anything else. It is not self-evident that economic tendencies have this clear predominance in history, or indeed that anything has it. History might have no 'driving forces' or 'basic movement' at all, because the kind of intelligibility Marx is looking for in it might simply not exist.

Not only is it not self-evident whether historical materialism is true or false, but it is difficult to say precisely what empirical facts would verify or falsify the materialist hypothesis. This point is widely recognized by Marx's critics. But they have a deplorable tendency to infer from this that historical materialism is a 'metaphysical' theory in some pejorative sense, not an empirical hypothesis at all. It is an elementary mistake to dismiss a theory as nonempirical simply on the ground that its claims are too far reaching and complex to make its verification or falsification an easy or simple matter. Historical materialism is a proposal or outline for a certain kind of explanatory theory about the structure of societies, the nature of their institutions and prevalent ideas, their changes over time. We may consider historical materialism verified to the extent that successful theories of this kind have been produced, and falsified to the extent that the empirical facts have resisted explanation along materialist lines.

For several generations, Marxist and non-Marxist historians have debated the merits both of Marx's own theory and of various attempts to extend or supplement it. If these debates have still not established any firm conclusions, this is easy enough to explain in terms of the inherent difficulty of the issues, the low level of theoretical understanding on which they have often been discussed, and the obvious partisanship of the participants. There is no need to explain it by supposing that empirical evidence is not relevant to the evaluation of materialist social theories.

2 *Materialist explanations are teleological*

I have described the basic explanatory postulates of historical materialism as 'tendencies'. In Chapter V, I suggested that materialist explanations are typically not *causal* explanations. I now suggest that they are *teleological* explanations.

There is a large and sophisticated body of philosophical litera-ture on the nature and scientific function of teleological explanations. The defensibility of historical materialism, as I am interpreting it, may well depend on some of the issues debated in this literature. What I am about to say does not pretend to contribute to the discussion of those issues. My purpose is only to explain, within the limits of the space available, what I mean by describing materialist explanations as 'teleological'.[5]

Teleological explanations arise in connection with what are sometimes called 'goal-directed systems': systems which exhibit a persistent tendency to achieve or maintain a certain state, or to change in a specifiable direction. By calling the tendency 'persistent' I mean that it is relatively independent of conditions external to the system, so that the system shows some ability to adapt to potentially disturbing influences, and maintain its characteristic tendency in the face of them. We explain some element or aspect of such a system teleologically when we show how it manifests or contributes to the persistent tendencies which characterize the system, and provide reasons for thinking that this element or aspect exists *because* it manifests or contributes to those tendencies. The behavior of living organisms and many features of their internal structure are explained teleologically when it is shown how this behavior or these features contribute to the organism's tendency to remain alive and in good health. This tendency is such a basic and pervasive fact about living things that it explains the existence in living things of behavior or structures which are necessary for their survival and health. A more elaborate account of the reasons for thinking that teleological *explananda* exist because they contribute to this tendency might be provided by a theory of natural selection. But I doubt that the legitimacy of teleological explanations is necessarily dependent on the availability of a true account of this sort. (Darwin's theory shed light on the teleological explanations biologists had been using for centuries, but did little to legitimate − and nothing to discredit − these explanations.)

The explanations proposed by historical materialism are typically teleological in the sense just described. Marx proposes to explain the social relations prevailing in a community by showing how they manifest or contribute to its tendency to make efficient use of its productive powers. And he takes this tendency to be a sufficiently basic and pervasive feature of societies to account for the existence of the phenomena which manifest it. Productive powers 'determine' production relations in the sense that these relations exist *in order to* bring about an efficient use of productive powers, and *because* they bring about an efficient use of productive powers. Historical materialism proposes to account for large scale changes in social relations either by showing how they serve to adapt these relations to new productive powers or by showing how they contribute (at that stage of history) to the persistent expansive tendency of humanity's productive powers. Social relations change *because of* the development of productive powers, that is, *in order to* accommodate or effect that development.[6] Further, Marx proposes to explain the character of a society's legal system, politics and moral or religious beliefs by showing how they serve to sanction its social relations. The 'economic structure' of a society is thus the 'basis' of its legal, political and ideological 'superstructure' in the sense that many features of the superstructure can be explained in terms of their ability to make the basic economic relationships work. Finally, Marx proposes to explain the power of certain political groups and the prevalence of certain ideas by showing how they serve class interests. In other words, he means to explain them by showing how they manifest the tendency of people living under similar conditions to organize into movements with general interests, and to get these interests satisfied as far as the class's historical situation permits. Revolutions occur and class struggles have the outcome they do, *in order that* the productive powers of society may continue to expand, and the social relations of production may be suited to them.

Many caricatures and misguided criticisms of Marx's theory have come from the (usually hazy) recognition that the theory involves teleological thinking, combined with various misconceptions about what teleological explanations are. To provide a teleological explanation of something is not to assert that some events have temporally later events as their efficient causes, nor is it to attribute what is explained to the intentions of a human or superhuman agent. A teleological explanation accounts for its *explanandum* in terms of the (already existing) persistent tendency of a system to achieve a certain result or move in a certain direction. Such tendencies are often found in unconscious things, and even in conscious beings they are usually not the result of conscious intentions. To recognize the existence of teleological tendencies (as Aristotle already knew quite well) is not to commit oneself to saying that they result from the deliberations of a conscious agent. To hold, for instance, that humanity has a persistent tendency to expand its productive powers is not necessarily to hold that the human race or its members are moved by the 'idea of progress', or that human beings consciously have any universal or collective motives or aims at all.

Neither does the recognition of teleological tendencies require that one should hypostatize them as entelechies or occult agencies of any sort. (To see history as governed by certain basic tendencies does not require us to believe in a 'force of destiny'.) Marx's view, from very early in his career, was always that the 'social history of men is never anything but the history of their individual development, whether they are conscious of it or not'. *The German Ideology* makes this very plain:

> The philosophers have represented the outcome of the historical process as an ideal under the name 'man' and have grasped history as the process of 'man's' development, so that at each historical stage 'man' is substituted for individuals as the driving force of history. . . . The communists in practice treat the conditions generated through production and intercourse as conditions of social unity but without imagining that it was the plan or destiny of previous generations to provide them with these materials.[7]

Why do people so often regard teleological explanations as necessarily involving either the attribution of events to the intentions of conscious agents or the belief in occult forces? Putting aside religious and metaphysical motives, I think the chief reason is a propensity to confuse teleological explanations with efficient cause explanations. Explanations generally may be viewed as tracing the *explanandum* to some sort of regularity or abiding feature of the world. Causal explanations (as they are now commonly understood) work by tracing an event to some lawlike regularity in the behavior of things. The efficient cause of an event is the set (or some prominent subset) of conditions upon which the event follows in accordance with a certain causal law. Teleological explanations work by tracing the *explanandum* to a persistent tendency of some system to which it belongs. The tendency, however, does not function in the explanation like an agent or efficient cause, bringing about the *explanandum* in accordance with some law. The tendency is rather more analogous to the causal law itself, for it is the regular or abiding feature of the world to which the *explanandum* is traced. To look at the tendency itself as an occult causal agent or to hypostatize an intentional agent behind it is to confuse teleological explanations with causal ones, and in effect to insist that teleological explanations must be causal in spite of themselves.

Of course, it may be reasonable to ask for a causal explanation of the existence and workings of the persistent tendency which grounds a teleological explanation.[8] It is a matter of controversy whether such tendencies can always be causally explained, and it is also debated whether teleological explanations can, as regards what they assert, always be 'reduced to' (or translated into equivalent) nonteleological explanations. I know of no basis for guessing at Marx's opinion on the latter issue, and doubt that he has one. On the former issue, the indications are that both Marx and Engels do regard all teleological tendencies as causally explicable in materialistic terms (biological ones, for instance, by Darwinian evolutionary theory).[9]

However such issues are decided, there seems to be no good reason for thinking of teleological explanations as necessarily 'unscientific' or at odds with Marx's generally 'materialistic' view of the world. If there are causal explanations for the existence of organized systems and their persistent tendencies, these systems and tendencies are not the less objective features of the world for that. Even if the content of teleological explanations can always (at least in principle) be stated in nonteleological terms, teleological explanations nevertheless succeed in focusing our attention on the internal structure and global tendencies of organized systems in a way that nonteleological explanations do not. As long as we lack complete causal explanations for the workings of complex organized systems (as we obviously still do both for biological organisms and for human societies) teleological explanations may be our only mode of scientific access to certain phenomena. Even after we acquire the needed causal explanations (if we ever do) teleology still provides an illuminating perspective on

107

organized systems. There is widespread agreement about this among contemporary philosophers of science. As one influential writer has put it: 'The use of teleological explanations in the study of directively organized systems is as congruent with the spirit of modern science as the use of nonteleological ones.'[10] Of course there is always room for objection to the particular teleological explanations Marx suggests. And there may be general objections to them, from those who deny that societies are really 'directively organized systems' or that they exhibit the persistent tendencies Marx attributes to them. But we are not on solid ground if we want to object to Marx's historical explanations simply because they are teleological in form.

3 Is Marx a historical teleologist?

Marx does not reflect philosophically on the form of explanation his materialist theory employs. I do not say that historical materialism involves teleological explanations because Marx ever announces an intention of providing explanations of this form.[11] Rather, I say it because (as I interpret his theory) the form of the explanations it offers is in fact teleological. But it would be a serious objection to my interpretation if Marx disavowed the kind of explanations I attribute to his theory. There are a few passages in which Marx might appear to be doing just this, and my interpretation ought to confront such passages. In every case, I contend, careful inspection reveals that Marx is not criticizing or repudiating teleology generally or the kinds of teleological explanations I have attributed to his theory, but only the abuse of teleology by natural theists or speculative philosophers. I will try to show this by discussing the two passages where it seems to me least evident.

The first passage is found in *The German Ideology*:

> History is nothing but the succession of single generations, each of which exploits the materials, capital and productive powers made over to it by the previous ones, thus on the one side continuing the traditional activity under changed circumstances and on the other modifying the old circumstances with wholly changed activity. This can be speculatively distorted so that later history is made the purpose of earlier. . . . Thereby history becomes a 'person beside other persons', having its own purposes, . . . signified by the words 'destiny,' 'purpose,' 'germ' or 'idea'.[12]

Marx's target in this passage is not teleological thinking generally, but only views which represent later stages of society as the goal (conscious or unconscious) of earlier ones. Marx's theory involves nothing of this kind. Marx does not, for instance, explain capitalism teleologically by saying that it makes communist society possible (though Marx does hold that capitalism *in fact* makes communism possible). Instead, he explains capitalist social relations teleologically by showing how they serve to make efficient use of existing productive powers and to stimulate the further development of these powers. Marx's theory rests on the idea that there is a general historical tendency for productive powers to be used efficiently, and to expand. But Marx does not hold that there is a general historical tendency for a certain kind of society (such as communist society) to come about. It is the belief in historical tendencies of this latter kind that is being attacked in the above quotation.

The second passage comes from an 1861 letter from Marx to Ferdinand Lassalle, where Marx says of Darwin's theory of evolution that 'not only does it strike a death-blow to "teleology" in the natural sciences, but also empirically explains its rational meaning.'[13] This remark might be read as saying that Darwin's theory has rendered teleological explanations in general obsolete (at least in the natural sciences) and that such explanations have 'rational meaning' only insofar as there exist causal explanations (such as those provided by natural selection) for the tendencies on which they are based. Even so, the remark would not entail that teleology is obsolete in historical studies (where no correspondingly successful causal theories have yet emerged).

But I do not think even this is a correct reading of the remark. Marx and Engels's respect for Darwin (which is not unbounded) does not rest on the fact that Darwin provided causal explanations of biological organization. It rests on the fact that he exhibited a progressive historical movement in the natural world, and provided a purely naturalistic account of biological organization, undercutting explanations of natural teleology in theological or supernaturalist terms. In the letter to Lassalle, I think Marx means by 'teleology' what Engels elsewhere calls the 'old' or 'external' teleology, which explains teleological regularities by reference to the will of an extramundane creator. Engels correctly observes that the notion of 'inner purposiveness' employed by Kant and Hegel does not do this, and he is critical of Ludwig Büchner, Ernst Haeckel and other 'mechanistic materialists' for confusing the two types of teleology.[14] As we shall see in Part Five, dialectical thinking (whether Hegelian or Marxian) deals with organized systems, and deals with them teleologically. Engels recognizes this fact.

Once we consider the teleological character of materialist explanations, we can see clearly what is wrong with many common misinterpretations and criticisms of historical materialism. In general, when we explain something teleologically by showing how it manifests or contributes to the tendency of a system to achieve a certain result, this does not exclude (on the contrary, it positively implies) that the teleological *explanandum* figures as a causal *explanans* of the result. Thus when Marx (teleologically) explains social relations in terms of productive powers, or political and ideological phenomena in terms of economic structure of society or the class struggle, this does not exclude (on the contrary, it positively implies) that certain features of social relations figure in causal explanations of the state and development of productive powers, and that superstructural phenomena causally influence the economic basis of society. Marx's theory is thus fundamentally *incompatible* with any form of 'economic determinism' which holds that law, morality, politics or religion exercise no causal influence on material production or economic relations. In fact, it is precisely these influences which Marx's theory tries to understand, to explain in terms of the economic tendencies they manifest. The causal influence of superstructural phenomena begins to threaten Marx's theory only when these phenomena exhibit tendencies of their own which diverge from the 'basic' economic ones. Marx and Engels do not deny (indeed, they explicitly affirm) that these other tendencies exist, but they believe (for plausible if not decisive reasons we have already examined) that 'in the last instance' the economic ones must predominate over them.

The same considerations also suffice to dispatch all criticisms which say that there cannot be one 'basic' or 'predominant' factor in society or history because society and history involve the reciprocal interaction and mutual determination of many different factors.[15] Marx agrees that there is no single 'predominant factor' in history if this phrase refers to economic, political or ideological facts regarded as *efficient causes*. But that does not commit him to denying that certain persistent tendencies traceable to material production predominate in determining the general character and result of the interaction of different causal factors. Of course, it might be that the interaction of various tendencies in history is just as complex and indeterminate as the reciprocal interaction of causal factors. But to admit that there is no predominant causal factor in history does not commit Marx to saying that there is no predominant teleological tendency in it.

VIII

Materialism, Agency and Consciousness

---

1 *Is Marx a determinist?*

Many writers say historical materialism holds that the thoughts
and actions of individual human beings are causally determined
by economic factors. They take historical materialism to be a
species of causal determinism, and incompatible with libertar-
ianism, the view which affirms that human choices are free and
denies that they are determined. I know of no text where Marx
explicitly addresses the issue of free will and determinism, and
doubt that he has any firm opinion on this issue. The belief that
historical materialism involves a species of causal determinism
about human actions probably derives from the erroneous idea
that the 'determination' of production relations by productive
powers and of the social superstructure by its economic basis are
cases of efficient causes determining effects. Now that we have
(I hope) disposed of this idea, we can take a new look at the textual evidence which might lead us to think that historical materialism is committed to causal determinism.

Marx says that economic relations are 'independent of the will'
of those who enter into them, and he often asserts or implies that
people are controlled or tyrannized by 'alien' economic conditions. But no philosophical determinism is implied in these claims.
Marx holds that economic circumstances dominate people by
placing obstacles in the way of their achieving a fulfilling way of
life and by subjecting them to illusions which prevent their setting
meaningful goals for themselves. Even extreme libertarians admit
that people are sometimes prevented by external obstacles from
doing what they want to, and that ignorance or error sometimes
stands in the way of their formulating rational aims. One of

Marx's primary objectives is to free people as much as possible from the social relations and ideological illusions which dominate and imprison them. If Marx's belief that people in class society are so dominated is a species of determinism, then it is one of Marx's chief practical aims to make this determinism cease.

Marx is convinced that a violent class war between the bourgeoisie and the proletariat is virtually inevitable, because the bourgeoisie is incapable of accepting the truth that capitalism is an obsolete system. But he is not convinced of this because he believes that the consciousness of each individual bourgeois is determined robot-like by economic facts. Marx explicitly asserts that 'as earlier a part of the nobility went over to the bourgeoisie, so now a part of the bourgeoisie is going over to the proletariat, namely the part of the bourgeois ideologues which has worked itself up to a theoretical understanding of the whole historical movement.'[1] If Marx is persuaded that this part of the bourgeoisie must remain a minority, that is because he respects the powerful social influence of bourgeois ideologies, which even the most evident scientific knowledge cannot wholly overcome before the practical abolition of the social conditions on which they rest. Once again, it is Marx's aim to counteract this influence as far as he can.

Some of Engels' remarks do appear to endorse the thesis that the volitions of individuals are causally determined by economic circumstances. 'Individual wills', he says, 'will as they are driven to by their corporeal constitution and by external, in the last instance economic circumstances (either their own personal circumstances or general social ones).'[2] Does Engels really believe that individuals are always caused ('driven') to will as they do by economic circumstances? Not consistently, anyway. For he also believes, as we saw earlier, that individual wills are determined by 'passion or deliberation', and these in turn are moved directly not by economic factors but 'levers of various kinds' including 'purely individual crotchets'. Thus perhaps in the above remark Engels means to say only that a satisfactory explanation of the historical efficacy of an individual's action must always invoke 'external and in the last instance economic circumstances', and does not mean that economic circumstances always 'drive' individuals to perform the particular actions they do.

Whatever Engels may believe, it is only the latter conclusion which is implied in historical materialist explanations. Historical materialism seeks to explain political events or socially prevalent ideologies teleologically by showing how they contribute to basic social or historical tendencies. Explanations of this sort are in general not deterministic. They do not imply that the tendency in question had to be manifested in just that way, or that it required the contribution of that particular *explanandum* in order to exist at all. In fact, a 'basic historical tendency' which required (that is, depended on) certain particular events or the performance of certain actions by particular individuals would *eo ipso* be too flimsy and brittle to deserve the name. A materialist explanation of the French Revolution, for example, might show that the events of 1789 and the actions of such men as Mirabeau and Sièyes served to bring about political changes required by the economic conditions of France and the state of the class struggle. But the explanation need not show that economic conditions required these changes to take place at just that time or in just that manner, and almost certainly could not show that they had to be effected by just those individuals. To say that the Revolution came about on account of a basic historical tendency is precisely *not* to say that it had to happen in just the particular way it did.

A materialist theory may attempt historical explanations of greater or less detail. But however detailed they may be, they are concerned with the thoughts and actions of particular individuals only insofar as these individuals happen to be especially influential or to represent some important social type. Such a theory might (for instance) try to show how Napoleon's political objectives suited the balance of class power in France at the beginning of the nineteenth century, and in this way to explain both why France was likely to have a ruler with those objectives and why a skillful and ambitious leader with those objectives was politically successful. But historical materialism offers no explanation for the fact that this individual, Napoleon Bonaparte, had the particular desires and objectives he did. Materialist explanations are perfectly consistent with the supposition that Napoleon's aims were at the mercy of his causally undetermined choices. Again, historical materialism offers no explanation for the fact that a singular personality such as Jean-Jacques Rousseau espoused petty bourgeois republicanism rather than divine right monarchy, or indeed for the fact that Rousseau chose to write about politics at all, instead of spending his whole life copying music or being kept by neurotic gentlewomen. What historical materialism might try to explain is why some individual (no matter who) invented a political philosophy like Rousseau's, and why this philosophy was prominent or influential. (It might do this, for instance, by showing how this philosophy served as vehicle for the development of bourgeois and petty bourgeois class consciousness.) This means that a materialist account might do much towards explaining the currency of Rousseau's philosophy in various bowdlerized forms but have little or nothing to say about Rousseau's actual thought insofar as it has been widely misinterpreted and has had little or no social impact. Even supposing that Rousseau was causally determined to think and write as he did (whether by economic conditions or by anything else) this fact could not play a significant role in the kind of explanation historical materialism might give of his ideas or actions.

One reason which is sometimes given for saying that Marx is a causal determinist is that he believes certain historical developments are *inevitable*. But it is not immediately evident why this belief should commit him to causal determinism. Perhaps the most reasonable way of making the connection is this: Marx bases his belief in historical inevitability on the existence and predominance of certain social tendencies. It is reasonable to think (even if it is not wholly evident) that these tendencies in Marx's view must be causally explainable in terms of the influence of economic conditions on individual human beings. Hence we may conclude that Marx regards the actions of individuals as causally determined by economic conditions.

This is a bad argument. There might very well be causally sufficient conditions for a certain historical tendency, even for a certain inevitable result, even if no individual's behavior is causally determined. Libertarians usually admit (what is obvious) that we often can accurately predict what people will do. One standard account they give of this ability says that people's actions are influenced or inclined to a certain course of action by motives or circumstances, without being determined to choose that course or prevented from choosing another. By knowing which influences or inclinations are operating on a person, we can often guess (with a high degree of probability) what the person will choose to do, even though these choices are free and not causally determined.

If we are libertarians who accept some such account as this, then we have all the philosophical beliefs anyone needs not only to provide causal accounts of the tendencies postulated by historical materialism, but even to convince ourselves that some courses of events are historically inevitable. For suppose we know (1) that a large number of individuals will be strongly inclined to perform actions of a certain sort; (2) that nothing will prevent them from doing so; and (3) that a certain number of these actions will be causally sufficient to produce a certain result. Then we know enough to provide a causal explanation for the fact that there is a tendency for this result to be produced, and even enough to justify the belief that this result is inevitable. Yet we remain

114

libertarians in good standing all the while.

Consider the following example. The manager of a theater knows that certain theater seats will tend to be sat in more often than others, because not all performances play to a full house, and some seats provide a better view of the stage than others. She also knows that when a given seat has been used a certain number of times, its upholstery will become worn and will need repair. From this she infers that certain identifiable seats will *inevitably* need repair sooner than others. In order to reason in this way, the manager surely does not need to be a determinist about human actions. No sensible person could accuse her of denying that theater-goers are free to choose which seats they sit in.

The reasoning behind Marx's belief in the historical inevitability of the rise and fall of capitalism in Western Europe is not so very different from that used by the theater manager. Suppose a historian believes that people are generally inclined to expand their productive powers and adjust their social relations to accommodate the exercise of these powers. For this reason, the historian thinks there is a general tendency for a given set of production relations to be adopted when they are sufficiently conducive to the development of productive powers and when the already existing relations have ceased to be conducive to this development. Now suppose our historian also believes that during the early part of their history capitalist relations were highly conducive to productive development as compared with feudal or petty industrial ones, but more recently they have become fetters on development in ways that socialist relations would not be. The historian therefore infers that the general inclination of people toward social relations which favor productive development made it inevitable that capitalism should triumph over feudalism and petty industry, and will make socialism's triumph over capitalism equally inevitable.

This is an oversimplified but basically correct account of Marx's reasoning. But it is reasoning which does not differ in any philosophically interesting respect from the reasoning of our theater manager, and it is reasoning in which most libertarians could comfortably engage. I conclude that there is nothing in Marx's belief in historical inevitability which prevents him from being a libertarian. If some people are disposed to view Marx's belief in the historical inevitability of capitalism's rise and fall as committing him to controversial metaphysical doctrines, I think this is only because they are dazzled by the ambitious scope (and possible disturbing implications) of Marx's predictions. I doubt that the same people would see any metaphysical difficulties in

115

similar (but more socially innocuous and empirically modest) predictions like the theater manager's prediction that certain seats will inevitably need reupholstery sooner than others.

There is nothing in Marx's historical materialism, I submit, which requires him to hold that human thoughts and actions are causally determined. It is a separate question whether he actually is a determinist, a question which I doubt we can answer with any degree of certainty. Marx seems to endorse the 'materialistic' thesis of Condillac and Helvetius that 'men are made by circumstances', and this thesis is presumably intended to assert some form of causal determinism about human character and action.[3] But Marx also insists that previous materialism has erred by overlooking the 'active side', ignoring the complementary truth that 'men change their circumstances'.[4] It is not clear whether or how this revision is supposed to bear on the determinist aspect of the earlier materialists' views. In any case, it seems quite likely that if Marx is a determinist he is also a compatibilist, that is, he believes that causal determinism with regard to human actions does not imply that people are unable to choose freely. When Engels endorses the Hegelian doctrine that 'freedom is necessity comprehended', he probably intends (among other things) to subscribe to some form of compatibilism.[5] Frankly, I doubt Marx and Engels ever gave much thought to the issue of free will and determinism. Why should they? Nothing in their theory of history turns on this issue.

There is another charge sometimes brought against Marx which really has nothing to do with free will and determinism, but tends to be closely associated with the free will issue in people's minds and probably contributes to the idea that Marx holds some scandalous doctrine in this area. This is the charge that historical materialism fails to comprehend individuals in their unique individuality, that Marx 'minimizes the individual and his significance' in history, and 'drowns the individual in the class and the movement of history'.[6] There is quite a bit of truth in these charges, though not, I think, in the idea that they locate a defect in historical materialism. Materialist explanations are teleological explanations. Teleological explanations generally focus attention on the contribution made by elements of an organized system to its global tendencies. Accordingly, they tend to ignore the properties of these elements which are not relevant to their function in the system. Historical materialism proposes a teleological theory about the careers of social forms, political movements and prevalent or influential ideas. Its aims and methods require historical materialism to view individuals from the perspective of their

116

relation to these social forms, and thus deliberately to ignore their 'unique individuality'. Historical materialism is not (and was never meant to be) a good guide to the writing of personal biography or the history of some individual's inner spiritual development.

2 Three senses of 'ideology'

'Ideology', like 'alienation', has become one of the most fashionable concepts in Marxian thinking, despite (or rather perhaps because of) the fact that Marx is conspicuously unclear as to what he means by 'ideology' and what he does say is beset with dangers of confusion and inconsistency. I think we can discern three basic uses of 'ideology' and its cognates in the writings of Marx and Engels, and we can acquire a basic grasp of what Marx thought about ideology if we understand how these three uses are related to each other and to historical materialism.

Marx derived the term 'ideology' from Destutt de Tracy, though it had also been used by other writers. Marx's first use of it apparently occurs in *The German Ideology* of 1845-6. In that manuscript, the term refers primarily to a certain sort of philosophical belief, the belief in the 'dominion of thought' (*Gedankenherrschaft*), the thesis that 'the world is ruled by ideas, that ideas and concepts are the determining principles.'[7] 'Ideologists' are philosophers who hold and teach this doctrine. In this use, 'ideology' means the same as 'idealism' (in one of the many senses given the term by Marx and Engels). For the sake of a convenient terminology, I will call 'ideology' in this sense 'historical idealism'.

Needless to say, 'ideology' or 'historical idealism' is taken by Marx and Engels to be a *false* doctrine. But it is not immediately evident what views they count as 'belief in *Gedankenherrschaft*'. One view they appear to include is any metaphysics which, like Hegel's, regards ultimate reality as a cosmic mind or spirit, and this spirit's 'determinate thoughts as the mystery of the world accessible to philosophers'.[8] But Marx and Engels also identify 'ideology' with a thesis about how progressive social change is to be brought about. Ideologists, they say, 'agree in the faith that their acts of critical thought must bring about the downfall of the existing order'.[9] Obviously, they have in mind Bauer, Stirner, Feuerbach and the other young Hegelians who believe that alienation consists in or is caused by false consciousness, and that the cure for it lies in the acquisition of a truer or more 'critical' world view. But it is misleading of Marx and Engels to imply that the young Hegelians' diagnosis of alienation and their strategies

117

for social change are founded on the metaphysical thesis that ultimate reality is mental, or even the thesis that the course of history is determined in Hegelian fashion by the conceptual dialectic of the world spirit. There is no need for 'idealistic' views about the strategy of social reform to be based on metaphysical idealism. [10]

The German Ideology's attack on historical idealism seems to be aimed chiefly at two points: first, the idealists' repudiation of any materialist account of their own philosophical ideas (a repudiation Marx and Engels take to be implicit in the young Hegelians' contemptuous aloofness from political struggles); and second, the idealists' belief that progressive social change can be brought about merely by a conversion of people's consciousness, irrespective of the material conditions of production. If we make these two points the identifying features of 'ideology' in the sense of 'historical idealism', then it is clear that the object of Marx's attack is by no means a straw man. For a good part of liberal and reformist thinking even today is 'ideological' in this sense.

'Ideology' in the sense of 'historical idealism' is not a useful concept for social analysis. Even in *The German Ideology*, however, and almost exclusively elsewhere in the Marxian writings, 'ideology' is used to propose a materialist explanation of widely held or influential beliefs and forms of social consciousness. The *Critique* describes jurisprudence, politics, religion, art and philosophy (other accounts add morality to the list) as 'ideological forms in which men become conscious of conflicts [between productive powers and production relations] and fight them out'. *The German Ideology* says that historical science must 'present the development of ideological reflexes and echoes from the actual life process of men. Even the foggy images in men's brains are necessary, empirically confirmable sublimates of their life process, and are bound up with material presuppositions.' [11]

In these passages, the term 'ideology' is used to express the materialist thesis that socially prevalent or influential ideas can be explained by showing how they either sanction the social relations determined by the existing stage of productive powers or express and promote class interests. An 'ideology' is any belief, theory or form of consciousness whose prevalence can be explained materialistically by the way it contributes to basic social and historical tendencies. Let us call ideology in this second sense 'functional ideology'. When Marx describes jurisprudence, politics, religion, art, philosophy or morality in general as 'ideological', he means that most of the socially prevalent and influential thoughts that occupy people's heads and fall under these rubrics can be so explained.

Many passages in Marx's writings, however, suggest that ideology must not only be materialistically explainable, but must also involve some sort of false consciousness or illusion. Engels even asserts flatly that in order to be ideology, a belief or form of consciousness must be unaccompanied by any awareness of its own economic basis. Ideology following these passages is consciousness which is ignorant of its own real social and historical significance.[12] Let us call ideology in this third sense 'ideological illusion'.

This term, however, may be misleading. For we normally apply the term 'illusion' only to positive errors, and not merely to gaps of ignorance, even self-ignorance. It is perfectly possible for a justified belief, and even a piece of full-fledged knowledge, to be an 'ideological illusion' in the sense just specified, if it has a materialist explanation and if this explanation remains unknown to those who have the belief or knowledge. But Marx obviously thinks that this ideological self-ignorance is often supportive of many 'illusions' in a more straightforward sense. As long as they are ignorant of the fact that their beliefs are socially prevalent on account of the social function the beliefs fulfill, people are likely to think that these beliefs are so widespread because they are justified (that they are either self-evident or authenticated by the experience of humanity through the ages). Ignorance of the material basis for beliefs can lend credibility to a great many commonly held moral, religious and philosophical ideas which would otherwise be recognized for the plain rubbish they are. These beliefs, if Marx is right, do count as illusions in an unproblematic sense.

Between 'ideology' in these three senses (historical idealism, functional ideology and ideological illusion) there are some clear affinities and relationships. Historical idealists, as Marx conceives of them, repudiate a materialist explanation of their own consciousness. Hence if that consciousness can be explained as functional ideology, then it is also ideological illusion. Marx and Engels apparently believe that historical idealism is a form of functional ideology, which serves the interests of ruling classes by diverting people's attention from the real causes of their alienation. If so, then historical idealism is also a pervasive, even paradigmatic form of ideological illusion, since in effect it promotes ideological illusion to a general principle.

The three senses of 'ideology', however, still refer to three distinct things. Historical idealism is not *eo ipso* either a form of functional ideology or ideological illusion. If it is either of these, that must be established empirically. Ideological illusions, moreover, need not involve historical idealism in any of its forms. We can be ignorant of the economic basis of our consciousness, and even have illusions about its social significance, without holding any philosophical view to the effect that it lacks an economic basis. Ideological illusion is always functional ideology, but functional ideology need not be ideological illusion. In principle at least, it seems that historical self-knowledge, even the doctrine of historical materialism itself, might be functional ideology, that is, it might become influential or socially prevalent because it serves the interest of a class. Marx in fact apparently thinks just this about historical materialism in relation to the interest of the proletariat.

3 Ideology and science

Marx and Engels rarely describe their own views as 'ideology'.[13] This is perhaps evidence that they do not really intend to use 'ideology' in the sense of functional ideology, but always mean it in the pejorative senses of historical idealism and ideological illusion. Yet of the three senses of 'ideology' it is functional ideology which captures the most important concept for materialist social analysis. The fact that there is a materialist explanation for a widely held belief is of more theoretical significance than the fact that this explanation is unknown to or denied on principle by those who hold the belief. This would serve to justify the usage of more recent Marxists (including Lenin) who do not hesitate to speak of 'proletarian ideology' and even apply this term to Marxism itself.

Perhaps someone might try to justify Marx's usage against that of the more recent Marxists by arguing that all functional ideology must in fact be ideological illusion. One such argument might be this: In order to be functional ideology, a belief or form of consciousness must not only serve an economic system or class interest, but its existence must be explained by the fact that it does so. Now someone may say that it makes no sense to explain knowledge or a rationally justified belief in such a way, since in such a case the rational grounds for the belief always suffice to explain why we hold it, and render a materialist explanation superfluous. For functional ideology not to be ideological illusion, it would have to be the case that knowledge or justified belief could rest not on the objective grounds for thinking the belief true, but on the fact that our holding this belief serves a certain economic or class purpose. It would also have to be the case that we could know of our own beliefs that they serve such a purpose, and yet consciously hold them not on objective grounds but because of the class interests they serve. We would in effect have to place a higher priority on serving class interests than we do on objective truth, and be justified in so doing. This may be good bolshevism, but it is such flagrant intellectual dishonesty that it does Marx no credit to associate him with it.

If Marx's usage is based on arguments like this one, however, then it is based on a mistake. For the argument confuses the grounds on which an individual may hold a true belief, and which may render the belief knowledge for that individual, with the explanation which a historical materialist might give for the fact that a certain truth has come to be widely known. The historical materialist might explain the fact that some true doctrine (such as historical materialism) has come to be widely known by the way in which its coming to be known serves the class interests of the proletariat. His explanation might (in effect) take the form of showing how the development of proletarian class consciousness involves their coming to attend to this truth for the first time, and the removal of ideological obstacles to their clear and objective perception of it (obstacles such as the cultural indoctrination of the masses by religion, historical idealism, and other superstitions.) Historical materialists who did explain the social prevalence of historical materialism in this way might, without the least intellectual dishonesty, be explicitly aware of all the following things: (1) that their own acceptance of historical materialism is justified on purely objective grounds; (2) that the acceptance of historical materialism by people like themselves serves the class interest of the proletariat; and (3) that (2) explains the widespread acceptance of historical materialism, even (4) that without the proletarian movement they themselves would probably never have come to know that historical materialism is true. For such historical materialists, historical materialism would be functional ideology, but also objective historical science, and not ideological illusion. It is, moreover, quite reasonable to think that Marx regards himself as just such a historical materialist.

Many writers lay stress on the alleged fact that for Marx ideology and science are mutually exclusive, and they make this thesis axiomatic for their interpretation of Marx's concept of ideology. As we have just seen, these writers may be largely justified by the actual usage of Marx and Engels, but their view is belied on a deeper level by the role which the concept of ideology has to play in historical materialism. A few of these writers have even gone so far as to conclude that for Marx 'science' (as a general department of social life) must be treated simply as a 'productive power',

121

apparently on the ground that there is no other place where it can be consistently fit into Marx's scheme.[14] Of course science can be considered as a productive power insofar as scientific knowledge contributes to society's capacity to produce. But this does not prevent science from also being a form of social consciousness, and even an ideology. I see no adequate textual basis for saying that for Marx 'it is a defining property of ideology that it is unscientific.'[15]

Historical idealism, of course, cannot be science, for the simple reason that Marxian historical science knows it to be a false doctrine. But there is no reason why science cannot serve class interests (as Marx obviously supposes a materialist science of history serves the interests of the proletariat).[16] Hence there is no reason why science may not be functional ideology. But there is also no reason why science may not be ideological illusion, or at least contain significant elements of ideological illusion.

Darwin's theory of natural selection is obviously regarded by both Marx and Engels as an epoch-making contribution to natural science. Yet they also see in it some clear evidence of bourgeois ideological illusions: 'It is remarkable how Darwin recognizes again among beasts and plants his own English society with its division of labor, competition, opening up of new markets, "inventions" and the Malthusian "struggle for existence".'[17] Perhaps no ideological illusion, *qua* illusion, is science. But genuine science for Marx may be closely allied to and intertwined with ideological illusion (as Darwinian biology is with detestable Malthusian superstitions). In any case, there is obviously nothing to prevent science, in any usual sense of the term, from being ignorant of its own historical materialist foundations. From this point of view, there is no basis for any distinction between ideology and science which precludes one and the same intellectual contribution from being simultaneously a genuine part of a living scientific theory and also a functioning ideological illusion.

PART THREE

Marxism and Morality

IX

Marx on Right and Justice

---

1 *Does Marxism have moral foundations?*

From one point of view, Marx is very explicit about his reasons for condemning capitalism. He describes and documents the miserable conditions to which the working class is subject: their grinding poverty, the degradation and emptiness of their mode of life, the precariousness of their very existence. And he argues that these conditions of life are by no means natural or unavoidable, but are rather the artificial products of an obsolete and irrational social system which is not recognized as such only because it serves the interests of the privileged minority. Whether we agree or disagree with what Marx says on this score, it is at least fairly clear what he means, and it is difficult to deny that if what Marx says is correct, he has powerful grounds for attacking capitalism and advocating its overthrow.

But from another point of view, Marx has dissatisfyingly little to say about his reasons for denouncing capitalist society. He does not ask the sorts of questions philosophers are fond of asking about the assessment of social institutions. He takes no pains to specify the norms, standards, or values he employs in deciding that capitalism is an intolerable system. Marx may exhibit his acceptance of certain values in the course of attacking capitalism, but he seldom reflects on what these values are, or on how they might be justified philosophically. Whether or not this silence constitutes a serious lacuna in Marx's thought, it has certainly given rise to puzzlement on the part of his readers, and to diverse theories about the 'moral foundations' of Marxism. In the next two chapters, I will try to say something about Marx's treatment of moral norms (especially right and justice) and the relation of

125

morality to Marx's historical materialism and critque of capitalism.

In Part One, I argued that Marx's views about alienation and the human essence involve some definite views about the conditions under which human beings can sustain a justified sense of self-worth and meaning in their lives. More specifically, I argued that these views involve a recognizably Aristotelian conception of human self-actualization, the development and exercise of our 'human essential powers'. Further, I argued that Marx conceives of these powers most fundamentally as our powers of social production. These views (or some version of them) are regarded by many writers as constituting the 'moral foundations' of Marxism, or at least as an important part of these foundations. I think there are some good reasons why we should be reluctant to accept this common idea.

For one thing, alienation, or the frustration of human self-actualization, is not the only evil Marx sees in capitalism. Perhaps it is not even the primary evil denounced in his mature writings. Marx is at least as concerned about philosophically less interesting evils to which the working class is subject: hunger, disease, fatigue, and the scarcity and insecurity of the means of physical survival. Aristotle regarded all other goods (including the necessities of life) as good only insofar as they are accessories to the final human good of happiness as the actualization of our human potentialities. But there is no sign that Marx followed Aristotle at this point. Hence there is no reason to treat self-actualization through social production as fundamental to Marx's value system. The most we can say with assurance is that self-actualization is prominent among the elements of human well-being which Marx sees as frustrated by capitalism.

Thus we may doubt whether Marx's views about alienation and self-actualization are *fundamental* moral views. But it is also questionable whether these are *moral* views. No doubt there is a sense in which any far-reaching views about human well-being count as 'moral' views, and in this sense I would not deny that Marx's conception of human self-actualization is a 'moral' conception. But there is a narrower and I think more proper sense of 'moral' in which we distinguish *moral* goods and evils from *nonmoral* ones. We all know the difference between valuing or doing something because conscience or the 'moral law' tells us we 'ought' to, and valuing or doing something because it satisfies our needs, our wants or our conceptions of what is good for us (or for someone else whose welfare we want to promote — desires for nonmoral goods are not necessarily selfish desires). This difference roughly marks off 'moral' from 'nonmoral' goods and evils as I mean to use those terms here. Moral goods include such things as virtue, right, justice, the fulfillment of duty, and the possession of morally meritorious qualities of character. Nonmoral goods, on the other hand, include such things as pleasure and happiness, things which we would regard as desirable and good for people to have even if no moral credit accrued from pursuing or possessing them.[1]

As I read him, Marx bases his critique of capitalism on the claim that it frustrates many important *nonmoral* goods: self-actualization, security, physical health, comfort, community, freedom. Of course the distinction between moral and nonmoral goods is never explicitly drawn by Marx, but it is a familiar one (both in philosophy and in everyday life) and it is not implausible to think that Marx might be tacitly aware of it and even make significant use of it without consciously attending to it.

Marx's condemnations of capitalism are often based quite explicitly on its failure to provide people with the nonmoral goods listed above, together with the claim that the existing powers of social production could provide them to all members of society if production were organized more rationally and democratically (i.e., socialistically). But Marx never claims that these goods ought to be provided to people because they have a *right* to them, or because *justice* (or some other moral norm) demands it.[2] In fact, as we shall see presently, Marx positively denies that capitalist exploitation does the workers any injustice or violates their rights. There is some evidence that Marx's own concern with the working class movement may be prompted in part by moral considerations (or at least by a distaste for the sort of person he would be if he were indifferent to human suffering).[3] But Marx seldom or never appeals to such considerations in urging others to support the movement. He is evidently persuaded that the obvious nonmoral value of the goods to which he appeals is sufficient, quite apart from appeals to our love of virtue or sense of guilt, to convince any reasonable person to favor the overthrow of a social order which unnecessarily frustrates them and its replacement by one which realizes them.

On the other hand, Marx consistently avoids social criticism based on moral goods or norms, and consistently shows contempt for those who do engage in such criticism. He attacks the 'moralizing criticism' of such people as Pierre Proudhon and Karl Heinzen, and rejects as 'ideological shuffle' (*ideologische Flausen*) the Gotha Program's demand for a 'just distribution'.[4] Likewise, he is angered by those who (like Adolph Wagner) interpret Marx himself as putting forward a critique of capitalism which is morally based.[5]

127

Marx never really makes explicit his reasons for taking these attitudes. Any attempt to expound these reasons must be to some extent speculative. For my interpretation I claim only that it provides the best explanation I can think of for what Marx actually says, and it is not explicitly contradicted by anything in the texts.

The interpretation is this: Marx's conception of nonmoral goods is different from his conception of moral goods. Marx believes that judgments about the nonmoral good of men and women can be based on actual, objective (though historically conditioned and variable) potentialities, needs and interests of human beings. But he sees moral norms as having no better foundation than their serviceability to transient forms of human social intercourse, and most fundamentally, to the social requirements of a given mode of production. Marx's attitude toward social criticism based on appeals to the two sorts of goods varies accordingly. Capitalism can be condemned without any ideological mystification or illusion by showing how it starves, enslaves and alienates people, that is, how it frustrates human self-actualization, prosperity and other nonmoral goods. But Marx rejects moral norms (such as right and justice) as acceptable vehicles of social criticism or apologetics (at least in situations of fundamental social revolution, where the entire framework of a given mode of production is to be challenged or defended.) He does so because such norms are for him only the juridical and ideological devices by which a given mode of production enforces its social relations, or a class attempts to promote its own interests. Moral consciousness, moreover, typically masks the real basis of its norms: it represents them as proceeding not from historically transient social forms but from the will of God, or *a priori* laws of reason, or our natural moral sense, or the general happiness of sentient creatures. When morality is detached from its real social basis (as by reformers who attempt to represent capitalist distributions as unjust) it becomes both irrational and impotent. Even when moral judgments are founded on this basis, their content is best understood not in morality's own mystified language, but in terms of the social structures they serve and the class interests they represent.

This rather negative attitude toward the rational foundation of morality is implied in Marx's unrelenting contempt for morally based social criticism. But it is also made more explicit in several places. *The German Ideology*, for instance, claims that historical materialism has 'broken the staff of all morality', by exhibiting the connection between morality and the conditions of life out of which it arises. When an imaginary bourgeois critic charges that 'communism does away with religion and morality instead of forming them anew', the *Communist Manifesto* does not deny that the charge is true, but replies to it by observing only that 'the communist revolution is the most radical break with traditional property relations; no wonder that in the course of its development there is the most radical break with traditional ideas.'[6] Presumably 'doing away with morality' is part of this radical break.

The distinction between moral and nonmoral goods is certainly one of which moral philosophers have been aware. Kant is cognizant of it when he distinguishes the 'moral' from the 'natural' (or 'physical') good, or the 'good' (*Gut*) from 'well-being' (*Wohl*). Mill acknowledges it when he distinguishes the 'utilitarian theory of life' (a hedonistic theory of the nonmoral good) from the 'utilitarian theory of morality' (which holds that the moral good consists in what is conducive to the greatest nonmoral good).[7] The distinction even makes possible two of the most basic issues on which Kant and Mill disagree:

A. Does the pursuit of moral good ultimately diverge from the pursuit of nonmoral good?

B. Which good is the more fundamental and (if the two ever do conflict) the overriding human good?

On issue A, Kant returns an affirmative answer, while Mill gives a negative one. Kant, of course, does not think the two kinds of good are incompatible or diametrically opposed, only that what morality demands is sometimes in conflict with the greatest nonmoral good (which Kant sees as the welfare only of the sensuous part of our nature). Mill recognizes that the moral good may conflict with particular lots of nonmoral good (a particular pleasure, or the happiness of a particular person or group). But since what is morally good is determined by what is conducive to the greatest total nonmoral good, there can be no ultimate divergence.

On issue B, Kant holds that the moral good is the unconditioned good, which must take precedence whenever the two goods conflict. Mill, since he sees morality as merely a device for maximizing the total nonmoral good, holds the nonmoral good to be fundamental.

As I read him, Marx agrees with Kant on issue A and with Mill on issue B. But this means that unlike either of them, Marx holds that the nonmoral good can systematically override the moral good in certain situations. (I think this is in effect what Marx is doing when he advocates the overthrow of capitalism while agreeing – at least verbally – with its bourgeois apologists that it is just.) Another way in which I think Marx differs from both Kant and Mill is that their theories of the nonmoral good are hedonistic, while Marx's is not.

The idea that Marx does not regard capitalism's inhuman exploitation of the workers as unjust or as a violation of their rights may be a hard one to accept, or even to understand. Yet at the same time, Marx's view on his point and his reasons for holding it constitute important evidence for my interpretation of Marx on morality. Hence although I have treated Marx's conception of right and justice more fully elsewhere, I will devote the remainder of this chapter to a brief discussion of it.[8]

2 Marx's concept of justice

According to historical materialism, people's moral beliefs and the motives to adhere to them are part of the 'ideological super-structure' of society. Engels says: 'Consciously or unconsciously, men create their moral intuitions in the last instance out of the practical relations on which their class situation is founded – out of the economic relations in which they produce and exchange.'[9] Historical materialism proposes to explain the social influence of moral beliefs by the way in which they contribute to the basic economic tendencies in the society in which they are found. And it proposes to account for the content of these beliefs by the way it helps to stabilize a social system or to promote class interests.

Historical materialism tries to explain why people have the moral beliefs they have. To do this, however, is not yet to say which (if any) of these beliefs are correct, or to provide any basis for answering questions of this kind. There are indications, however, that materialist explanations do for Marx have implications for the correctness of moral beliefs and moral judgments. More specifically, Marx seems to regard the correctness of some moral judgments as turning on the way in which people's conduct is related to the prevailing production relations.

One important moral notion which Marx treats in this way is that of right (*Recht*) or justice (*Gerechtigkeit*). In *Capital*, he says:

> The justice of transactions which go on between agents of
> production rests on the fact that these transactions arise out
> of the production relations as their natural consequences.

The juristic forms in which these economic transactions appear as voluntary actions of the participants, as expressions of their common will or as contracts that may be enforced by the state against a single party, cannot, being mere forms, determine this content. They only express it. This content is just whenever it corresponds to the mode of production, is adequate to it. It is unjust whenever it contradicts it.[10]

When Marx says that a just transaction is one which 'corresponds' or is 'adequate' to the mode of production, he means, I think, that it harmonizes with and performs a function relative to it. An unjust transaction, by contrast, is one which 'contradicts' the prevailing mode, which clashes with it or is dysfunctional relative to it. To make a scientific judgment on the justice or injustice of a particular transaction or practice therefore requires both that we understand the workings of the productive mode we are dealing with, and appreciate the functional relationship this transaction or practice has to this system of production. Thus Engels says that 'social justice or injustice is decided by the science which deals with the material facts of production and exchange, the science of political economy.'[11]

Marx's concept of justice is not relativistic. Whether a given transaction is just or unjust does depend for Marx on its relationship to the mode of production of which it is a part, so that transactions which are just in the context of one mode of production would be unjust in the context of another. But one does not have to be a relativist to believe that the justice of an act depends on the circumstances in which it is performed. A relativist is someone who holds that certain specific actions are right or wrong, just or unjust only 'for' (as judged by) some individual or culture or epoch, that there is no saying whether an act is right or just unless we specify the subject relative to which the judgment is made. The Marxian concept of justice, however, involves no view of this kind. If, for example, a historical analysis of the role of slavery in the ancient world shows that this institution corresponded to the prevailing mode of production, then in the Marxian view the holding of slaves by the ancients was a *just* practice, not only 'for them' but also 'for us', and indeed 'for' anyone. The judgment that ancient slavery was unjust, whether it is made by contemporaries of the institution or by moderns reading about it in history books, would simply be wrong.[12] When Marx and Engels say that people at different times and places have held diverse views about the nature of 'eternal justice', they are not espousing relativism; they are rather arguing that there are no 'eternal' rational principles or formal criteria of justice, applicable irrespective of time and circumstances. As Engels puts it, truths about morality 'belong to the domain of human history'. They are objective, empirical truths about the functional relation of acts or practices to the social structures in which they take place.[13]

Marx gives no argument for his conception of justice, but the reasoning behind it is probably something like the following: Historical materialism holds that the concept of justice is socially important and socially potent because of the way in which standards of justice sanction the production relations corresponding to the current state of a society's productive forces. It also holds that these standards have the content they do at a given time because of the way in which that content sanctions the particular form of production then prevailing. To the extent that materialists are successful in making a case for these claims, they can show that if a society adopted standards of justice different from its actual ones, treating as just what it currently treats as unjust, then production under the existing conditions could not function as smoothly or efficiently as it does, and as it must tend to do if the postulates of historical materialism are to hold. Consequently, there is a strong tendency, founded on materialist considerations, for those standards of justice to prevail which sanction practices corresponding to the existing mode of production. Further, it is only insofar as moral standards serve the function of sanctioning social relations that they exist. Standards which are at odds with prevailing relations do not fulfill the function proper to moral standards. Hence they must be not only socially impotent but also wrong, because they are at odds with the proper social function of morality. Material production thus provides a basis for moral standards, the only real basis Marx thinks they can have. For Marx, as for Hegel, the morally rational is determined by the socially actual.

3 Capitalism and commodity exchange

We can see Marx's concept of justice in operation when we turn to his treatment of the question whether the appropriation of surplus value by capital involves any injustice to the workers, or any violation of their rights. A number of socialists in Marx's day (Pierre Proudhon, Thomas Hodgkin, John Bray, among others) argued that capitalism involves an unequal (and hence unjust) exchange of commodities between worker and capitalist.

Their argument was based on Ricardo's principle, adopted in a slightly modified form by Marx himself, that labor is the sole creator of exchange value and that 'the value of a commodity . . . depends on the relative quantity of labor necessary for its production.'[14] Workers, these socialists pointed out, hire themselves out to the capitalist for a definite wage, and are supplied by the capitalist with means of production which are productively consumed in the labor process. At the end of this process, however, a worker has produced a commodity of greater value than the combined values of the wages paid and the means of production consumed. That the 'surplus value' (as Marx calls it) should be appropriated by the capitalist is an injustice, according to these socialists. For according to Ricardo's principle, the worker's labor is responsible not only for the value paid in wages, but for the surplus value as well. Hence surplus value must arise because capitalists pay workers less in wages than their labor is worth. If capitalists paid workers the full value of their labor, no surplus value would result, and the demands of just and equal commodity exchange would be satisfied.[15]

Marx rejects both this account of the origin of surplus value and the claim that surplus value involves an unequal exchange between worker and capitalist. He sees this explanation of surplus value as at bottom no different from the one given by Sir James Steuart and others before the physiocrats, that surplus value originates from selling commodities above their value.[16] The socialists merely turned things around and explain surplus value by supposing that labor is purchased below its value. Both explanations make surplus value appear the result of mere accident, and are therefore inherently unsatisfactory.

The main flaw in the argument that surplus value involves an unequal exchange, as Marx sees it, relates to the phrase 'the value of labor'. Strictly speaking, according to Marx, labor itself cannot be said to have value.[17] In the socialists' argument, the phrase 'value of labor' is used to denote two different values. It denotes, on the one hand the *value created by labor*, the socially necessary labor time expended on the commodity and added to the value of the means of production consumed in making it. It is in this sense that the capitalist pays the worker less than the 'value of his labor'. But as Marx points out, it is not the value created by labor that the capitalist pays for. The capitalist does not buy finished commodities from the worker, less the amount of means of production consumed. Rather, capitalists buy, in the form of a commodity, the workers' capacity to produce commodities for them, they buy what Marx calls 'labor power' (*Arbeitskraft*).

In the capitalist labor process, capital is merely making use of what it has bought antecedent to the process. 'As soon as [the worker's] labor begins, it has already ceased to belong to him; hence it is no longer a thing he can sell.'[18]

The *value of labor power*, like the value of any commodity, depends on the quantity of labor socially necessary for its production. In other words, the value of labor power depends on the quantity of labor necessary to keep a worker alive and working, or to replace a worker who dies or quits. Now Marx's theory of surplus value *postulates* that all commodities, including labor power, are bought at their values.[19] Hence Marx's theory of surplus value postulates that the exchange between capitalist and worker is an exchange of equal values, and hence, on the very principle of justice used in the socialists' argument, a *just* transaction. Surplus value, to be sure, is appropriated by the capitalist (as Marx often says) without paying the worker an equivalent for it.[20] But there is nothing in the transaction which requires any payment for it. The exchange of wages for labor power is the only exchange between capitalist and worker. It is an equal exchange, and it is consummated long before the question arises of selling the commodity produced and realizing its surplus value.[21] The capitalist buys a commodity (labor power) and pays (Marx postulates) its full value; by using, exploiting, this commodity, capital acquires a greater value than it began with. The surplus belongs to the capitalist; it never belonged to anyone else. 'This circumstance', says Marx, 'is peculiar good fortune for the buyer [of labor power], but no wrong or injustice (*Unrecht*) at all to the seller.'[22]

Nevertheless, it might still seem that Ricardo's principle could be used to argue that the appropriation of surplus value by capital does an injustice to the worker. Ricardo's principle says that labor is the sole creator and the very substance of value, that means of production only increase in value insofar as labor time is expended on them. It seems to follow that the entire increase ought to go to the worker, since it is through labor alone that it comes about. 'The labor of a man's body, and the work of his hands,' as Locke puts it, 'are properly his.'[23] By appropriating surplus value, capitalists may not be engaging in an unequal exchange with workers, but they are (in Marx's own words) 'exploiting', even 'robbing' them, reaping the fruits of their 'unpaid labor'. Surely Marx must regard this exploitation and robbery as unjust. I think it is really this argument that we attribute to Marx when we are tempted to take his denunciations of capitalism as denunciations of injustice.

134

The argument has two main premises. The first is that surplus value arises from the appropriation by capital of part of the value created by labor for which the worker receives no equivalent. The second is that each person's property rights are based on that person's labor, so that each person has a right to appropriate the full value created by that labor, and anyone who deprives a worker of this value can be said to have done the worker an injustice. Marx plainly accepts the first premise. Does he accept the second? We saw in Chapter III that Marx, like Locke, views appropriation as a basic function of human labor. But unlike Locke, Marx does not regard this appropriation as determining any particular form of social property or (what is the juridical expression of the same thing) any determinate property rights.

Marx recognizes, of course, that the notion that property rights are based on one's own labor is common among bourgeois ideologists, and he even sees reasons why this notion should seem plausible.

> Originally property rights appeared to us to be based on one's own labor. At least this assumption must be made, since only commodity owners with equal property rights confronted each other, and the only means of appropriating an alien commodity was by alienating one's own commodities, which could only be replaced by labor.[24]

In a mode of production where individual producers own their own means of production, property rights would be based exclusively on one's own labor, and surplus value would not exist. But the reason for this would simply be that since there is no separation of labor from the means of production, there would be no need for these means to take the social form of capital, and no need for labor to take the form of a commodity, labor power.

In capitalism, however, labor power appears as a commodity on an ever-increasing scale. Labor power, however, is only purchased to be used, and cannot function as a commodity if it is not useful to its purchaser. If the entire value of the commodity produced were expended by capital in wages and means of production, then the capitalist would have received no use from the labor power he purchased, and would have done better simply to convert his purchasing power into commodities he could consume. If capital realized no surplus value, capitalists would have no incentive to develop the forces of production, and no occasion to engage in that prudent abstinence for which they are rewarded by God and man alike. Hence the appearance of labor power as a commodity brings about what Marx calls a 'dialectical reversal' of the pre-

135

viously assumed rights of property: under capitalism

> property turns out to be the right on the part of the capitalist
> to appropriate alien unpaid labor or its product, and on the
> part of the worker the impossibility of appropriating his own
> product. The separation of property from labor has become the
> necessary consequence of a law that apparently originated
> in their identity.[25]

4 *Capital exploits justly*

Given Marx's concept of justice, capital's exploitation of the
worker is just. The justice of transactions in capitalist production
rests on their adequacy and correspondence to the capitalist mode
of production. The exploitation of labor by capital not only harmonizes with the capitalist mode of production, but without it,
capitalism would not even be possible. Consequently, capitalist
exploitation is just.

Marx is quite explicit about this. In the *Critique of the Gotha
Program*, he replies to the Program's demand for 'a just distribution' with a series of rhetorical questions:

> What is a 'just distribution'?
> Do not the bourgeois assert that the present distribution is
> just? And isn't it in fact the only just distribution based on
> the present mode of production? Are economic relations ruled
> by juridical concepts (*Rechtsbegriffe*), or do not, on the con-
> trary, juridical relations arise out of economic ones?[26]

I take it that the second and third questions are to be answered
affirmatively. The bourgeois *do* assert that the present distribution
is just, and it *is* in fact the only just distribution based on the present mode of production. Lest we think that the justice or injustice of a system of distribution might be judged on some other
basis, the implied answer to the fourth rhetorical question reminds
us that juridical concepts do *not* rule economic relations, but, on
the contrary, juridical relations (the actual justice or injustice
of transactions between agents of production) *do* arise out of
economic ones.

Adolph Wagner's interpretation of Marx elicits from him some
even more emphatic statements:

> This obscurantist foists on me the view that 'surplus value,'
> which is produced by the workers alone, remains with the
> capitalist entrepreneurs in a *wrongful* manner (*ungebührlicher*

Weise). But I say the direct opposite: namely, that at a certain point, the production of commodities necessarily becomes 'capitalistic' production of commodities, and that according to the *law of value* which rules that production, 'surplus value' is due (*gebührt*) to the capitalist and not to the workers.[27]

In my presentation, the earnings of capital are not in fact [as Wagner alleges] 'only a deduction or 'robbery' of the worker.' On the contrary, I present the capitalist as a necessary functionary of capitalist production, and show at length that he does not only 'deduct' or 'rob' but forces the production of surplus value, and thus helps create what is to be deducted; further I show in detail that even if in commodity exchange *only equivalents* are exchanged, the capitalist — as soon as he pays the worker the actual value of his labor power — earns *surplus value* with full right, i.e. the right corresponding to this mode of production.[28]

In reading these passages, there still may be a temptation to think that Marx does not mean to say that capitalist exploitation is really just, but only that it is commonly considered just, or that it is just only by (false) bourgeois standards. But to think this is to make the assumption that there might be standards of justice which are 'truer' than those dictated by adequacy or correspondence to the prevailing mode of production, or another (and better) basis for calling practices just or unjust than the one provided by their actual economic function. Marx's concept of justice involves the rejection of precisely these assumptions.

The Wagner notes also lay to rest the idea that Marx must believe capitalist exploitation is wrongful or unjust because (in language reminiscent of the early Proudhon) he describes it as 'robbery' and 'theft'. For in the above passage Marx agrees that his theory says capital robs the worker, but nevertheless insists (in the very same sentence) that the capitalist 'earns surplus value with full right'. Plainly the sort of 'robbery' involved in capital's exploitation of labor is not one which Marx sees as constituting a wrong or injustice to the workers. What sort of robbery is this? In a number of places, Marx indicates that the capitalist class stands to the proletariat in a relation somewhat analogous to that of a conquering people to a less organized and less well-armed (but more productive) population which it regularly plunders or from which (in lieu of this) it exacts tribute.[29] If this is the analogy, then it is not so clear that robbery has to be unjust, given Marx's concept of justice. For Marx, the relation between plunderers or conquerors and their victims or tributaries is not something economically accidental, but must constitute a regular production relation as determined by the stage of development of the victims' productive powers.[30] Hence there is good reason to think that the transactions (ranging from military incursions to tax collection) between plunderers and plundered correspond to the prevailing mode of production, and are just according to Marx's concept of justice. Likewise, there is good reason to think that when capitalists plunder their workers in an analogous fashion, they are acting fully within their rights, as the Wagner notes say they are.

As we will see in Chapter XV, an essential feature of all economic exploitation for Marx is coercion. In capitalist exploitation, this coercion is masked by the *fictio juris* of a voluntary contract between capitalist and worker. This is the point of Marx's frequent insinuations that capital not only robs but also cheats or defrauds the workers. Yet Marx never infers from this that capital does the workers an injustice, and there is no reason why he must draw such an inference. Very few people would hold that all coercion as such is unjust, and there is no sign that Marx holds this. Marx does mean to attack the illusions built into capitalist production, and in particular its illusion that wage laborers are freer than slaves, serfs or other oppressed classes. One of the reasons why Marx attacks the juridical conception of the capital-labor relation is that it is a prominent vehicle for this illusion. But the illusion here is not in the belief that the transactions between capital and labor are just (this belief is quite true). The illusion is in the false, moralistic idea that this justice guarantees liberty to the workers, or protects them from exploitation, or gives them any reason to be content with their lot.

Another temptation may be to suppose that Marx might condemn capitalist exploitation as unjust by applying standards which would be appropriate to some postcapitalist mode of production. No doubt capitalism could be condemned in this way, but since Marx holds that such standards would not be applicable to capitalism, there is no reason to think he would agree with the resulting moral judgments. 'Right can never be higher than the economic formation of society and the cultural development conditioned by it.'[31] Marx does believe that a communist revolution will introduce a new mode of production, and with it new standards of right and justice — or rather a succession of such standards, as postcapitalist society itself develops. If Marx speaks of these standards as 'higher' than those of bourgeois society, he does not mean that they approach more closely to some timeless moral ideal, but only that they belong to a society which as a whole is higher as measured by its productive powers and the non-moral goods they furnish to people. New moral or juridical standards do not create a new mode of production, they only express and support it, just as the old standards did for the old society. A higher mode of production is not 'more just' than a lower one; it is only just in its own way.

Engels does of course speak of the 'proletarian morality of the future' and its competition with the 'Christian feudal' and 'modern bourgeois' moralities. He interprets competing moral codes as class ideologies, 'either justifying the domination and the interests of the ruling class or else, as soon as the oppressed class becomes strong enough, representing the indignation against this dominion and the future interests of the oppressed'. He even says that there has been 'progress in morality largely and on the whole, as in all other branches of human knowledge'.[32] These remarks might lead us to expect that Marx and Engels would envision 'proletarian' standards of justice whose imposition on capitalist society would give expression to the proletarians' indignation against their condition and serve to promote their class interests. Engels, however, explicitly denies that the 'proletarian morality of the future' is 'true' as contrasted with its feudal and bourgeois predecessors. And neither Marx nor Engels ever employs the standards of 'future' or 'proletarian' morality to condemn the present social order.

But why not? The reason, I believe, is this: The fact that capitalism is just (by the standards appropriate to capitalist production) provides no real defense of capitalist society. Likewise, the fact that it could be condemned as unjust by applying some foreign standard constitutes no valid criticism of capitalist relations. The rational content of proletarian moral ideologies consists in the real proletarian interests represented by these ideologies, and the nonmoral goods which will come about as a result of the victory of these interests in the historical struggle. Marx prefers to criticize capitalism directly in terms of this rational content, and sees no point in presenting his criticisms in the mystified form they would assume in a moral ideology.

Marx does not hold that an idea is correct just in case it is a proletarian idea. If Marx had condemned capitalism by measuring it against 'proletarian' standards of justice, then it would still be pertinent to inquire after the rational foundation of those standards, and the grounds for regarding them as applicable to capitalism. These questions are not settled for Marx merely by calling the standards 'proletarian', or even by showing that their dissemination or satisfaction serves proletarian interests. For

139

Marx, standards of justice based on correspondence to the prevailing mode of production can be given some sort of rational foundation. Alternative 'proletarian' standards could not. The most that could be said for them is that people whose heads are stuffed with such ideological fluff would be easier converts to the proletarian cause. But one of the chief aims of that cause, as Marx pictures it, is to enable people to disenthrall themselves of ideological illusions, to cast off the need for them. To create a 'proletarian morality' or 'proletarian concept of justice' by disseminating a set of ideas which working class agitators find politically advantageous would strike Marx as a shortsighted and self-defeating course for the movement to adopt. It is far safer and more efficacious in the long run to rely simply on the genuine (i.e., nonmoral) reasons people have for wanting an obsolete and inhuman social system to be overthrown and replaced by a higher one.[33]

X

Morality as Ideology

1 *The social function of morality*

Given Marx's concept of justice, it is obvious that for him the question whether capitalist exploitation should be abolished or not does not turn on whether it is just or unjust. Instead, it turns on whether capitalist social relations correspond to the existing stage of society's productive powers and whether they are conducive to the further development of these powers. If (as Marx believes) capitalism is fast becoming obsolete, and has already become a fetter on human development, then the more swiftly and painlessly capitalism is done away with, the better it will be for humanity. The laws and moral precepts which arise out of the existing order, however, are charged with the function of protecting that order; they will probably forbid some of the steps necessary to overthrow it. Once we recognize that moral defenses of capitalism have this material basis, these defenses will no longer have the power to mystify us. We will be like those proletarians to whom, according to Marx, 'laws, morality, religion are only so many bourgeois prejudices, behind which hide just as many bourgeois interests.'[1]

For Marx, in revolutionary situations, morality is more an obstacle to human progress than one of its weapons. Against Proudhon, he insists that in history 'it is always the bad side which finally triumphs over the good side. For the bad side is the one which brings movement to life, which makes history by bringing the struggle to fruition.'[2] At this point, as Engels makes quite explicit, Marx is following Hegel, for whom 'evil is the form in which the driving force of historical development presents itself. . . . Each new progress necessarily steps forward as a crime

against something holy, as rebellion against conditions which are
old, dying, yet hallowed by custom.'[3]

Engels' interpretation of Hegel is correct. Hegel sees morality
as basically a conservative social force, an aspect of human culture
which periodically must be violated and overthrown by the movement of history to make way for what is novel, higher and more
rational. The essential function of morality for Hegel is to preserve
a spirit, a culture, a people, a way of life. When history has rendered
a form of spirit obsolete, it must destroy this form to make way
for a higher one:

> Here is just where there arise the great collisions of subsisting,
> recognized duties, laws and rights with those possibilities
> which are opposed to this system, which violate it, and even
> destroy its foundations and actuality. . . . These possibilities
> now become history; they include a universal of another species
> than the universal which constitutes the basis of the people's
> or state's subsistence.[4]

The world-historical possibilities, in Hegel's view, are seized upon
by 'world-historical individuals', by extraordinary and ambitious
men such as Alexander the Great, Julius Caesar or Napoleon
Bonaparte, who 'grasp the higher universal, make it their own
purpose and realize this purpose in accordance with the higher
law of the spirit'. The effectiveness of these individuals as vehicles
of historical reason consists largely in the fact that they are driven
by powerful 'passions' which 'respect none of the limitations
which law and morality would impose on them', and consequently
are not deterred by the powerful conservative forces which try to
block the progressive movement of the world spirit.[5] As Engels
says (again expounding Hegel): 'it is precisely the bad passions of
men, greed and love of dominion, which have become the levers
of historical development.'[6]

Of course Marx does not view 'reason' or 'spirit' or 'history'
as historical agents, and he does not think that individual 'great
men' are the prime movers of history. But he does agree with
Hegel in viewing human history as consisting of a series of epochs,
with each one succeeding the next through a tumultuous period of
transition in which society is shaken to its very foundations. And
he does think that moral standards, as they are actually recognized
and lived, are generally on the conservative side in such historical
struggles. A rising social class for Marx is of course not driven by
'passion' but by its class interests. Yet these interests (like the
ambitions of Hegel's great men) are fundamentally aspirations
to nonmoral goods, which are able to effect fundamental social

142

changes precisely because they are opposed to and more powerful than the moral and legal superstructures of the old social order.

The *Communist Manifesto* emphasizes this 'immoralist' aspect of the bourgeois revolution when it points out how the bourgeoisie has abolished the 'political and religious illusions of feudalism', and 'drowned the holy fervor of pious enthusiasm, of chivalrous inspiration, of philistine sentimentality, in the icy water of egoistical calculation'.[7] Marx exhibits the same attitude in behalf of the revolutionary proletariat when he asserts that the movement will not be deterred by 'bourgeois prejudices, hiding bourgeois interests', and condemns those who would base the proletariat's conception of its historical aims on 'ideological shuffles' and 'outdated verbal trivia' such as the notions of 'just distribution' and 'equal right'.[8] For Marx, the socially effective norms of right and justice (if correctly understood in their actual social function) are largely weapons of the oppressing class. Far from being carried out in their name, the proletarian revolution can only succeed through 'despotic encroachments on property rights'.[9]

Marx regards moral consciousness generally as ideological, and moralists in general as ideologists. Granted Marx's views, morality may be described as 'ideology' in all three of the senses we distinguished in Chapter VII. Engels decries the concern with achieving 'social justice' in post capitalist society as 'idealistic'.[10] I think Marx and Engels regard social criticism based on moral norms as a form of 'historical idealism'. That is, they regard the moralistic approach to social criticism as predicated on the belief that the faithful adherence by individuals to the correct moral precepts is the proper way to effect progressive social change and to remove social oppression, whatever the state of society's productive forces or economic relations. It is not evident that social critics are necessarily committed to this belief when they base their criticism on 'justice' or other moral ideals, but it is undeniable that the belief is commonly held (often tacitly and uncritically) by people who do adopt a moralistic approach to social issues. And the belief is clearly inconsistent with some of the main tenets of historical materialism.

Marx also holds that moral ideas, beliefs and sentiments are functional ideologies. As we have seen, he holds that the content of recognized moral norms can be explained by the way in which they sanction existing social relations. Even where moral consciousness turns revolutionary, its content is determined by the class interests it sanctifies. And finally, moral consciousness is typically ideological illusion, in that people are normally unaware

143

of the social function fulfilled by the moral convictions they hold, and ignorant of the real basis of the highminded sentiments which motivate them. As a consequence of this ignorance, moral consciousness often involves illusions: ignorant of the real basis of their moral duties and impulses, people are easy prey for philosophical or religious ideas which represent these duties and impulses as having some holier or more rational basis than transient social forms and class interests.

Marx's critique of moral consciousness at this point clearly involves some assumptions which historical materialism by itself can never fully justify, no matter how successful it may be empirically. Perhaps historical materialism can show that Christian, Kantian or utilitarian moral theories have social functions of which their proponents are unaware, and that it is these social functions rather than the philosophical proofs offered in their favor which explain their wide social appeal. But historical materialism cannot (all by itself) show that recognized moral duties are *not* commanded by God or pure reason, or enjoined by some principle built into our nature as pleasure-loving, pain-avoiding and naturally sociable beings. Nor can it show that there is not some quality of overriding disinterested goodness which attaches to just and virtuous actions, even when these actions can be shown systematically to contribute to a social system based on class oppression. By itself, historical materialism can at most confound the moralists, by showing them that their disinterested moral good is in the end historically impotent because it is always finally at odds with the long term nonmoral interests of human development which govern the basic tendencies of history.

The German Ideology claims that historical materialism has 'broken the staff of all morality'; the *Communist Manifesto* declares that in view of the fact that people's ideas are products of their material conditions, 'the charges raised against communism from a religious, philosophical and in general from an ideological standpoint deserve no detailed examination.'[11] In these passages, Marx and Engels may be expressing the mistaken belief that historical materialism alone suffices to justify their contemptuous rejection of a long and broad tradition of moral thinking. But their attitude, while it may be rendered much more plausible by a materialist account of the social function of morality, also requires some *philosophical* defense. Marx may owe some argument (which he never really gives) to those who believe that standards of right and justice have a broader scope or stronger rational basis than his materialist theory allows for. Certainly a defense of his view requires that some sort of reply be made

144

to those philosophers who have pretended to supply such a basis. But Marx is probably right in thinking that if he can explain the content of morality materialistically in terms of its social function, then this raises deep and troubling questions for moralists, and suggests that a radical reassessment of moral values and moral consciousness is in order.

2 Marxism and utilitarianism

The claim is often made that the moral basis of Marxism is some form of utilitarianism. While I disagree with this claim, I think it is true that Marx's thoughts about morality have more in common with utilitarianism than with any other familiar position in moral philosophy. These thoughts can be illuminated by exploring their differences with utilitarianism.

Marx's explicit statements about utilitarianism do not give us much to work with. They express contemptuous rejection of the doctrine, but give little evidence that Marx understands what he is rejecting. *The German Ideology*'s attacks on Stirner's utilitarianism, which include criticisms of the French and British tradition behind it, rely heavily on Hegel's criticisms of the 'standpoint of utility' in *The Phenomenology of Spirit*. They attack only caricatures of utilitarian thinking, and betray some fairly elementary misunderstandings of what utilitarianism (at least in such philosophers as Bentham, Mill, Austin, and Sidgwick) is all about.[12] Marx's well-known comments in *Capital* about Bentham ('that insipid, pedantic, leather-tongued oracle of the ordinary bourgeois understanding') and his principle of utility ('at no time and in no land has a homespun commonplace ever swaggered so complacently') are abusive enough, but on closer inspection they exhibit even less substantive disagreement with Bentham's principle than comprehension of it.[13]

Utilitarianism holds that what is fundamentally desirable is the nonmoral good of all human (perhaps all sentient) beings, and that the moral good is determined by what is conducive to maximizing this nonmoral good. The determination of the moral good by the nonmoral can be conceived of in a variety of ways (directly in terms of particular acts, or via rules, moral codes or the imposition of sanctions), and this variety marks off the main forms utilitarianism takes. Most utilitarians (especially early in the doctrine's history) have held a hedonistic theory of the nonmoral good, though some have not. All utilitarians, however, hold that the nonmoral good is measurable and summable, so that at least in principle it makes sense to compare acts or policies on the basis of a precise measurement of the total nonmoral good which will result from them.

Marx and utilitarians agree in according supreme value to the nonmoral good of human beings, and in denying that this good can be overridden by moral considerations allegedly having a higher claim on us than this good. I think these points of agreement constitute the principal element of truth in the claim that Marx is a utilitarian. But there are further affinities as well. Like utilitarians, Marx views morality as a device for securing the compliance of individuals with social requirements. Marx's account of what is right or just as what corresponds to the needs of the existing mode of production has some resemblance to the utilitarian account of morality as laying down the conditions for maximizing human welfare.

But Marx is not a utilitarian. There is no sign at all that Marx's conception of the nonmoral good is hedonistic. Further, Marx appears disinclined to regard the nonmoral good as quantitatively measurable and summable in the ways required by utilitarian theories. I think this is part of what *The German Ideology* means to express when it criticizes utilitarians for 'merging all relations in' or 'reducing all relations to' the 'abstract category of utility'.[14] Of course, if Marx were asked whether he would prefer a society with *more* of what he considers nonmorally good (self-actualization, prosperity, community, freedom) to one with *less*, I suppose he would answer affirmatively. He even says in one passage that 'in future society the time of production devoted to different objects will be determined by their degree of social utility.'[15] In *Capital*, however, Marx peremptorily dismisses the use-value of commodities as a basis for their exchange value on the ground that the utility of different commodities cannot be quantitatively compared at all: 'As use-values, commodities are before everything of different quality, while as exchange values they can only be of different quantities.'[16] As the *Critique* makes clear, Marx regards different use-values as comparable quantitatively only relative to others which are qualitatively the same, and can be measured against them in terms of gross physical quantities, such as length or weight or volume: 'Different use-values possess different measures according to their physical properties: a bushel of wheat, a quire of paper, an ell of linen.'[17] To utilitarians, these remarks will no doubt seem philosophically naive. But I think they are conclusive evidence of Marx's disinclination to treat utility in a utilitarian way.

Marx's deepest disagreements with utilitarianism, however, have to do not with his conception of nonmoral goods, but with his conception of morality. Marx regards moral norms (for instance, right and justice) as determined by correspondence to the prevailing mode of production, and not by what is conducive to the greatest nonmoral good. Given Marx's theory of social change, this leads to systematic divergences between his account of what morality demands and a utilitarian account, especially during periods of social revolution.

According to Marx, the primary function of moral standards is to sanction existing production relations which, during periods of social stability, constitute the social conditions under which society's productive powers, at the existing stage of their development, can be most efficiently employed and developed further. It might be (though it is not self-evident) that during such periods, morality does prescribe conditions under which the total welfare of humanity will be maximized. Even supposing this is so, in societies based on class oppression, morality would prescribe the conditions for the systematic subordination of the welfare of the oppressed to that of the oppressors. Utilitarianism conceals this fact by considering only the aggregate good or 'general happiness', thus conspicuously exemplifying the tendency of moral ideologies to represent the interests of the ruling class as universal human interests, which even the oppressed have a stake in promoting. During periods of social revolution, when existing social relations have become fetters on human development, the dictates of morality on Marx's theory will systematically diverge from the path prescribed by the good of humanity as a whole; Marx's account of morality will flatly contradict the utilitarian one. Of course Marx and the utilitarian agree that in such situations the nonmoral good of humanity is preferable to the dictates of morality (conceived in the Marxian fashion as correspondence to the prevailing mode of production). But they differ in that Marx regards these dictates as *morally valid*, whereas the utilitarian is committed to denying this.

I am sure that to many Marx's position here will appear perverse. Utilitarians will doubtless argue that when a mode of production has become obsolete (for the utilitarian: has ceased to promote the general happiness of humanity) then the moral code which sanctions it has also ceased to be valid, and a new moral code (perhaps one appropriate to the next form of society and serving the interests of the oppressed classes) should be regarded as the binding one. Most utilitarians (like Mill) will admit, or rather earnestly maintain, that people still have much to learn as to the effects of actions on the general happiness. They agree with Marx that the received codes of morality are not of divine right.

147

The force of their utilitarianism is only that moral standards conducive to the greatest happiness *should* prevail, whether they have done so up to now or not.

At this point utilitarianism betrays its commitment to some definite assumptions which are distinctly at odds with Marx's historical materialism. First, utilitarians generally assume that the social function of morality is and always has been to promote the general happiness, and that its failure to do so adequately in the past has always been due to the unfortunate effects of ignorance and superstition. (Utilitarians are nearly always inclined to beat a cowardly retreat to the conservative assumption that received morality is utilitarian whenever opponents threaten them with morally repugnant consequences which appear to follow from utilitarianism.) But second, even in their more reformist moods, utilitarians betray their espousal of views which Marx would condemn as 'ideological' or 'idealist'. When utilitarians tell us that moral standards conducive to the greatest happiness *should* prevail, the 'should' must not be construed morally. If it were, the utilitarians would be appealing to some (as yet unjustified) moral standard to ground the moral standards they claim to be giving a nonmoral foundation. But in that case, why do they have to mention morality at all? Why don't they say directly (with Marx) that social relations (including those to which the actually valid moral standards correspond) 'should' be revolutionized so as to promote people's nonmoral good? The main reason, I think, is that utilitarians still believe that the right way to bring about economic change is to reform the moral ideas people carry around in their heads. Marx holds, on the contrary, that both the prevailing moral ideologies and the moral or juridical relations which are valid for a given society arise out of the economic relations belonging to its mode of production. Changes in prevailing standards of right and justice do not cause social revolutions, but only accompany them.

This of course is not to deny that bringing about changes in the moral, legal and political superstructure of society is for Marx an important subordinate moment of revolutionary practice. As we saw earlier, superstructures have economic power, and on Marx's theory they exist because they serve the needs of the mode of production to which they correspond. An economic revolution therefore probably could not take place without a revolution in the political and ideological sphere. But on Marx's theory, new standards of right and justice come to be valid *because* revolutionary changes occur in economic relations. It is *not* the case that revolutions do occur or should occur because postrevolutionary

148

moral standards are already valid for prerevolutionary society.

Marx's point is that morality is not a blank tablet on which we can write whatever commandments seem best to us. Morality, like every other artifact of human history, is made by people under definite conditions and presuppositions. To command, require or forbid a certain act *morally* is to command, require or forbid it in a determinate way, to say something about it with a definite social meaning. It is not an analytic proposition or trivial truth to say that the just, the virtuous or the morally right thing is the thing which, all things considered, should be done. For Marx, in fact, it is sometimes a pernicious falsehood. Marxism explicitly parts company with all views which hold that moral standards (such as right and justice) constitute 'the fundamental principle of all society', 'the standard by which to measure all things human', 'the final judge to be appealed to in all conflicts'.[18]

The very existence of moral concepts (right, justice, duty, virtue) and sentiments (the love of virtue, the motive of duty, the sense of justice) is on Marx's materialist theory to be explained by the social functions they perform. More specifically, the theory proposes to explain the specific content of moral norms by their correspondence to the prevailing mode of production. For Marx, what is right and just simply *is* what performs this function at this time, whether or not the valid norms of right and justice happen just then to serve the long run interests of humanity, and even if these interests require us to disregard and violate these norms. To suppose, as utilitarians do, that a moral norm or moral code is actually valid wherever its adoption would promote the greatest nonmoral good is (on Marx's social theory) to entertain a false and fantastic conception of the actual role morality plays in human society. And since on Marx's theory the nature of any social factor is determined by its social function, this is to entertain a false and fantastic conception of what morality *is*.

3 Is Marx an immoralist?

So far, I have been emphasizing the 'amoralist', even 'immoralist' side of Marx. I believe the best way to account for Marx's explicit statements about right and justice, as well as a number of other things he says about morality, is to suppose that he observes a distinction between moral and nonmoral values, and that (following Hegel) he views moral values as normally on the conservative side in revolutionary situations.

Marx's view of morality may also be fruitfully compared with Nietzsche's. Marx and Nietzsche both approach morality by attempting to identify the role it actually plays in human life, and to evaluate moral values themselves according to the way they promote or impede the development of humanity's nonmoral potentialities. In Nietzsche's case, the nonmoral values in question include such things as strength, creativity and abundant life. Nietzsche attacks morality's basic conceptions and everything that has so far been esteemed in its name insofar as he thinks morality has proven detrimental to (even hostile to) these non-moral goods. Like Nietzsche, Marx is a critic of morality. He too rejects morality insofar as it represents blind submission to en-trenched customs and stands in the way of human development by protecting outmoded social structures.[19]

Some of Nietzsche's harshest criticisms of morality are directed toward the way in which he believes it expresses and encourages illusions and self-deception about the meaning of people's feelings and actions. Marx's theory does not necessarily ascribe uncon-scious psychological motives to people, or self-deception about their motives. But it does hold that moral ideologies typically perform their social function by hiding that function from people, providing a religious, metaphysical or bogus humanitarian ratio-nale for observing morality's commands. These ideologies falsely represent the interests of one social class as universal human inter-ests, or what serves the interests of a class as something disinter-estedly good. And they typically encourage false, idealistic beliefs about what progressive social change consists in, and how it can best be achieved. Insofar as morality does these things, Marx believes that it is one of the chief tasks of historical materialism and the working class movement to undermine moral conscious-ness, along with other mystifying ideologies.

But Marx's 'immoralism' cannot be the whole story. For what-ever his social theory may say about morality, Marx is far from avoiding moral judgments about particular individuals and about commonly held social attitudes. His writings seethe with moral indignation, apparently directed against the bourgeoisie and its apologists. It is not difficult to find him attacking bourgeois governments or his political foes for cruelty, unscrupulousness or dishonesty, and defending the honor of the individuals and move-ments of which he approves. Like most everyone else, Marx mor-ally condemns stock-market swindling, mendacity and venality in politicians, and disloyalty or opportunism in his fellow radicals. He is not even above being scandalized by Ferdinand Lassalle's liaison with the Countess von Hatzfeldt.[20]

How are we to square the apparent 'immoralism' of Marx's social theory with the otherwise humdrum fact that Marx moralizes like the rest of us? One possibility, of course, is that my interpretation of Marx on morality is mistaken. But to adopt this solution, I submit, would require us to ignore or give a tortured interpretation to nearly everything Marx says explicitly about the nature of morality, the content of moral norms and the relation of moral consciousness to historical materialism.

Another option, more viable in my opinion, would be to say that Marx's views are simply incoherent: more precisely, that Marx's common sense moral judgments are undermined by the things he says about morality from a theoretical standpoint. Marx's theoretical reflections on morality are not extensive or well-developed in his writings. It is not unthinkable that even so acute a mind as his might not have realized that if these reflections were carried through consistently they could not be reconciled with the common-sense moral consciousness Marx takes for granted most of the time. If we decide to adopt this solution, it might justify us in dismissing the account of morality I have drawn from Marx's texts as a line of thinking too little developed by Marx himself to be counted as part of his genuine doctrine at all. To do this, however, would commit us to abandoning altogether the quest for Marx's moral views, or for the 'moral foundations' of his critique of capitalism. For it would be in effect to admit that Marx has no views about morality at all, that what he says on the subject amounts to nothing coherent enough to be called a definite doctrine.

But I doubt that we are forced to any such conclusions. For I doubt that there is any obvious incoherence between Marx's everyday moral judgments and his theoretical pronouncements about morality. Marx consistently refuses to attack capitalist social relations themselves as unjust or morally wrong in any way. These relations, which are always his primary target, are consistently attacked on exclusively nonmoral grounds, for the nonmoral evils (poverty, alienation, unfreedom) they impose on the workers. Undoubtedly the 'oppression', 'exploitation' and even 'robbery' inherent in capitalist relations are prominent objects of Marx's attacks. But there is no sign that Marx sees anything morally wrong or unjust about these features of capitalism; that they are wrong or unjust is precisely what Marx consistently denies. I think we find no contradiction or incoherence in Marx if we proceed on the assumption that he attacks social oppression and exploitation simply because he regards them as nonmoral evils or as the cause of nonmoral evils.

But what of the unmistakeably moral tone which pervades Marx's writings? The *Communist Manifesto* openly professes that

the communists 'never cease for a moment to educe from the workers the clearest possible consciousness of the hostile opposition
between bourgeoisie and proletariat'.[21] At least part of this hostility, as Marx expresses it, seems to consist in moral indignation
and blame, apparently directed against the bourgeoisie, and
against those who share bourgeois attitudes. But what can be
the target of this blame if not the oppressors, and how can Marx
treat oppressors as blameworthy if he finds nothing wrong or unjust in what they do?

Marx, however, explicitly disavows the intention to condemn
individual bourgeois morally for the social fact of class oppression. Not only does he deny that they are guilty of injustices, but
he also explicitly denies that they are morally responsible for
the exploitation from which they benefit. In the Preface to
Capital, Marx says:

> In order to prevent possible misunderstanding, a word. By
> no means do I paint the forms of capitalist and landowner in
> a rosy light. But here it is a question of persons only insofar
> as they are the personifications of economic categories, the
> bearers of determinate class-relations and class-interests. Less
> than any other can my standpoint, which grasps the develop-
> ment of economic social formations as a process of natural
> history, hold individuals responsible for the relations whose
> creatures they remain socially, however much they may rise
> above them subjectively.[22]

Here Marx denies that individual capitalists and landlords are
to blame for the exploitation from which they benefit, because
they as individuals do not create exploitative social relations but
only live out the role in which these relations cast them. But the
passage must be read carefully. For Marx is *not* saying that the
exploiters are blameless because they 'know not what they do'
(on the contrary, he explicitly excludes from blame those who
'subjectively rise above' their class position, who understand the
terrible consequences of the social relations in which they are
involved). Nor, I think, is Marx saying that the exploiters have
no choice because their actions are all causally determined (as
by economic facts). His point, I think, is that under capitalism
the individual exploiters should not be blamed because the economic system gives them no viable option but to exploit. If an
individual capitalist, in order to avoid being an exploiter, should
withdraw his capital from production (a choice which, as far
as I can see, Marx does not deny he is free to make) the result
would be only that he would lose the profit on his capital, and

152

the social power he refused to exercise would be wielded by some-one less high-principled (and less ineffectual). Marx never urges capitalists to practice such 'voluntary poverty' or tries to make them feel guilty for playing the economic role in which the system casts them. Certainly Marx never urged Engels to give up his textile mills in Manchester or prodded his conscience about them. Some writers have professed to find something hypocritical in the fact that Marx and Engels condemn capitalist exploitation while Engels (and Marx too, for many years) live off its fruits. Perhaps the behavior of Marx and Engels does violate moral principles held by these writers; but there is no evidence that it violates principles held by Marx and Engels themselves.

Marx has nothing but praise for those who, whatever their source of income, see the evils of capitalism and devote their time, energy and resources to its revolutionary overthrow. I suggest that he does not blame exploiters as such, but only those exploi-ters whose class interests blind them to the inhumanity of the system, people who remain callous and complacent in the face of the needless misery and alienation it causes. I think we can account for the tone of Marx's writings quite well if we suppose that his indignation is directed primarily against those 'oxen', who 'turn their backs on the torments of humanity and care only for their own hides'.[23] Callousness in the face of suffering may be morally evil even if suffering is a nonmoral evil. Marx falls into no inconsistency if he morally condemns an attitude of complacency in the face of massive and remediable nonmoral evil, while refusing to condemn morally the nonmoral evil itself.

4 Why should a Marxist be moral?

Perhaps what worries us, however, is not the threat that Marx's theoretical pronouncements about morality directly conflict with the specific moral judgments he makes. Instead, the suspicion may be that Marx's theory undermines morality in general, leaving Marx with no basis on which to be indignant over callousness, dishonesty, opportunism (or anything else) without succumbing to what he himself attacks as ideological nonsense.

But it will take some argument to show that this suspicion is well-founded. Marx holds that the rational basis for our moral beliefs and attitudes, insofar as there is one, consists in the way in which these beliefs and attitudes serve the prevailing mode of production or promote the interests of a certain social class. Once we see how they do this, we may very well find parts of morality dispensable or even objectionable. But it requires further argument

153

to show that the destructive impact of materialist self-awareness on our moral consciousness must be radical and wholesale, rather than limited and selective.

One such argument might be drawn from the Marxian claim that all morality is class morality, and the Marxian view that valid moral standards (e.g., of right and justice) consist in what corresponds to the prevailing mode of production. These ideas might be taken to imply that all valid moral standards in capitalist society promote bourgeois class interests and serve to protect what Marx regards as an inhuman system. Marx himself says that in bourgeois society morality is only 'bourgeois prejudice' masking 'bourgeois interests'. There is no reason for a proletarian, or indeed anyone else clearsighted enough to see capitalism as Marx sees it, to promote bourgeois interests or contribute to the stability of capitalist society. Therefore, such an individual has no reason at all to respect valid moral standards. They should appear as objectionable to him as capitalism itself.

This argument is sophistical. When Marx says that all morality is class morality and that justice consists in correspondence to the prevailing mode of production, he means that the effect of moral standards as a whole is to protect prevailing social relations and that certain distinctive features of prevalent moral ideas (e.g., the glorification of self-reliant individuality in bourgeois morals, or their emphasis on the sanctity of private property) can be explained by the way they promote class interests. But it does not follow from any of this that each and every element of bourgeois morality counts as distinctively bourgeois, considered in isolation from the whole, or that the moral precepts preached in bourgeois society always promote bourgeois interests whenever they are followed. Bourgeois morality, for instance, also teaches virtues such as kindness, generosity, loyalty and fidelity to promises. But there is no reason to think that these teachings in their bare, bloodless generality are peculiar to bourgeois society or necessarily serve bourgeois interests. They become specifically bourgeois only when united with other ideas and practices (for instance, when 'generosity' comes to mean socially inefficacious 'private charity' in place of genuine, revolutionary remedies for systematic poverty in society, or when 'loyalty' comes to mean devotion to the bourgeois state or to the 'free enterprise system'). Marx obviously expects proletarians to practice generosity and loyalty among themselves, and realizes that without these moral virtues the movement will neither succeed nor be deserving of anyone's support.

Of Michael Bakunin, Engels remarks: 'It is one of his chief principles that keeping promises and things of that kind are merely

154

bourgeois prejudices, which the true revolutionary must always treat with contempt in the interest of the cause.'[24] Engels obviously does not endorse Bakunin's (alleged) principle. There is nothing in Marxian theory which should incline him to do so.

When the *Communist Manifesto* says that to the proletarians, morality is only bourgeois prejudices masking bourgeois interests, we should not interpret this as saying any more than that proletarians should view in this light all moral appeals which would require or encourage them to sacrifice their class interests to those of the bourgeoisie, or place moral scruples in the way of overthrowing the capitalist system. Marx is not so desperately stupid as to regard every act of immorality or lawlessness as a blow against oppression, and he has only contempt for mindless terrorists who view their actions in this way.[25] He is always inclined to regard proletarian crime and immorality, like bourgeois crime and immorality, as a distasteful symptom of capitalism's decadence rather than as anything to be approved of. There is no reason why Marx should condone the violation of even so bourgeois a moral precept as respect for private property unless it serves some genuine purpose in the class struggle.

For Marx, morality is based on what societies require in order to function under the specific historical conditions where they are found. The fact that societies exist, and that moralities contribute to their success in the way they do, is clear evidence that people have a natural capacity to fulfill these requirements and a natural susceptibility to the demands morality makes on them, even where these demands run contrary to their personal whims or self-interest. For obvious reasons, Marx stresses the way in which morality in class society involves false consciousness and often commands people to act contrary to their real class interests. But Marx does not question the rationality of the basic human tendency on which the appeal of morality is founded: the tendency of people to fulfill the demands imposed on them by social life.

Of course this is not to say that Marx has any distinctive answer to the philosopher's question: 'Why be moral?' Marx does not even appear to hold that the moral thing always is the thing to do, so we should not expect a general answer from him in any case. But we might suppose that the question would be more difficult for him than for most philosophers, since his views pretty clearly involve a repudiation of some standard theological and metaphysical answers to it. Yet I see no reason why the question 'Why be moral?' should trouble a Marxist any more than it does most others who hold that the foundations of morality are made of mortal clay rather than of some celestial or transcendental stuff.

Marx's views ascribe to people a natural tendency to fulfill the substance of morality, that is, to satisfy the demands of social life corresponding to the stage of development of their productive powers. Although in class society the fulfillment of these demands may often depend on illusions, there is no reason to think that all acts of loyalty, honesty, generosity or self-sacrifice must depend on them. In particular, the fact that these acts may sometimes go against our self-interest creates no problem. Recall that for Marx egoistic actions are no more inherently natural or rational than altruistic or socially directed actions. The fact that the actions morality approves are sometimes not in the agent's own interest does not by itself show that there is any special problem about the rationality of these actions.

Marx sees historical materialism as 'breaking the staff of all morality' by showing people the real reason why moral ideologies appeal to them. In this way, it enables them to escape false or mystifying ideas which have held them captive. Because this new freedom gives them the power to reassess the rationality of morals, it is only to be expected that it will involve some changes in people's attitudes, less blind acceptance of what traditional morality dictates, and less susceptibility to fantastic motives and sentiments dreamed up by ideologues. In this sense, Marx must see a future society free of ideology as one which 'does away with morality instead of forming it anew'. But because the economic basis of morality is in itself fundamentally rational, there is reason to think that to a considerable extent the consequences of understanding morality materialistically will be that people will do 'consciously' and 'humanly' the same things they did before without understanding the real reasons for them. Hence there is also some reason to say (as Engels does) that in future society there will be an 'actual human morality' in place of the false, ideological moralities of class society.[26]

PART FOUR

Philosophical Materialism

XI

Materialist Naturalism

1 *What is materialism?*

Marx views his own social thought as involving some definite ideas about the nature of ultimate reality, the source of human knowledge and other matters which philosophers would place under the rubric of 'metaphysics and epistemology'. He does so because he regards his thought as a vehicle of the proletarian movement, and believes that a distinctively 'materialist' world outlook harmonizes with the historical practice of the proletariat and with the productive powers of modern scientific technology which make proletarian emancipation possible. There are indications of what Marx understood by his 'materialism' scattered through his writings, but chiefly in his earlier writings (produced between 1844 and 1846). Marx never wrote at length on the theme, however, or gave his own materialism any systematic focus. In the *Theses on Feuerbach*, Marx is at pains to distinguish *his* materialism from that of previous materialists, but he tells us very little about what 'materialism' itself is supposed to be.

More informative on this point are some of Engels' later writings, especially his essay on Feuerbach and his Introduction to the first English edition of *Socialism Utopian and Scientific*. Both expound Marxian materialism in some detail, though their substance does not depart very far from what Marx says explicitly (the Introduction quotes at length from an account of modern materialism written by Marx for *The Holy Family*). Unlike Marx, however, Engels does attempt to bring some degree of focus and system to the materialist world outlook. According to him, 'the great fundamental question of all philosophy, and especially of modern philosophy, is the relation of thinking and being', or (as he also puts it) of 'spirit and nature'. The question is: 'What is original or primary (*das Ursprüngliche*), spirit or nature? According as they have answered this question in one way or another, philosophers have divided themselves into two great camps', the 'idealists' and the 'materialists'.[1] Materialists assert the primacy of being or nature, while idealists hold that thought or spirit is primary. But what is it to believe in the 'primacy' of nature to spirit or of spirit to nature? At first reading, Engels' answers are bewilderingly diverse. Materialists, he tells us, hold that 'nature is the sole reality', that it 'exists independently of all philosophy', that 'nothing exists outside nature and man'.[2] Idealists maintain that God created the world, while materialists hold that the world has existed from eternity.[3] Idealists believe 'their thinking is an activity not of their bodies, but of a separate soul dwelling in the body and leaving it at death'; in contrast, materialists assert that 'matter is not a product of mind, but mind is only the highest product of matter,' and 'thinking is inseparable from matter which thinks.'[4] Further, materialists hold that motion is inherent in matter, and that the entire world is governed by natural laws, admitting of no miraculous intervention from without. Finally, we are told that the first form of materialism was scholastic nominalism.[5]

It is obvious that these characterizations of 'idealism' and 'materialism' involve a number of different philosophical issues. Engels' account suggests that there are really only two viable combinations of views on all these issues, each following from one of the two possible answers to a single basic philosophical question. (One is reminded of the opposition of 'idealism' and 'dogmatism' in the opening pages of Fichte's *Wissenschaftslehre*.) But I see no way in which Engels' suggestion could be made out. Without any obvious inconsistency, many philosophers have combined 'idealist' views on some matters with 'materialist' views on others. Hegel holds that nature is mind-dependent, but rejects a dualist account of the mind-body relation. Nominalists have believed in God and the separate existence of souls. Hobbes is a theist who holds both nominalism and a materialist theory of mind. Theists have held that motion is inherent in the (created) nature of matter, and atheists have denied that the world has always existed.

Yet perhaps there is something in Engels' way of putting things. Suppose we regard the fundamental tenet of Marxian materialism as what I will call *naturalism* (a term Marx also uses to describe his outlook). Naturalism says that the sole reality is the natural world, and this world is made up solely of matter. Naturalists will be atheists, since God is supposed to be a supernatural and an immaterial being. Naturalists will of course deny that the world was created by anything outside it, and that natural motion requires God (or any other supernatural agency) as its cause. Naturalism also implies realism, the thesis that material things are not dependent for their existence or nature on any mind or minds. For such minds would have to be external to and of another nature than the objects which depend on them. Naturalists will deny any theory of mind which treats thinking or sensing as operations of supernatural or immaterial substances, since naturalism denies the existence of such things. Nominalism may be regarded as a species of naturalism insofar as it denies the existence of platonic forms or other abstract entities (which are presumably supposed to be supernatural or immaterial).

Obviously there are many possible versions of materialist naturalism, and endlessly many ways of departing from it. Insofar as Engels' account suggests the contrary, it is philosophically naive and misleading. But Engels' real purpose is to focus attention on the opposition between a materialist outlook, based on naturalism, and its most popular, influential and adamant opponent, a traditional religious outlook, whose chief tenets are that the natural world was created by an extramundane Deity and that souls are immortal. If an 'idealist' is someone who believes that the world as a whole is mind-dependent (in other words, someone who rejects realism), then Engels is even within his rights in describing this dominant anti-materialist view as 'idealism'. For orthodox theism does hold that God is a mind and that everything besides God is wholly dependent for its being and nature on God's mental activity (his creative knowledge and will). Engels' rather manichean distinction between idealism and materialism may be simplistic and philosophically unsophisticated, but it is not wholly misguided.

Engels himself realizes that the materialist world outlook has other opponents besides idealists as soon as he turns to epistemological issues. 'The question of the relation of thinking and being has yet another side: How do our thoughts about the world surrounding us relate to that world itself? Are we capable of generating in our representations and concepts of the actual world a correct mirror image of actuality?'[6] On this question Engels admits that many idealists (Hegel, for example) join with Marxian materialism in returning an affirmative answer. Here the anti-materialists are the skeptics or 'agnostics' (such as Hume and Kant) who deny that the real nature of things is accessible to us, or assert that 'things in themselves' are unknowable.

161

The chief Marxian view about knowledge, apart from the insistence that human beings can attain it, is that none of it is *a priori*. In *The Holy Family*, Marx asserts that the whole tradition of modern materialism has been 'an open, explicit struggle against metaphysics', which in this context seems to mean the attempt to found science or philosophy on knowledge which is innate or *a priori*. In opposition to metaphysics, seventeenth century materialism was founded on 'Bacon's fundamental principle, the origin of all human knowledge and ideas from the world of sensation'. Bacon was the 'progenitor of English materialism and all modern experimental science' because he held that 'all science is based on experience', and 'experience is the source of all knowledge'.[7] In the Paris manuscripts, Marx presents the same views as his own: 'Sense perception must be the basis of all science. Only when it proceeds from sense perception . . . is it *true* science.' Even the propositions of logic and mathematics for Marx are empirical knowledge, knowledge of the way in which the structure of reality is 'reflected' or 'reproduced' in human thought. Even the 'purest' mathematical concepts, he insists, are only 'abstractions from characteristics of nature'.[8]

But although they hold that all knowledge is based on the senses, Marx and Engels never describe themselves as empiricists. For them, empiricism means a naive reliance on haphazard observation, an uncritical preoccupation with the surface appearances of things, which fails to grasp (or even ignores) the essence of reality beneath these appearances because it does not give sufficient attention to the concepts and theoretical structures needed to 'reproduce the concrete in thought'. All this makes empiricism a 'limited, metaphysical', a 'restricted method of thought'. Empiricists see the world as a 'collection of dead facts', devoid of organization and dialectical interconnection.[9] I think we convey the spirit of Marx's rejection of empiricism if we say that like scientific realists in our time, he criticizes empiricists for emphasizing observation too much at the expense of theory, and for treating scientific concepts and theories only as convenient mechanisms for relating isolated facts rather than as attempts to capture the structure of reality. We will see in later chapters that these epistemological convictions have important consequences for the theoretical structure Marx erects in *Capital*.

Engels sometimes writes as if *historical* materialism were another immediate consequence of accepting the 'primacy of being to thought'. It is of course quite natural for Marx and Engels to express historical materialism (or at least its theory of functional ideology) by saying that people's consciousness does not determine their being, but on the contrary, their social being determines their consciousness.[10] Perhaps historical materialism is a bit more plausible to a naturalist than to an idealist or orthodox theist, insofar as historical materialism rests on the idea that the deepest and most historically potent human interests lie in developing people's natural powers to shape the world, and not in looking after the supernatural destination of their souls. But the relationship of historical materialism to naturalism and related doctrines is really quite distant. Many philosophical materialists obviously do not accept historical materialism; conversely, it would involve no inconsistency, and probably no significant degree of intellectual tension, to combine a belief in God and immortality with a Marxian theory of social change.

'Historical materialism' may be so named by Marx and Engels partly because it emphasizes the degree to which human social behavior is explainable by people's orientation toward nature ('matter') rather than toward 'spirit'. But another (perhaps better) reason why they describe their doctrine in this way is that it proposes to explain the social relations or 'forms' in which people carry on productive activities in terms of the content (or 'matter') which inhabits those forms — in terms of *'what* [individuals] produce and *how* they produce'.[11] To the extent that this is the motivation, the 'matter' in historical materialism is to be contrasted not with 'mind' or 'spirit' but with (social) 'form', and there is no reason at all to associate historical materialism with any particular views about the 'primacy' of being to thought or of nature to spirit.

None of Marx's or Engels' views on metaphysical or epistemological topics are finely honed. For instance, Marx and Engels plainly hold that thought is a process occurring naturally in certain living organisms. But what sort of process? Engels' insistence that 'consciousness and thinking are the product of a material, corporeal organ, the brain', might be taken as any espousal of physicalism or central state materialism, while some prominent references to language as 'the sensuous element of thought' and 'the matter in which consciousness makes its appearance' might suggest some form of linguistic behaviorism.[12] But the only sensible thing to say here is that the texts do not justify ascribing any definite theory of mind to Marx and Engels.

The philosophical views of Marx and Engels do, however, have some characteristic (and at times surprising) wrinkles. Once again, the materialist theory of mind, at least in Engels's expression of it, is a good case in point. While insisting that thought is a 'form of material motion', Engels rejects any attempt to 'reduce' thought to mechanical, physical or chemical processes. Mechanistic reductionism, he says, 'blots out the specific character' and 'qualitative difference' of nonmechanistic forms of motion. The 'essence' of thought, he insists, is not 'exhausted' by the mechanical, chemical, thermal, and electrical motions which 'accompany' thought, and out of which thought 'develops'.[13] Behind Engels strictures against reductionism lies his adherence to the view (derived from the *Naturphilosophie* of Schelling and Hegel) that natural processes form a teleological hierarchy or 'inherent series', in which matter 'unfolds the whole wealth of its motion', rising from mechanical forms of motion through chemical and biological forms to 'matter's highest blossom, the thinking mind'.[14] To each form of motion, there corresponds a distinct science, with its own proper methods and concepts, but linked to all the other sciences by the dialectical development of their subject matter: 'As one form of motion develops out of another, so their mirror images, the different sciences, must arise with necessity one from another'.[15]

The rest of Part Four of this book will explore Marx's philosophical views on several points where they are distinctive and where their interpretation may be controversial. The remainder of this chapter will be devoted to two arguments for atheistic naturalism found in the Paris manuscripts. Chapter XII will discuss Marx's famous claim that the truth of human thinking is bound up with practice, and will defend against a body of modern interpretation the claim that Marx believes the nature of the objective world is independent of human thought about it.

2 Marx's atheism

There is no doubt that Marx was an atheist from the outset of his career as a writer and revolutionary. Equally clear is the general nature of Marx's reasons for his unbelief. The discoveries of modern empirical science have consigned the belief in everything supernatural to the category of primitive superstition. In a scientific picture of the world there is no room for any God or gods, no room even for the abstract possibility of such beings. Marx's habit is to regard these points as so far beyond rational doubt as to be unworthy of discussion. In the Paris manuscripts, however, Marx does make some approach to a philosophical defense of his atheism. His arguments are obscure, and it is not clear that in them Marx develops a single coherent position. But his arguments exhibit a striking reliance on some distinctively Hegelian metaphysical ideas and some interesting reasoning on the basis of these ideas.

In his manuscript 'Critique of the Hegelian Dialectic', Marx's chief concern is to attack Hegel's notion that 'absolute knowledge' involves 'surmounting the object of consciousness', 'superseding externality and objectivity as such'.[16] Marx's foremost aim is to show that Hegel's favored attitude toward external, sensible objects, the attitude which treats them as phenomenal manifestations of the knowing mind, is an alienated attitude, a symptom of an alienated mode of life. In order to do this, Marx presumably must hold that this attitude embodies a falsehood. Hence he must also attack the Hegelian idea that ultimate reality is an all-embracing divine mind or spirit, which recognizes every finite object as the appearance of its own creative power and by this recognition cancels or supersedes the 'externality' or 'otherness' of its objects. Hegel's God or absolute spirit is described by Marx as a 'nonobjective being', in contrast to human beings who are 'objective', and even have 'objectivity in their essential determination'. According to Marx, only 'objective beings' really exist; 'a nonobjective being is a nonbeing (*Unwesen*)', an 'abstraction'.[17]

By an 'objective being' in this context Marx means a being which 'has objects outside itself'. But he also means a being which 'has objects that it needs', is 'passive' (*leidend*) to these objects, and 'has its nature outside itself' in them.[18] An objective being, in other words, is a being whose normal activities and even whose very existence is dependent on external things, and a being which is open to their causal influence. If Marx shows that everything which exists is an 'objective being', that 'a nonobjective being is a nonbeing', then he has shown that there is no such thing as Hegel's cosmic spirit. But he has also shown that there can be nothing having the attributes of 'all-sufficiency', 'impassibility' and 'aseity' or 'self-existence' which are part of the orthodox conception of God. Hence if Marx is successful, he has also shown that there is no God in the orthodox monotheist sense.

Marx's argument that 'a nonobjective being is a nonbeing' is presented in the following passage:

> Suppose a being which neither is an object or has an object.
> First, such a being would be the *only* being. There would
> exist no being outside it, it would exist solitary and alone. . . .
> Thus to suppose a being which is not an object for another
> being is to suppose that *no* objective being exists. As soon as
> I have an object, this object has me for its object. But a *non-
> objective* being is a nonactual, nonsensible, an only thought,
> i.e., only imagined being, a being of abstraction. To be *sensible*,

i.e., to be actual, is to be an object of sense, to be a sensible object, hence to have sensible objects outside itself, to have objects of its sensibility. To be sensible is to be *passive*.[19]

As I read this argument, it is meant as an immanent critique of Hegel: an argument against Hegel's theistic monism, drawn from principles Hegel himself supposedly accepts. The basic structure of the argument is quite simple:

(A) If there were a nonobjective being, it would be the only being; there would be no objective beings.

(B) But there are objective beings.

Therefore, (C) there is no nonobjective being.

This argument is formally valid. What we need to understand is the meaning of premises (A) and (B), and Marx's reasons for asserting them.

We saw above that an objective being is one which needs other beings, is dependent on them for its existence and open to their causal influence. By contrast, then, a nonobjective being is one which stands in no need of others, is independent of and not causally influenced by them. Hence what (A) says is that if there is an all-sufficient, impassible and self-existent being, then this is the only being; there are no beings whose nature admits of their needing others, or being dependent on them, or being influenced by them. Hegel in a sense does accept (A). For he holds that only God or spirit is ultimately real; finite things are merely appearances of spirit, having in themselves no unqualified reality or truth. Considered in abstraction from their metaphysical ground, they have a being which is 'phenomenal', they constitute a realm of nonbeing or half-being, just as the transitory world of sensible particulars does for Plato. More orthodox theists, however, will need convincing about (A). For they hold that God creates real things different from himself, which are causally dependent on, causally influenced by and stand in need both of God and of other finite things.

Marx's reasons for asserting (A) are Hegelian. Hegel thinks that the world is an organic system, that each finite thing is a part or organ of this system, intimately dependent on the whole and thus on other finite things. For any two things, each ultimately needs, depends on, is affected by, the other. In Marx's language, each 'has the other for its object'. For any two things a and b, if a has b for its object, then b has a for its object as well. 'As soon as I have an object, this object has me for its object.' To be 'sensible' (to be able to act on the sensible faculties of other things) is to be 'passive' (to be acted on in turn by them). Let us call this idea the *reciprocity principle*.

(A) is based on the reciprocity principle. For suppose, first, that there is more than one nonobjective being. Then the reciprocity principle says that each nonobjective being is part of an organic system in which it is reciprocally dependent on others. But this violates the hypothesis that the beings in question are nonobjective. Or again, suppose that there exists a nonobjective being n and also an objective being o. By the reciprocity principle, n and o must be reciprocally dependent, and if o needs, depends on or is influenced by n, then n must also need, depend on and be influenced by o. Hence n is objective after all, contrary to hypothesis. A nonobjective being could therefore coexist neither with another nonobjective being nor with an objective being. It would have to exist 'solitary and alone'.

Hegel accepts the reciprocity principle for finite things, but he would obviously wish to deny that absolute spirit is causally dependent on or influenced by finite things. Yet Hegel does hold that there is a sort of reciprocity between them. Spirit is the very being of finite things, which are nothing without it. But spirit also needs these things for its own essential self-completeness, since only through them does spirit achieve manifestness, actuality and concrete existence. As Hegel says: 'Without the world, God would not be God.'[20] What Hegel might question in (A) is Marx's narrowly causal interpretation both of the reciprocity principle and of the dependence involved in 'objective being'. Such an interpretation is obviously implied in Marx's choice of sensibility as his paradigm for the reciprocal dependence between things.

The same response would not be open to more orthodox theists. For they want to hold that finite beings depend causally on God and are causally influenced by him, while God is self-existent, self-sufficient and impassible. Their only recourse is to deny the reciprocity principle altogether. The effect of Marx's argument is to call attention to the serious theological unorthodoxy, even the implicit naturalism, latent in certain aspects of Hegel's metaphysics, such as the reciprocity principle.

Once we understand what Marx means by 'objective being', (B) turns out to be difficult to deny unless one is prepared to adopt the view that the sensible world is a mere shadow or illusion. It is some such mysticism that Marx scornfully attributes to Hegel. Perhaps this is not quite fair, since Hegel would prefer to say that the sensible world is real insofar as it is viewed as an

167

aspect or manifestation of spirit, and illusory only when considered (in vulgar realist fashion) as a realm of things existing in their own right. But it is noteworthy that in asserting (B), Marx is using some of Hegel's own doctrines against him. Hegel does hold that it is only by manifesting himself in finite, sensible things that God ceases to be a mere 'abstraction' and attains to genuine 'actuality'. When Marx stigmatizes nonobjective being as an 'abstraction' and equates what is 'actual' with what is 'sensible', he is basing what he says on Hegelian doctrine, even if he is deliberately ignoring parts of it which he finds uncongenial.

3 The essentiality of man and nature

Marx attacks theism once more in the Paris writings, late in the manuscript 'Private Property and Communism'. Here again his main concern is to expose the theistic world view as symptomatic of alienation, and his chief philosophical motivations are (selectively) Hegelian. But Marx's target this time is the religious sense of 'creatureliness', of the dependence of human beings and the whole natural world on God, and the cosmological proof for God's existence in which this sense finds philosophical expression. Marx interprets the religious intuition of dependence as a mystified awareness of the unfreedom people experience in capitalist society, their consciousness of the fact that the course of their lives is not determined by them but is at the mercy of social forces which are beyond human control.

> A being counts as independent for itself only when it stands
> on its own feet, when it owes its existence to itself. A man
> who lives by the grace of something else considers himself
> a dependent being. . . . *Creation* is therefore a notion which it
> is very hard to dislodge from popular consciousness. That man
> and nature have their being through themselves is incomprehensible to this consciousness, because it contradicts everything *palpable* in practical life.[21]

Marx's interpretation of the religious sense of creatureliness and contingency is shared to a considerable extent by many religious thinkers, who also emphasize that our most intimate awareness of God's presence comes through a sense of the poverty and insufficiency of nature, and especially of our own being, a feeling of need for God's presence and the emptiness of life apart from it. Modern theologians such as Maritain and Tillich say that our sense of the world's dependence on God is founded on our 'primordial intuition' of the 'loneliness and frailty' of our own existence, our sense that this existence is incomplete and inadequate, threatened with absurdity and (as these thinkers are fond of putting it) encumbered with 'nothingness' or 'nonbeing'.[22]

Marx's only real disagreement with these theologians is over the veracity of the religious sense of creaturely dependence. For Marx, religious intuitions are perniciously false as guides to our cosmic predicament, and contain truth only when interpreted as an expression of the social conditions to which people's lives are presently subject. The defense of this position naturally leads Marx to a critique of the cosmological proof. This proof, he says, depends on a 'progression' from reasonable questions about the causes of particular natural things to the cosmological question about the cause of nature as a whole. This question, however, is 'a product of abstraction'. 'It cannot be answered because it proceeds from a perverted standpoint', because it is based on

> a progression which does not exist for rational thought. When you ask about the creation of nature and man, you posit them as *not being* and yet you want me to prove them to you as being. But I say to you: give up your abstraction and you will also give up your question. Or if you want to hold fast to your abstraction, then be consistent. If you who are thinking think of man and nature as not being, then think of yourself as not being, since you too are nature and man.[23]

On first reading these remarks may seem silly. Proponents of the cosmological proof do not 'posit nature and man as *not being*'. On the contrary, they insist that natural things have being, but stand in need of ontological support or causal explanation. And they ask for an adequate explanation not only for particular natural things, but for nature as a whole. To understand Marx's thinking in this passage, we must appreciate the Hegelian presuppositions which lie behind it. For Hegel, only cosmic spirit is ultimately real, because only it is 'self-complete' (*bei sich*) or 'essential' (*wesentlich*, *wesenhaftig*), that is, something whose being is self-dependent or (as Marx puts it) something which has 'being through itself' (*Durchsichselbstsein*). Everything else is only the appearance of spirit, having only a phenomenal being or partial reality.

In the passage just quoted, I think Marx is subscribing to the Hegelian thesis that only what is essential or has its being through itself is truly and ultimately real. Let us call this thesis the *essentiality principle*. Given the essentiality principle, it follows that to require a supernatural ground for nature as a whole is in effect to 'posit nature as not being', that is, to regard the objects of our senses (and even ourselves, insofar as we are finite, natural beings and not identical with absolute spirit) as not ultimately real. Marx's argument against cosmological theism is directed at those who are prepared to accept the essentiality principle but cannot accept Hegel's 'mystical' belief that the being of nature and man is merely phenomenal.

What does Marx mean when he claims that 'man and nature' are 'essential' or 'have their being through themselves'? Pretty clearly this claim involves the thesis that the natural world does not exist contingently, but is in some sense self-existent or metaphysically necessary. It may surprise us to see a materialist accepting the notion of necessary existence, but the idea that the material world is necessarily existent was not uncommon among eighteenth century materialists, based chiefly on their reading of Descartes and Spinoza.[24] The obvious advantage of this view is that it permits one to be an atheist and a materialist while accepting the principle of sufficient reason in a form strong enough to be useful to cosmological theists. Such theists argue that unless there is a necessary being, things cannot have the sort of complete explanation which they must have if they are to be part of an intelligible universe. A materialist may concede all this if he is prepared to argue that the material world itself is necessary or self-existent.

But why is the being which exists 'essentially' or 'through itself' described as 'man and nature'? Why is 'man' especially included? Here again, Marx's thought is very Hegelian. For Hegel, the processes of nature form a sort of hierarchy, in which spirit rises from the simplest forms of objectivity and sensuousness (mechanical motion, physical and chemical processes) through life and consciousness to human thought, in which the world spirit attains to rational self-understanding. The Paris manuscripts contain a parallel doctrine, though already Marx places the emphasis not on people's theoretical comprehension of the world but on their practical shaping of it to human purposes. Through creative labor, says Marx, man 'makes the whole of nature into his inorganic body, both insofar as it is his immediate means of life and to the extent that it is the object and tool of his life activity. . . . Man reproduces the whole of nature.'[25] In a truly human or communist society, 'objective actuality everywhere comes to be the actuality of human essential powers, a human actuality', or 'objective man'.[26] Only in such a society, says Marx, 'has man's *natural* existence come to be his *human* existence, and nature come to be man for him'. Communist society is 'the completed essentiality of man with nature, the true resurrection of nature'.[27]

Marx's language here is highly metaphorical and hyperbolical.

When he says that nature becomes 'man himself' or 'objective man', Marx is clearly referring to the way in which labor imposes a new form on objects, fashioning them to human use and transforming them into vehicles of human self-expression. It is an exaggeration, putting it mildly, to say that 'the whole of nature' is 'humanized' or 'reproduced' by man. Obviously it is only a tiny speck of the natural universe which is or ever will be shaped by human labor, and surely Marx realizes this. Yet Marx is also impressed by the capacities of modern industry to harness natural forces in man's behalf, and to reshape people's surroundings, producing an essentially humanmade world for human beings to live in. He looks forward to a time when the processes of nature can be more fully harmonized with human needs, so that men and women will be completely at home both with nature and with themselves as natural beings. It is not difficult to see how such hopes could find expression in the hyperboles and metaphors Marx uses.

For Marx there is a kind of reciprocal dependence between man and nature, though the dependence is not causal in both directions. Men and women are a part of nature; they live upon it, and depend on it both for their physical survival and for the means and objects of their self-actualization and self-expression. At the same time, however, human labor 'resurrects' nature by 'humanizing' it; through human labor, nature becomes something which acquires a significance for itself. Only the human being 'knows how to apply the inherent standard everywhere to the object', and hence 'to form it according to the laws of beauty'.[28] Man is a part of nature and depends on nature for existence and power; nature depends on man for its fulfillment, its sense of meaning. Taken together, 'man and nature' thus form a self-sufficient or 'essential' totality. This totality requires nothing outside itself, no immanent spirit or transcendent God, either to explain the system of natural processes or to give meaning and fulfillment to nature.

Marx is convinced that this reciprocity between man and nature is implicit in the practical consciousness of all men and women who participate in the life-activity made possible by modern science and industry. The final aim of his discussion of cosmological theism is to make this consciousness explicit, and set it at war with the sense of 'inessentiality' which we derive from the inertia of old superstitions and the alienated consciousness of an inhuman society.

Now that the *essentiality* of man in nature, of nature as the being of man and man as the being of nature, has come to be

171

something practically, sensibly intuitable, the question about an *alien* being, a being above nature and man — a question which includes the admission of the inessentiality of nature and man — has become impossible in practice.[29]

Once the 'essentiality' of man and nature has penetrated practical consciousness, we can raise the old cosmological questions only by turning away from this consciousness, by 'abstracting' ourselves from it. Marx thus insists that these questions must disappear as soon as the abstraction is given up. To press the question consistently is to deny what we must implicitly affirm every moment, in our every sensation, our every action, our every self-conscious thought:

> If you want to hold fast to your abstraction, then be consistent, and if you who are thinking think of man and nature as *not being*, then think of yourself as not being, since you too are nature and man. Don't think, don't ask me, for as soon as you think and ask, your *abstraction* from the being of nature and man has no sense.[30]

Once again Marx's views have strong echoes in twentieth century religious thought. The idea that modern humanity cannot choose but possess a view of the world profoundly at odds with that of traditional theistic religion is axiomatic to a whole wave of modern theologians and religious thinkers, from respectable academics such as Rudolf Bultmann and Paul Tillich to more popular writers such as Bishop Robinson, Leslie Dewart and the 'death of God' school. Even religious conservatives often do not oppose this characterization of our consciousness, but reject only the modernists' tolerant attitude toward it. This is nicely illustrated by a remark of C. S. Lewis concerning the tacit naturalism of modern biblical scholarship:

> When you turn from the New Testament to modern scholars, remember that you go as a sheep among wolves. Naturalistic assumptions . . . will meet you on every side — even from the pens of clergymen. This does not mean (as I was once tempted to suspect) that these clergymen are disguised apostates. . . . [Rather it is that] we all have Naturalism in our bones and even conversion does not at once work the infection out of our system. . . . And this means that you must really re-educate yourself: must work hard and consistently to eradicate from your mind the whole type of thought in which we have all been brought up.[31]

In this chapter we have looked at two different arguments against theism presented by Marx in the Paris manuscripts. Neither is very clearly expressed, but both seem to rely on Hegelian metaphysical ideas. Unless my reading of the arguments is very wide of the mark, however, the two lines of thought they contain are pretty clearly incompatible. The argument from 'Critique of the Hegelian Dialectic' tries to show that there cannot exist an 'nonobjective being', that is, an entity which is not causally dependent on others and is involved in no reciprocal interactions with them. The argument from 'Private Property and Communism' claims that 'man and nature' exist 'essentially' or have *Durchsichselbstsein*. The former argument rules out the possibility of any self-existent or necessary being, while the latter claims that 'man and nature' is just such a being.

One might try to save Marx from this open contradiction by claiming that it results merely from a (very understandable) indecisiveness about whether the world as a whole should count as 'a being'. Perhaps Marx means that it should for the purposes of the essentiality principle but not for the purposes of the reciprocity principle. But this will not do. It is important for Marx's critique of Hegel that there should be no beings, however peculiar, which are exempted from the reciprocity principle. For if 'man and nature' is exempted from it, then why should not Hegel's cosmic spirit be exempted too? As I see it, the basic problem is that one cannot without inconsistency hold simultaneously the reciprocity principle, the essentiality principle and the view that particular finite things are ultimately real. There are of course many ways in which the inconsistency might be avoided, but I think all of them would involve some modification of the views Marx appears to express in the Paris manuscripts.

XII

Materialist Realism

1 *Knowledge and practice*

Marx's writings have very little to say directly about epistemology. The main theme of the few passages there are is the close relation between human 'thinking' or 'theory' and practice. The most prominent passage on this is Marx's second thesis on Feuerbach:

> The question whether objective truth belongs to human thinking is not a question of theory but a practical question. It is in practice that man must prove the truth, i.e., the actuality and might, the this-sidedness of his thinking. The dispute over the actuality or nonactuality of thinking isolated from practice is a purely scholastic question.[1]

These obscure remarks have provided a fertile ground for creative interpretation. Perhaps the most common interpretation of them has been the 'pragmatist' one. According to John McMurtry, this passage 'directly defines the nature of knowledge' in the following manner: 'A conception, x, is knowledge if, and only if, x is used to materially alter the world in accordance with human needs.'[2] But it is surely inaccurate to say that Marx defines 'knowledge' in the passage, since no word meaning either 'knowledge' or 'define' appears in it. Marx does seem to *equate* 'the truth of thinking' with its 'actuality and might'. If the equation is meant as a definition, then it is a definition not of 'knowledge' but of 'truth' or 'the truth of thinking'. Leszek Kolakowski so interprets it when he says that for Marx 'the truth of a judgment is defined as a practical function of the usefulness of its acceptance or rejection.'[3]

It is difficult to exclude the possibility that Marx might agree with this definition, but harder still to convince oneself that he is expressing it in the second thesis on Feuerbach. Marx equates the truth of thinking with its actuality and might, and says that it is in practice that man must prove this actuality or might. In the equation, the emphasis is plainly on 'actuality', with 'might' as an afterthought. 'Might' presumably means whatever enables thought to achieve 'actuality', and can be glossed as 'practical usefulness' only if one has already decided that Marx's theory of truth is pragmatic. It seems most natural to read the passage not as a definition of truth, but as advice as to how we should proceed in deciding whether our thoughts have 'truth' or 'actuality' (however these terms are defined). The advice is that we should decide this on the basis of the practical efficacy of these thoughts. When Marx stigmatizes questions about 'thinking isolated from practice' as 'scholastic questions' he is recommending that we not trouble ourselves about such questions. But he is not necessarily saying that the notion of truth makes no sense in relation to thinking isolated from practice. What he says does not commit him to a specifically pragmatist dismissal of judgments lacking practical import as nonsensical, meaningless or lacking in truth-content.

Kolakowski's purpose in ascribing a 'pragmatist concept of truth' to Marx is to support an essentially idealist reading of Marx, according to which Marx holds that 'the existence of things comes into being simultaneously with their appearance as a picture in the human mind.'[4] The idea seems to be that since (Kolakowski alleges) 'the pragmatic concept of truth is clearly not compatible with the classical definition of "truth" as correspondence between our thoughts or judgments and a reality independent of them', Marx must not believe there is such a reality.[5] Later in this chapter we will consider whether Marx is an idealist. For now we may note that even if Marx does embrace a pragmatic concept of truth, Kolakowski's argument from this point on is rather dubious. It is not evident that a pragmatic theory of truth is incompatible with a correspondence theory. William James regards his own pragmatic theory of truth as a version of the correspondence theory, as supplying a criterion for the correspondence between judgments and reality.[6] Even if James is wrong about this, it is invalid to infer merely from the premise that truth does not consist in the correspondence of thoughts to an independent reality to the conclusion that no such reality exists. In any case, there is no sign that Marx reasons in any such way.

In the second thesis on Feuerbach, Marx is concerned in some way with philosophical skepticism, with 'scholastic' disputes over 'whether objective truth belongs to thinking'. This is evidently the spirit in which Engels interprets Marx's ideas about the relation of thinking to practice. He treats them as a reply to the 'agnostic' who admits that all knowledge is based on the senses, but doubts that 'our senses give us correct representations of the objects we perceive through them', and so holds that 'whenever he speaks of objects or their qualities, he does not in reality mean those objects or qualities, . . . but merely the impressions which they have produced on his senses.' Engels admits that

> this line of reasoning is hard to beat by mere argumentation. But [he replies] before argumentation there was action. *Im Anfang war die Tat*. Human action had solved the difficulty long before human ingenuity had invented it.

Clearly Engels' reply to skepticism is *not* based on a pragmatic definition of truth. For this would dismiss the skeptic's doubts as meaningless, and so defeat skepticism 'by mere argumentation'. Besides, it is not plausible to think that Engels believes that pragmatic definitions of truth were themselves invented by human action, or that they antedate skeptical difficulties. Engels' reply to skepticism is rather this:

> From the moment we turn to our own use these objects, according to the qualities we perceive in them, we put to an infallible test the correctness or otherwise of our sense perceptions. If these perceptions have been wrong, then our estimate of the use to which an object can be turned must also be wrong, and our attempt must fail. But if we succeed in accomplishing our aim, . . . then that is positive proof that our perception of [the object] and of its qualities, *so far* agrees with reality outside ourselves.[7]

It is well that Engels adds the qualifying 'so far' in the last sentence, since even theories which agree very poorly with reality may serve adequately as practical guides within certain limits. But with this necessary qualification, it is not clear that anything is left of Engels' claim that practice provides an 'infallible test' of our perceptions. The practical applications of a theory are in any case only one sort of test to which it might be put, often a less demanding test than could be devised in the laboratory.

Of course as we accumulate a larger and more varied body of evidence for a theory (including evidence drawn from everyday practical applications) doubts about it raised by philosophical skeptics become increasingly hard for a person of common sense to take seriously. I think Engels is right when he elsewhere suggests that the relatively undeveloped state of natural science in the seventeenth and eighteenth centuries was partly responsible for the appeal of empiricist arguments for the unknowability of real essences, primary qualities, causal powers and things in themselves.[8] But insofar as skepticism is a challenge to common sense itself, Engels' reply to it is not to the point. If there is a philosophically interesting reply to skepticism in Marx's second thesis on Feuerbach, then we still have to discover what it is.

2 *The contemplative attitude*

Marx's second thesis on Feuerbach must be read in light of the others, especially the first. Marx complains that in *The Essence of Christianity* Feuerbach 'considers only the theoretical attitude as genuinely human, while practice is grasped and fixed only in its dirty Jewish form of appearance'.[9] Feuerbach's chief criticism of 'the essential standpoint of religion' is that its attitude toward the world is engaged, interested, 'practical', and so 'biased', 'egoistic' and 'unaesthetic', grasping things only 'subjectively' in the form of mere 'appearance'. In contrast, he advocates the 'objectivity' and 'purity' of the theoretical or contemplative attitude.[10] Marx rejects this because for him the integral exercise of the human essential powers is to be understood in terms of the practical relation of men and women to nature as laboring and self-expressing beings. Social labor is the basic expression of human life. But 'one basis for life and another for science is a lie from the start.'[11] If human beings are essentially practical, then knowledge must be treated as an integral part of their practical relation to the world and not traced to an attitude which is supposed to involve a suspension of this relation.

For Marx, contemplation is one aspect of genuinely human practice, which reaches fulfillment when man 'duplicates himself not only intellectually as in consciousness but actively, actually, and so contemplates (*anschaut*) himself in a world he has created'.[12] For Feuerbach, on the other hand, the attitude of 'theory' or 'contemplation' (*Anschauung*) is distinct from and opposed to practice. When Marx disparages 'thinking isolated from practice', he is not advocating a pragmatic definition of truth or knowledge, but rejecting a false and fragmented view of the human essence, which would set the 'genuinely human' attitude toward the natural world in opposition to people's necessarily practical relationship to nature as living parts of it. If the second thesis has anything to say about skepticism's 'scholastic' questions, it is that these questions proceed from a false and fragmented view of men and women as knowing beings.

How is skepticism rooted in a false view of the human essence? Marx tells us very little about this, but we may form some reasonable conjectures. First, it is notoriously difficult to take skeptical doubts seriously while engaged in the practical affairs of life. (This point is particularly emphasized by such famous skeptical doubters as Descartes and Hume; it seems to be an important ingredient in Engels' rejection of skepticism in the passage we examined above.) It is therefore possible for us to treat skepticism as a serious philosophical position only insofar as we are disposed to regard the detached, contemplative attitude (in which skeptical arguments seem compelling) as somehow epistemically privileged, 'purer', more 'genuinely human' than the practical attitude (in which such arguments seem strained and ridiculous). If we refuse to grant this privileged status to the contemplative attitude, if in fact we resolve to treat the practical attitude as the only genuinely human one, then we will have no trouble dismissing all skeptical questions as idle and 'scholastic'.

I think this is the basic critique of skepticism which we find in the writings of both Marx and Engels. In the form just presented, however, this critique may seem open to the charge that it is philistine and even anti-intellectual. It may be legitimate to criticize skeptical arguments by attacking the pictures, conceptions or epistemic priorities they presuppose. The Marxian critique, however, does not show us clearly how skeptical arguments presuppose the contemplative attitude or why this attitude is wrongheaded. It seems to consist merely in urging us to shut our eyes to skeptical arguments, or at any rate in urging us to adopt an attitude in which it is psychologically impossible to consider them seriously.

I believe these charges can be given a tolerable rebuttal. Marx's critique of skepticism is based on the general idea (championed by such precursors as Schiller and Hegel) that human beings have a healthy attitude toward themselves only if they conceive their powers and functions as an integral unity. More specifically, it is based on the distinctively Marxian idea that this unity is captured by the notion of labor or social practice. Any viewpoint which (like Feuerbach's) treats the 'genuinely human' attitude as something isolated from this practice can thus be treated as an unwholesome, even alienated viewpoint. Marx provides no rigorous proof for these ideas, but he does expound them in a way which makes them plausible and appealing. If he could show how skeptical doubts are rooted in the contemplative attitude advocated by Feuerbach, then Marx would have provided a respectable critique of skepticism.

It could be objected that by stigmatizing the contemplative attitude as alienated or unhealthy, Marx is begging the question against the skeptic. For as Marx conceives it, the 'practical' attitude is one which in effect takes it for granted that human beings are material beings interacting with other material beings and that their practical success in these interactions is largely due to the knowledge of these things which they have. But the whole question at issue, it may be claimed, is whether these assumptions can be given a firm epistemic foundation. In Marx's behalf we may reply that it is not clear we have any conception of 'firm epistemic foundations' independently of some notion of healthy human functioning. Good grounds for believing something are simply the grounds which would persuade a healthy-minded and properly functioning man or woman of it. We cannot have a conception of good grounds for belief without presupposing a conception of what a normal, well-functioning person would believe. Marx's conception of healthy human functioning may very well rule out the skeptic's epistemological scruples from the start, but it is not clear that there is anything illegitimate or question-begging about this. It may be merely a case of applying sane priorities to philosophical issues.

The main sort of skepticism Marx and Engels are concerned to attack is skepticism about the existence and nature of material objects. I believe a careful reading of the first thesis on Feuerbach enables us to see how they might have traced some standard forms of this skepticism to the contemplative attitude.

> The chief defect in all previous materialism (including Feuerbach's) is that the object (*Gegenstand*), actuality, sensibility, is grasped only under the form of the object (*Objekt*) or contemplation (*Anschauung*); but not as sensuous human activity, practice, not subjectively. Hence the *active* side was developed *abstractly* by idealism. . . . Feuerbach wants sensible objects (*Objekte*) as really distinct from thought objects (*Objekte*): but he does not grasp human activity itself as *objective* (*gegenständlich*) activity.[13]

The key to this passage is the distinction Marx draws between *Gegenstand* and *Objekt*. I think Marx is doing here what he elsewhere describes as 'using a germanic word for the immediate thing and a romance word for the thing reflected' in human consciousness.[14] What he is saying is that when a real, sensible object is regarded from the standpoint of mere contemplation (*Anschauung*, literally, on-looking), it is grasped only as an *Objekt*, a mental

179

reflection of reality. Just as contemplation is severed from its relation to practice, so its objects are cut off from the real world, and the images of that world in our consciousness are for that consciousness epistemically separated from the realities which it is their proper function to represent. Contemplative materialists, along with empiricists generally, thus hold that our only commerce as knowers is with *Objekte*, mental reflections or ghostly appearances of real, material objects (*Gegenstände*). Consequently, they can only regard themselves as forever separated epistemically from the real world, if indeed there is such a thing at all. They are tempted to draw the conclusion that their knowledge must consist only in entertaining the appearances of things, and can never extend to the things themselves and their 'inner' natures.

Of course Marx and Engels also speak of our ideas as 'reflections', and 'copy images' or 'offprints' (*Abbilder*) of material things. The standard description of knowledge in both thinkers is that it is thought 'reflecting', 'mirroring' or 'reproducing' the structure of the real.[15] But Marx and Engels never threaten us with the alleged skeptical consequences of this way of talking, and they never infer from it that we cannot properly be said to know or be acquainted with extramental things. For them to say that a person has a faithful image, copy or reflection of a real thing in thought is precisely to say that the person is acquainted with or knows the real thing itself (at least, I suppose, when the mental reflection has come about in the right way). This is because Marx and Engels always view our mental reflection of reality as an integral part of our practical commerce with it, and so cannot raise general questions about the ability of our thoughts to serve their practical function. Only when we adopt the contemplative attitude and isolate our thinking from practice can we begin to view the relation between real things and our mental reflections of them as one of indifference instead of a living reciprocity. For the contemplative attitude, the natural harmony experienced between thought and reality in practice can all too easily give way to the unnatural alienation of skeptical doubt.

Marx thus regards the contemplative attitude, and the epistemological problems to which it gives rise, as expressions of alienation, and describes contemplative materialism as the 'standpoint of bourgeois or civil (*bürgerliche*) society'.[16] The contemplative attitude expresses alienation because it transforms the simple, natural difference between real things and our thoughts about them into what Marx calls the 'opposition between subjectivity and objectivity', a destructive tension or unbridgeable gulf between our consciousness and the real things we experience. Instead of affirming our cognitive powers in their natural, positive relation to objects outside us, the contemplative attitude uses the distinction between our thoughts and their real objects as an occasion for questioning and doubting our powers. In this way it provides an outlet for the underlying sense of frustration and self-doubt which alienated men and women experience in real life.

A new materialism which is capable of grasping sensuousness as practice requires the perspective of a new society, 'human society or social humanity'. As with alienated religious consciousness, alienated philosophical consciousness cannot be overcome except by changing the conditions of life which are the basis of its appeal.

> We see how it is only in the social condition that subjectivity
> and objectivity, spirituality and materiality, activity and pas-
> sivity, lose their opposition and thus their existence as oppo-
> sites. We see how the resolution of *theoretical* oppositions is
> possible only in a *practical* way, and hence that this resolution
> is by no means a task of knowledge but a task of *actual* life,
> which philosophy could not resolve just because it grasped
> the task *only* as a theoretical one.[17]

In this passage, the distinction between 'theory' and 'practice' is not merely the distinction between Feuerbach's 'contemplative attitude' and a more encompassing and integral 'practical' attitude. Here 'theory' is the idea that alienation (and its intellectual expression in philosophical oppositions and perplexities) can be overcome merely by correct thinking, by 'interpreting the world' in a different way. 'Practice' is the commitment to changing the social conditions which give rise to alienation in real life. As in his treatment of cosmological theism, Marx here shows that he, like some more recent philosophers such as Wittgenstein, thinks that many philosophical problems should not be solved by arguments and theories but rather dissolved by abandoning the false view of things which generates them. For Marx, however, this abandoning of a false perspective is not just a matter of philosophical conversion or 'seeing the world aright'; it involves a change in our everyday life, fundamentally an alteration of our social relationships.

We may well question whether Marx's diagnosis of skepticism attends to the whole, or even the chief motivation behind skeptical doubts about the knowability of the material world. For instance, at least part of what leads people to take skeptical doubts seriously is the Cartesian aspiration to base all knowledge on something indubitably certain, and the resolve to dismiss all pretenses to knowledge which cannot be given such immovable foundations. It is not evident that Marx's diagnosis helps us at all to understand this motivation or to see what (if anything) is wrongheaded about it. But Marx's treatment of contemplative materialism does provide an original perspective on the social and human significance of familiar epistemological issues, and the philosophical attitude which takes them seriously. English speaking philosophers especially would do well to take this perspective on their enterprise more seriously than they do.

The contents of Marx's new or practical materialism, as far as epistemology is concerned, are not startling or revolutionary. They seem to consist only in the familiar tenets of common-sense realism. What would be new for Marx is the ability of people to feel entirely at home with a healthy common-sense view of themselves and of nature, to have no need to becloud this view with idealistic theories and no temptation to undermine it with skeptical doubts.

3 Is Marx an idealist?

Common-sense realism holds that material objects and the natural world generally have an existence distinct from anyone's consciousness of them and that the qualities they have do not depend on the mental activity through which they may be conceived or known. In light of Marx's frequent and vehement attacks on all forms of 'idealism' it might seem obvious that he is a common-sense realist in this respect. Astonishingly, however, there is a considerable body of commentary on Marx's writings which argues that Marx does not believe in a reality independent of man's practical consciousness of it. Perhaps the fountainhead of this line of interpretation was Georg Lukács' *History and Class Consciousness*, whose obscure but very unmarxian notion of practice condemned the distinction between 'thought and existence' as a 'false and rigid duality'.[18] Since more recent anti-realist interpretations of Marx rely heavily on the Paris manuscripts, it is interesting to note that it was Lukács' first acquaintance with them in 1930 which convinced him that his earlier standpoint had been fundamentally unmarxian in rejecting the 'ontological objectivity of nature' upon which Marx's concept of practice is based.[19]

Essentially idealist interpretations of Marx are now widespread, and are held by some very reputable commentators. Shlomo Avineri, for instance, says that for Marx 'actuality is not an external, objective datum.' Engels' materialism, unlike Marx's, is thus 'not dialectical at all', because it 'divorces [nature] from the mediation of consciousness'. According to Avineri, 'Marx's epistemology holds that the process of recognizing reality changes both the observed object and the observing subject.' Sidney Hook ascribes to Marx the view that 'the idealists saw correctly that in what-was-given-to-knowledge something was involved about the subject-to-which-it-was-given.' According to Nathan Rotenstreich, Marx believes that 'reality is not given. . . . Man creates reality with the strength of his being. . . . Marx's theory is based on the assumption that there is a fundamental identity between man and reality.' For Marx, says A. James Gregor, 'an object without the subject is as inconceivable as the subject without the object.' Jean-Yves Calvez ascribes to Marx the view that 'nature without man has no sense, it has no movement, it is chaos, undifferentiated and indifferent matter, and thus ultimately nothing.'[20]

None of these writers comes right out and says that Marx is an idealist (that would be too absurd). But all of them seem to hold that for Marx either there is no natural world apart from human beings and their subjectivity as practical beings, or else apart from man natural things have no determinate properties. Such views may in some ways be novel and hard to classify, but I think they are 'idealist' in a sense accepted by philosophers both in Marx's day and in our own.

The textual evidence for this reading of Marx is very thin. It is true that Marx's talk about nature as man's 'creation' or 'objectification' is reminiscent of Hegel's notion that nature is 'posited' by cosmic spirit as its 'externalization'. But the resemblance hardly justifies ascribing idealist views to Marx. Marx is emphatic that the process by which human beings 'create' nature or objectify themselves in it is labor, and he attacks Hegel for reducing this labor to 'abstract mental labor'.[21] Plainly the only way in which Marx thinks of nature or its properties as dependent on human beings is that the properties of natural objects can be changed by the direct or indirect action on them of human fingers (or other bodily parts) guided by human intelligence. Both before and after their transformation by human labor, natural objects exist independently of the existence of human beings, and the properties they have do not depend on anyone's being conscious (practically or otherwise) of these properties.

One passage which is often cited in support of idealist readings of the Paris manuscripts is one near the end of them which says that 'nature, taken abstractly for itself, fixed in separation from man, is *nothing* for man.'[22] The context of this remark (which

183

is never considered by those who make this use of it) is an immanent critique of Hegel's philosophy of nature, and it is not clear
how far Marx is speaking for himself and how far he is merely
representing things as they must look from the wrongheaded
Hegelian standpoint. Marx is clearly speaking from the latter
standpoint a paragraph later when he says: 'Nature *as nature*,
i.e., insofar as it is still distinguished sensuously from the secret
sense hidden within it — nature separated and distinguished by
these abstractions is *nothing*, . . . is *senseless*.'[23] But even if Marx
is expressing his own view when he says that 'nature . . . in separation from man is nothing for man', the most he could be saying is
that nature viewed apart from human self-objectification has no
significance *for man*. He is not saying that in the absence of human
consciousness or labor nature would cease to exist or that it would
be 'an undifferentiated chaos, without movement'. Earlier in the
same manuscript, Marx avows a vulgar realist position very bluntly
when he says that the objects of human consciousness and human
drives 'exist outside [man] as objects independent of him'.[24]

Proponents of idealist readings of Marx seldom make explicit
the line of reasoning which is supposed to lie behind Marx's rejection of realism. We are indebted to Kolakowski for bringing into
the open the train of thought which I suspect motivates most of
these readings. 'The basic point of departure for all of Marx's
epistemological thought', says Kolakowski, 'is the conviction
that the relations between man and his environment are relations
between the species and the objects of its need; it also concerns
the cognitive contact with things.' Thus:

> Nature appears as the opposition encountered by human drives,
> and all possible cognition is man's realization of the contact
> between conscious man and his awareness of external oppo-
> sition. . . . This means that it is fundamentally futile to hope
> that man . . . can come to know . . . pure 'externality', and
> thus existence in itself.

From these considerations, Kolakowski concludes that there can
exist only 'things for us' and not 'things in themselves' which are
'not given to anyone'. The very 'existence' of things, he says,

> comes into being simultaneously with their appearance as a
> picture in the human mind. . . . In this sense the world's pro-
> ducts must be considered artificial. In this world the sun and
> stars exist because man is able to make them his objects. . . .
> Nor are the qualities of things forms or attributes of reality
> 'in itself'. . . . They are subjective — or rather socially subjec-

tive -- as long as they bear the imprint of the organizational power of man, who sees the world . . . from such points of view as are necessary for him to . . . transform it usefully. . . . No division, not even the most fantastic as compared with what we are accustomed to, is theoretically less justified or less 'true' than the one we accept in actuality.[25]

In these comments I think we see pretty clearly how Marx can be transformed into an idealist (even a rather demented one) simply by attributing to him a requisite degree of the commentator's own philosophical confusion. Marx does hold that human knowledge is the result of people's exercising their cognitive capacities on nature. He also holds, against empiricists and 'contemplative materialists' that people are active in knowing, that knowing is always an integral part of their practical transformation of the world, and that knowing involves a creative process in which we construct concepts and theories in terms of which the structure of reality is to be ideally reproduced or mirrored. But none of this implies that reality itself is created or structured by our cognitive activity, or that human knowledge is anything but an attempt to mirror, copy or reproduce the structure of a reality which exists, and is what it is, independently of the manner in which we conceive of it. Quite possibly Marx would think it pointless to ask what reality is like 'in itself' if this is a question about what *we would know* reality to be like if we knew it without exercising our cognitive faculties or employing any of our concepts or theories. For on this account, 'reality in itself' is defined as the object of a kind of 'knowledge' whose very concept is unintelligible. Genuine knowledge, however, is the active use of our faculties and concepts to produce an image or conceptual reproduction of reality, and would have no meaning if this reality had no existence or structure 'in itself'. Of course skeptics have long wondered how we can know the nature of reality by means of thoughts which are distinct from the things they represent. And idealists have tried to avoid the problem by saying that reality, or at least all knowable reality, is identical with the thoughts or ideas in someone's mind. But this is not the only viable response to skepticism, or at any rate it is not Marx's response.

Hegel does infer from the premise that knowing is an active process which creates a concept of the known to the conclusion that the known is itself a creation of the knowing subject: 'Since the true nature of the object comes to light in reflective thought, and since this thought is my activity, it follows that this nature

185

is a product of my mind as a thinking subject.'[26] Marx agrees with the premise, but declines to draw the conclusion. The correct scientific method, he says, involves a

> reproduction of the concrete by way of thought. Thus Hegel fell into the illusion of taking the real as a result of self-moving thought . . . whereas the method of mounting up from the abstract to the concrete is only the manner in which thought appropriates the concrete for itself, reproducing it as mentally concrete. . . . After this process as before the real subject remains subsisting in its independence outside the head.[27]

Many commentators who give an idealist reading of Marx also insist that Marx could not have embraced Engels' 'reflectionist' conception of knowledge on the ground that such a conception is 'undialectical' and represents the knower as 'passive'.[28] The texts do not support this. Marx not only speaks of our knowledge as 'reproducing' the real in thought, but also describes his own 'dialectical method' as 'reflecting back ideally the life of the material'.[29] In addition, the interpretation is not warranted by any reasonable reading of the metaphors of copying and reflection as Marx and Engels use them. As far as I can see, these metaphors involve no more than an insistence of the difference between the real world and our thoughts about it (thus a repudiation of idealism) conjoined with some form of the traditional correspondence theory of truth (which Marx pretty clearly holds whether or not he also holds a pragmatic theory of truth). There is nothing in these metaphors which is incompatible either with the idea that human knowledge is an integral part of human practice or with the idea that the reflection of reality in thought comes about through the creative exercise of our cognitive capacities.

PART FIVE

The Dialectical Method

XIII

The Hegelian Dialectic

1 *Hegel's vision of reality*

Probably the most confusing aspect of Marx's thought is his use of the 'dialectical method'. What is this method? What is the relation between the Marxian dialectical method and its Hegelian precursor? How far is Marx really a Hegelian?

In *Capital* Marx 'openly avows [himself] a pupil of that mighty thinker [Hegel] '.[1] Some of Marx's readers have believed (and others have hoped) that this remark is a mere gesture, as is Marx's frequent use of Hegelian jargon in expressing his ideas. Yet Marxists as different as Lenin and Karl Korsch have insisted that the Hegelian component of Marx's thought is fundamental to it, and some have even held that one cannot truly understand Marxism without understanding Hegel's philosophy.

Like any really original intellectual creation, Marx's social theory must be understood on its own, and should be intelligible to sensitive students whether they know Hegelian philosophy or not. But Marx's debt to Hegel is not superficial. An account of it can be illuminating, especially when our purpose is to focus on the philosophical side of Marx's thought. The mistake to avoid is regarding the Hegelian dialectic as some sort of esoteric wisdom (or obscure hokum), and seeing the issue as whether one must master (or swallow) this body of murky metaphysical doctrines before one can understand Marx. Hegel's philosophy is difficult, and parts of it may be hard for a sober mind to take seriously. But its basic tenets are not hopelessly unintelligible if we approach them with patience and an open mind. The brief sketch I will provide in this chapter does not pretend to do full justice to the subtlety and complexity of Hegel's philosophy. My aim is to

189

present as simply and straightforwardly as I can those parts of it which are most useful in understanding Marx's dialectical method.

The terms 'dialectical method' and 'dialectical logic' are apt to mislead. Neither in Hegel nor in Marx is dialectical thinking really a set of procedures for inquiry, still less a set of rules for generating or justifying results. Only harm can be done by representing dialectic as analogous to formal logic or mathematics (witness Alexander Herzen's famous but asinine description of the Hegelian dialectic as the 'algebra of revolution'). Instead, dialectic is best viewed as a general conception of the sort of intelligible structure the world has to offer, and consequently a program for the sort of theoretical structure which would best capture it. But this means that the Hegelian dialectic cannot be separated from Hegel's vision of reality, and is best presented in terms of it.

The German idealists of Hegel's generation are usually thought of (and think of themselves) as followers of Kant. But at least as important for understanding their philosophies is the revival of interest in Spinoza among late eighteenth century Germans, through the writings of such men as Lessing, Mendelssohn, Jacobi, Herder and Goethe. The German idealists read (or misread) Spinoza as a speculative monist, for whom ultimate reality is a single, indivisible divine substance, while the plurality of finite, particular and sensible things is a realm of mere appearance having the absolute substance as its true being or metaphysical ground. The idealists accept Spinoza's monism, and for them the fundamental question of philosophy is how to conceive of or characterize the metaphysical absolute.

Fichte views the basic issue as a choice between two possible answers to this question. One answer (which Fichte calls 'dogmatism') is the conception of the absolute as 'object' or 'substance', determined and determining everything causally, through the necessity of its nature. The other answer is idealism, which grasps the absolute as 'subject' or 'ego', creating both itself and its objects through freedom. The choice is between seeing ourselves (and the rest of the world) as products of lifeless objectivity or as manifestations of a free creative self or ego. Fichte of course opts for idealism, since (he alleges) only it can do justice to the experience of our own spontaneity as knowing subjects or to our sense of dignity as free moral agents. Fichte interprets his idealism as essentially Kantian, despite the fact that Kant rejects both Fichte's question and his answer to it as dangerous philosophical extravagance.

190

Schelling and Hegel continue the 'Kantian' tradition of regarding the absolute as fundamentally mind's free creative activity, but both reject Fichte's idealism as too one-sidedly subjectivist, and attempt to do greater justice to the role of objectivity in characterizing ultimate reality. Schelling's absolute combines or transcends subjectivity and objectivity, it is the ultimate 'identity' or 'indifference' out of which the original duality of subject and object emerges. Hegel's variation on the speculative theme is even more complex and original. For him, the absolute is 'a movement of self-positing', that is, a process through which 'the living substance which is subject' actualizes itself by becoming object to itself and then restores its unity with itself by coming to know this object as its own free expression or manifestation. For Hegel, mind or spirit (*Geist*) means this movement of 'self-restoring sameness'.[2]

For most of us, 'idealism' is the Berkeleyan view which holds that only minds and their contents really exist, that there is no matter or mind-independent reality and that what we erroneously think exists outside the mind is really an idea or image in some mind. As applied to Hegel's idealism this description may not be positively wrong, but it is only part of the truth and may mislead. Hegel attacks 'idealism' (he probably means Fichte) for merely making the empty 'assertion' that the rational ego is all reality but failing to 'comprehend' what this assertion means.[3] For Hegel mind or spirit is fundamentally an activity or process involving self-expression, self-actualization and self-knowledge. To say that spirit is all reality or the absolute is spirit is thus to say that this process is the most fundamental feature of reality. To 'comprehend' the truth of idealism is to see how the movement of spirit expresses itself in the details of the world, how all spirit's objects bear the mark of the creative process of which they are the manifestation. In Hegel's idealism, the emphasis is on this vision of the world.

Hegel's notion of a spirit is complex, and attempts to merge several important philosophical ideas into a single compelling vision. Spirit is like Aristotelian 'soul' in that it is a form-giving principle or potency inhering in things. To say that spirit 'posits itself' means in part that it gives expression, embodiment and actuality to itself, just as the form or essence of a living species does for Aristotle in a living organism. Spirit's 'forms', however, are 'concepts' or 'pure essentialities', universal natures which philosophers know by abstract thinking, and which are (in Platonic fashion) truer and more real than the transitory sensible particulars which exemplify them.[4] For Hegel, sensible particulars

191

are created or 'posited' by spirit as the necessary medium for actualizing itself; without them spirit's thinking would remain 'abstract', incomplete, not perfectly expressed, a mere potentiality lacking fulfillment. Concepts are what is truly real, but concepts demand exemplification for their full actuality. Hegel's metaphysics thus ingeniously reconciles Plato's thesis that forms or universals are more real than particulars with Aristotle's insistence that forms actually exist only in particulars.

Much depends on Hegel's conception of spirit's thinking activity and the characteristic mode of its self-expression in its objects. Hegel's conception of spirit's activity is based on Kant's notion that thinking is a synthetic activity, giving unity and intelligibility to the data of experience. But for his model of thought Hegel looks not to the *Critique of Pure Reason* and the Kantian faculty of 'understanding', but to Kant's *Critique of Judgment* 'in which alone [says Hegel] the Kantian philosophy shows itself to be *speculative*'.[5] Here alone, Kant 'opened up the concept of *life*, of the *idea*, and thus did *positively* for philosophy what the *Critique of Pure Reason* had done only in an imperfect, indirect or *negative* way'.[6] The conception to which Hegel is referring is that of a living organism or 'organized being' through which Kant introduces the idea of natural teleology.

In a living thing, says Kant, 'the preservation of any one part depends reciprocally on the rest', so that 'the parts [of an organism] are all organs reciprocally producing each other'.[7] The same reciprocity holds between the organism and its parts. For a thing to be an organism, 'it is required *first* that its parts (as regards their existence and their form) should be possible only through their relation to the whole . . . and *secondly* that the parts should so combine in the unity of a whole that they are reciprocally cause and effect of each other's form.' In virtue of this, a living thing is not only an 'organized', but a 'self-organizing being'.[8]

It is not hard to see why Hegel found the notion of an organized being a promising model for his conception of spirit's activity. The organization of a living thing is precisely the Aristotelian self-actualizing and form-giving principle which Hegel takes to be the basic feature of spirit. Further, the structure of an organism appeals to Hegel as the highest conception of thought's synthetic activity and the rational intelligibility it gives to things. An organic whole not only exhibits the internal necessity and self-sufficiency which Hegel takes to be the mark of self-positing spirit, but it also admits of an endless variety of possible forms, and thus captures spirit's free creativity as well.

Finally, as Kant presents it the notion of organic totality seems well suited to express Hegel's idealist conviction that the source of the world's order is mental or spiritual, and even his thesis that the highest fulfillment of spirit consists in comprehending the identity between itself and the objects it has posited. The parts of an organism, says Kant, 'mutually depend on one another, . . . and thus produce a whole by their own causality'. Yet he also says that 'conversely the concept of the whole may be regarded as its cause according to a principle', and that 'the unity of the idea' of the organism 'serves as the *a priori* determining ground of . . . the form of its synthesis'.[9] Since Kant treats natural purposiveness as a regulative principle brought to nature by our reflective judgment, he even goes so far as to say that the 'idea' which 'causes' or 'grounds' an organism resides in the mind of the knower, for whom it serves as 'the ground of knowledge of the systematic unity of the form and combination of all the manifold contained in a given material'.[10] Together these points (as Hegel reads them) imply the ultimate identity of subject and object, of the knowable order of the world with the creative activity of the knowing mind.

To comprehend ultimate reality as spirit thus means comprehending reality as an organized system, a living whole exhibiting an endless variety of living forms in all its parts. Since the ground of any organized being is its tendency to manifest and preserve a certain form, the type of explanation best suited to comprehending spirit and its manifestations is teleological explanation. To comprehend reality as spirit is to show that it exists in order that the dialectic process of spirit might be, to explain its existence through spirit's tendency to fulfill itself. Hegel's philosophy is thus a theodicy, which reveals the world as a manifestation of God's creativity and its strict necessity which is at the same time the most perfect freedom.

To comprehend the world in this way is not only to comprehend spirit as fulfilled, it is simultaneously to bring spirit to its fulfillment. For the dialectical process of spirit is one which first posits a world expressing its nature and then restores its unity with itself by comprehending that world as its own creation. Spirit is essentially self-knowing, but its self-knowledge is achieved only through finite minds which rationally recognize themselves as spirit's expression. In short, spirit is a supremely perfect God whose perfection nevertheless extends only as far as that of the world he has created, and hence an omniscient Deity whose knowledge consists in the rational comprehension human minds have of him. God fully self-actualized is the Hegelian speculative philosopher. In Hegel's words: 'God is God only insofar as he knows himself. His self-knowledge is further his self-consciousness in men and men's knowledge *of* God, which proceeds toward the self-knowledge of men *in* God.'[11]

2 *Organic development or dialectic*

Hegel's model of spirit's creative activity is the organization of a living thing. But a living organism gives us only a first approximation to spirit, or rather is itself only an inadequate form in which the rational intelligibility of spirit manifests itself. 'Life', as Hegel puts it, 'is the immediate idea.'[12] In a plant or animal, the soul or rational principle must constantly struggle with the 'immediacy' of the matter in which it is embodied. 'The process of life consists in overcoming the immediacy with which it is still beset', and this is the 'finitude' of a living organism.[13] Spirit in its true form is like a living organism which is wholly master of the material in which it is embodied and finds nothing recalcitrant to its life-principle. The truer form is what Hegel calls the 'concept', 'a totality in which each of its moments is the whole that it is, and is posited as an indissoluble unity with it'.[14] A concept is at once a principle of rational intelligibility inhering in the actual world and the act of thought by which a knowing mind grasps this intelligibility.

The concept is possible only to a rational self-consciousness, which for Hegel is always at the same time a living human personality involved in its own commerce with the world and its own struggle for self-knowledge and self-actualization. Perhaps the best way to bring out the inadequacy of the living organism to serve as a model for spirit is to contrast a living thing with a self-consciousness:

> That which is limited to a natural life [says Hegel] has through itself no capacity to proceed beyond its immediate existence. But it is driven beyond it by something else, and this is its death. Consciousness, however, is for itself its own concept, it is immediately a proceeding beyond what is limited and, since this limit belongs to it, a proceeding beyond itself.[15]

A plant or animal organism, once it has grown to maturity, has a single, stable organic structure. Its whole life consists in the struggle to impose this structure on its matter, and when it ceases to be able to do so, it dies. Hegel views the personality, values and life-plan of a human self also as a kind of organic structure, but one which is self-aware. A self-conscious personality is therefore like an organism whose structure or idea is consciously self-imposed. (It is 'for itself its own concept'.) But a reflective human being, by living out a certain self-conception and a set of goals and values, can also bring about changes in that conception, in these goals and values themselves. Therefore, a self-consciousness is like an organism which can survive radical changes in its organic structure, and can even initiate these changes. (Its nature is to 'proceed beyond what is limited', and thus 'proceed beyond itself'.)

Thus a self-conscious being is like an organism whose final tendencies are not limited to the maturation and self-maintenance of its structure, but include systematic tendencies to overthrow and transform its structure through consciousness. Its life-processes not only struggle with 'immediacy' or 'finitude' but even with themselves. They tend to generate conflict among its elements or functional parts, and then to resolve this conflict (at least temporarily) by imposing on the organism a new structure which resolves the conflicts rendering the previous structure untenable. A model for this is the change and development of a personality which is simultaneously trying to realize an ideal for itself and to discover what ideal it wants to realize. As the personality strives to fulfill its goals, it learns more about itself and about what goals it should be striving for. Its conception of itself and of its goals therefore changes, sometimes passing through stages of crisis and deep spiritual conflict.

Hegel sees this pattern of organic development as fundamental to all change which expresses the nature of spirit, for instance, to the transformation of the culture and mores of a nation or people in history. 'A people must know the universal on which its mores (*Sittlichkeit*) rests. . . . The highest point in the culture (*Bildung*) of a people is this grasping in thought of its life and condition, the scientific knowledge of its law and mores.' But this self-knowledge is also the downfall of what is known and necessitates a new and higher mode of life for the people which achieves it: 'Thought as universal has a dissolving force. . . . Spirit is just this, the dissolution of all determinate content.' By reflecting on its mores and seeking the principle which justifies them, the people becomes conscious of their limitations 'and so consciousness discovers reasons for renouncing them. This lies already in the demand for reasons.' At the same time, however, 'this dissolution through thought is necessarily the arising of a new principle. . . . Spirit determined anew from within itself has other, further interests and ends.'[16]

The whole nature of a spiritual being (a human personality, a historical people, a philosophical vision) thus consists not in a single organic structure or idea, but in a definite series of such structures, the determinate stages of its inner organic development. Each of these stages is contained in its predecessor as a final tendency. If we are to comprehend the nature of such a being, we must do simultaneously two quite different and even opposite things: First, we must comprehend each separate stage according to its concept or self-sustaining organic structure; and second, we must attend to the process by which each of these structures in time undermines itself through its own workings and passes over into the next determinate stage. This means that we must view each stage in a double aspect, with a double teleology. We must see in it and in its elements both the short run tendency to self-maintenance and the long run tendency to conflict, dissolution and transition to a higher stage.

It is such a process of organic development that Hegel calls 'dialectic'. His choice of this term is natural. In more familiar philosophical parlance, dialectic refers to the activity of establishing or refuting ideas by arguments in the give and take of discussion. Hegel conceives of organic development as fundamentally a process of cosmic reason, a process by which spirit tests and 'refutes' the imperfect forms of its embodiment, rising successively to higher forms. For Kant, dialectic is a process in which reason falls into inevitable conflicts with itself and resolves them. Hegel thinks that a spiritual organism goes through such a process as it abandons each stage and rises to the next. (For Kant the resolution of dialectical antinomies comes not through higher insight but through abandoning the pretense to knowledge; for Hegel, of course, this is the chief defect of Kant's treatment of dialectic.)[17] In both Plato and Aristotle, the mark of dialectical reasoning is that it proceeds not from self-evident first principles but from mere 'hypotheses' or common opinions. By bringing out conflicts among these opinions and revealing their philosophical presuppositions, dialectic proceeds toward first principles with a firm rational basis. Likewise, organic development begins with some spiritual organism in its immediacy. It is the process by which an organism raises itself toward perfection by undergoing conflicts inherent in its nature and adopting new organic structures which enable it to resolve these conflicts.

The structure of all Hegel's major works and lecture courses is dialectical. In each of them, he arranges the content of his subject matter in a developmental series, presenting his starting point as the lowest or 'immediate' stage and trying to show how each successive stage is demanded by or arises necessarily out of the internal conflicts or inadequacies of the previous one. As Hegel emphasizes, the whole point of this method is to present 'the immanent soul of the content itself'. He strongly attacks a pretended dialectical method which falls into 'formalism', 'the shapeless repetition of one formula, applied only externally to different materials' (Schelling is the likely object of these criticisms).[18] Whether Hegel altogether avoids this pitfall himself is open to question. But his clear intention is to argue on the basis of the specific interconnections unique to each subject matter he treats, and not to follow some universal set of rules for 'dialectical logic' or to read into everything the same neat dialectical schematism. This intention is distorted in superficial discussions of dialectic which reduce it to the tedious and uninformative jargon of 'thesis-antithesis-synthesis'. (In fact, the use of this particular jargon is not only uninformative and distorting, but even inaccurate, in that Hegel almost never uses it. Marx uses it only once, and solely for the purpose of parody. The principal philosophers who use it are Fichte and Schelling.)[19]

There are, roughly speaking, two species of dialectic in Hegel, which we may call respectively the *temporal* and the *hierarchical*. As we have pictured organic development so far, it is literally a temporal process. In his historical lectures, Hegel presents the history of social mores, political institutions, art, religion and philosophy as a dialectical series, representing the successive epochs in the history of a given subject matter as stages of development of spirit in time. *The Phenomenology of Spirit* develops the concept of philosophical knowledge from its most immediate forms up to the standpoint of Hegel's speculative logic, presenting different philosophical viewpoints as if they were different phases through which a philosophical mind might pass in its search for the truth. The dialectic does not literally trace a temporal process, but its presentation is quasi-temporal, and the *Phenomenology* contains extensive allusions to the history of Western philosophy, religion and culture which are supposed to exhibit this history as following the inherent series of philosophical views which Hegel is expounding.

There is a different kind of dialectic in *The Science of Logic*, the *Encyclopedia* and *The Philosophy of Right*. In these works, Hegel is not concerned with temporal deveopment at all. His aims in presenting things dialectically are to exhibit the rational structure of his subject matter and to insure a systematic treatment of it. Here the dialectical stages are not phases of a temporal process but rather a hierarchy of successively more adequate viewpoints on a subject matter, or of successively more adequate forms in which a single idea actualizes itself in the world. Hegel's system of logic is an inventory of the conceptions through which thought grasps reality (these conceptions, Hegel tells us, 'may be regarded as definitions of the absolute, as the metaphysical definitions of God').[20] The inventory is dialectical because the concepts or definitions are not all equally adequate to reality, but form a hierarchy running from the poorest and emptiest (such as *being* and *nothing*) to the truest and most articulated (*life, knowledge, the absolute idea* which is object to itself). Hegel's method is to generate successively the richer definitions by exhibiting each of them as solving the particular difficulties inherent in the one which precedes it. In this way, Hegel's logic presents us with a series of viewpoints on reality, each of which is a closer approximation to the truth than the one out of which it is generated. A hierarchical dialectic of this sort is of some importance for Marx since in its general conception (though not of course in its finer details) it distinctly resembles the theoretical structure of *Capital*. (There is good evidence that this resemblance is intentional.)[21]

The last two parts of Hegel's *Encyclopedia* present nature and finite mind or spirit as the stages of cosmic spirit's return to itself out of the objective world. Although the various processes of nature (mechanical, physical, chemical, biological) exist simultaneously and show no temporal development (Hegel is entirely undarwinian in this respect) they do form a hierarchy and philosophy can present them as successively more adequate attempts to actualize the idea of spirit in external objectivity. The same sort of thing can be done for the stages of subjective mental life (sensation, consciousness, desire, knowledge, practical reason) and the stages of 'objective spirit' or social life. *The Philosophy of Right* presents the modern state as an unfolding of the principle of free volition through an entire hierarchy of stages: the free person as a subject of abstract rights, the forms these rights take in property, contract, crime and its punishment; the moral subject, concerned about purposes, intentions, responsibilities and the dictates of conscience; and the social system in which morality has its place, the family, the economic realm, ('civil society') and the political state. Hegel treats these moral and social structures, which exist side by side in the modern state, as a developing series of ways in which the same basic principle expresses itself. Each successive (and more 'concrete') expression of this principle is understood as a necessary development of the stage which precedes it, a way of satisfying the demands or solving the difficulties to which this stage gives rise. (As we will see, there is more than a casual resemblance between Hegel's program in *The Philosophy of Right* and Marx's method of moving from the 'abstract' to the 'concrete' in *Capital*.)

Obviously the value of Hegel's particular dialectical theories consists wholly in the specific interconnections and developmental tendencies he is able to establish between the particular elements and stages of his subject matter. Hegel would be the first to insist that there is no value at all merely in arranging a given subject matter according to triadic patterns or schematizing it in Greek jargon. The general conception of a dialectical system may be suggestive, illuminating, even inspiring (as it apparently is to Marx). But as far as the philosophical or scientific value of a dialectical system is concerned, everything depends on the details of its execution, on whether the 'life of the content' really displays dialectical interconnections and tendencies, and on how well the practitioner of the dialectical method is able to establish each specific connection and transition by good arguments.

Engels emphasizes this point in relation to the Marxian dialectic. Dialectic, he says, is not a technique for constructing proofs, or for producing explanations by fitting particular cases to general laws. The function of dialectical 'laws' for Engels is purely descriptive; the explanations which appeal to dialectical interconnections and tendencies depend 'on the particular nature of each case'.[22] In *Capital*, Marx describes the historical process leading from individual private property under petty industry through capitalist private property to socialist property as an example of the dialectical 'law' of 'negation of the negation' ('The capitalist mode of appropriation . . . is the first negation of individual private property, founded on one's own labor. But capitalist production generates with the necessity of a natural process its own negation. This is a negation of the negation.')[23] Engels criticizes Eugen Dühring for ascribing to Marx the intention of 'proving that the process was historically necessary' by subsuming it under a 'dialectical law'. 'On the contrary. After he has proved historically that in fact this process has in part already occurred, in part that it must yet occur, he adds a description of it as a process which follows a determinate dialectical law. That is all.'[24]

3 Dialectic and formal logic

Perhaps the most baffling side of Hegel's philosophy is his repudiation of traditional logic, his avowed denial of the principles of identity, contradiction and excluded middle. Because Marx and Engels appear to agree with this point of Hegelian doctrine and because it is often a stumbling block to the understanding and acceptance of dialectical thinking, Hegel's rejection of formal logic merits at least a brief discussion here.

In this section, I will try to defend the view that Hegel does not deny (or see himself as denying) the principles of formal logic as logicians have usually meant them. Instead, Hegel's complaint against formal logic is best understood as a disjunction. Either we interpret the principles of logic as formal logicians have meant them: in that case they are true, but trivial, silly, and philosophically worthless because they employ concepts of identity and difference which do not express the real nature of anything; or else we give the principles of logic a philosophically interesting interpretation by substituting in them less artificial concepts: in that case, however, they turn out to be false because they are incompatible with the vision of reality presented in Hegel's speculative metaphysics. If the principles of formal logic are true, then they are unphilosophical; if they are philosophically interesting, then they are false.

An important thesis of Hegel's philosophy is that it belongs to the nature of everything to be a 'unity of opposites'. Hegel even defines the 'speculative' or the 'dialectical' as 'the grasping of opposites in their unity'.[25] What are 'opposites'? Suppose you and I are playing the silly game where one of us says a word and the other says the word which means 'the opposite'. For many words ('hot', 'tall', 'up') there seems to be only one right answer, while for others there may seem to be none, or a number of possible answers. Suppose I say 'red'. If you are thinking of the system of complementary colors, you will answer 'green'. But this is not your only option. If you think of French wines or the Wars of the Roses or the Russian Revolution, you could answer 'white'; if you have just been playing cards or reading Stendhal, you could answer 'black'. You have these alternatives because when we think of any two things as opposites we do so relative to some system of categories or comparisons within which the two things count either as exclusive and exhaustive complementaries or else as extremes or poles which define the system. In the system of complementary colors, green is the opposite of red since it contains all and only the hues which red lacks. When we think of the Russian Revolution, white is the opposite of red because white represents the movement which stands at the opposite pole from the movement red represents.

Systems of organic totality and organic development constitute a fertile breeding ground for pairs of opposites. Further, they exhibit these opposites as a necessary unity. Organic structures typically sustain themselves homeostatically through the complementarity or equilibrium of activities or processes which count as functional opposites relative to the organism. Further, these opposites mutually sustain and condition one another. A warm-blooded animal, for example, has mechanisms both for generating body heat and for losing heat to its environment. Viewed in the abstract, it has two opposite tendencies, tendencies which even 'negate' each other, destroy each other's effects. Yet in the organism they are arranged so as to complement each other, to maintain the animal's body temperature at the maximal point for its life processes. Each of them is necessary to the life of the organism, and thus ultimately necessary for its own opposite. In organic development, the undeveloped or 'immediate' shape of a thing and its fully developed or perfected shape stand at opposite poles of a determinate process. The complete nature of the thing includes the entire process, to which both poles (as well as all the intermediate stages) are necessary.

Hegel believes that reality has an organic structure because it is the expression of spirit's thought. Accordingly, he believes he can confirm his vision of reality *a priori* in thought, by showing that in every pair of opposites the existence of each member logically or conceptually requires the existence of the other. All opposites, he says, 'are essentially conditioned through each other, and *are* only in relation to each other'.[26] Even the most 'trivial examples', Hegel says, confirm this: 'That *is* above which is *not* below; above is determined only as what is not below. And yet above *is* only *insofar* as there is a below, and conversely. In each determination lies its opposite.'[27]

In many cases, Hegel's point is correct. Many pairs of opposites (above/below, victory/defeat, front/back) are merely complementary sides or aspects of the same thing or same state of affairs. It is logically impossible for either opposite to exist without the other. No body can have a front side unless it has a back. No battle can be won unless it is also lost. As Heraclitus says, the road up and the road down are one and the same. Another class of opposites are pairs of comparatives (large/small, fast/slow, light/dark). Each comparative is supplied with a reference only by contrast with examples of its opposite. It makes no sense to suppose that the world might contain examples of one comparative without examples of the other: that there might be only fast motions and no slow ones, only large objects and no small ones.

But it is also evident that Hegel's point is not universally valid. Male and female are opposites, but it is at most a biological truth that the existence of each gender depends on the existence of the other. Right-handed and left-handed are opposites, but there is no inherent impossibility in a world containing only southpaws.

201

That there are mortal beings does not entail that anything is immortal. I think Hegel ignores such examples because his real purpose is not to make a conceptual point but to illustrate his organic view of reality, of which the unity of opposites is one aspect.

As Hegel interprets it, his principle of the unity of opposites has some surprising results. It implies that there are 'contradictions' in things, even that the essence of everything is constituted by the contradictions it contains. Further, it implies that nothing is simply identical with itself, but that everything is self-different, identical with its own opposite, the negation of its own self. An organic whole is essentially made up of different, functionally opposed and even reciprocally negating processes, which constitute the thing by their complementarity or homeostasis. Since these processes are not merely opposites but tend directly to negate or abolish one another, Hegel describes them as 'contradictories', and concludes that the nature of things is constituted by contradiction. Further, the essence of a thing which develops organically includes a series of different stages, each of which struggles with and eventually negates the one which precedes it. These stages, which all belong to the essence of the thing, are mutually contradictory. Developing things also contain contradictions in the sense that as one stage of their development passes over to the next, the elements of the collapsing stage cease to work in harmony. The relation between them gradually becomes not one of complementarity and reciprocal dependence, but instead one of conflict, incompatibility, and (in that sense) contradiction. Of course the conflicting elements are not incompatible in the sense that they cannot coexist for a time in the thing. But they are incompatible in the sense that the opposition between them directly undermines the stability of the structure, and eventually destroys it, along with the contradictions which constitute it.

The contrasting or opposite elements in an organic whole are reciprocally dependent, and cannot exist without one another. Further, in any pair of such opposites, both manifest the same essence, the same organic form or principle which animates the whole. In this sense, the opposites are *identical*, each is in its essence what its opposite is. Again, the stages of an organically developing thing are different, opposite, mutually negating, contradictory. Yet all of them belong necessarily to the selfsame essence which unfolds itself through them. Thus self-difference and self-negation constitute the essence of anything whose nature involves a developmental process. According to Hegel's meta-

202

physics, such a development (either temporal or hierarchical) belongs to the nature of every expression of spirit, and hence to all reality.

> The consideration of everything that is shows that *in itself* everything in its identity with itself is nonidentical with itself and self-contradictory; that in its difference, in its contra-diction, it is identical with itself, and that in itself it is this movement of transition of each of these determinations into the other.[28]

Hegel's language is deliberately paradoxical. But unless my interpretation of it is very wide of the mark, it should be clear that he is not denying the principle of identity or the principle of contradiction as traditional logicians have meant them. By the same token, once we penetrate Hegel's paradoxical modes of ex-pression, his metaphysics, even if it is not wholly clear or un-controversial, cannot be convicted of incoherence of unintelligi-bility as judged by these principles.

The principle of contradiction as formal logicians normally understand it does not deny that things may be composed of different parts or elements with contrasting functional values. It does not deny the natural fact of homeostasis among organic processes. The principle does not say that nothing may change its structure, nor even deny that things may have inherent or essen-tial tendencies to such changes. There is nothing 'contradictory' — in the formal logical sense — about real conflicts between things, or between the parts or elements of a single thing, or about a thing's having different structures or properties at different times or in different respects. The principle of contradictions says only that if we affirm a given predicate of a given subject, we cannot speak truly if we also deny that same predicate of that same subject at one and the same time and in one and the same respect.

Likewise, the logical principle of identity says only that we can-not speak truly if we deny that a given thing is the same thing as itself, or affirm that it is the same thing as something which is wholly diverse from it. This principle does not say that different things or tendencies cannot belong to a larger whole, or that they cannot manifest the same essence or explanatory principle. The principle of identity does not deny that one and the same thing may have different parts or aspects or stages. Formal logic pre-cludes no coherent account of the organic unity of things or their developmental tendencies, and poses no obstacle to a metaphysics which postulates organic essences and tendencies as the basic explanatory principles. Some philosophers (such as Bertrand Russell) have combined an enthusiasm for formal logic with a metaphysics Hegel would doubtless condemn as lifeless, abstract and atomistic. But the principles of formal logic themselves are neutral in disputes between Hegel and such metaphysicians.

I think Hegel is quite aware of all this. His metaphysical interpretation (or misinterpretation) of the principles of formal logic is not based on ignorance or misunderstanding. Hegel admits that as the formal logician *means* them, his principles are indisputable, in fact that they are 'empty tautologies'.[29] So understood, however, Hegel regards the principles of formal logic as worse than incorrect; he thinks of them as frivolous, 'empty', as 'trivialities leading nowhere'.[30] A deeper interpretation discovers that 'these laws contain more than is meant by them', a metaphysical content which, although it is false, is at least worthy of philosophical discussion. By reinterpreting its principles so that they turn out false, Hegel believes he is doing formal logic a favor.[31]

The shallowness of formal logic, according to Hegel, is due to the artificial notions of identity and difference (contradiction, negation) it employs. The formal logical notion of something's identity is what Hegel calls 'abstract identity'. This notion 'arises through a relative negating that goes on outside it, only separating from it what is distinguished, and otherwise leaving it as much as before something which merely *is*'.[32] With this notion of identity, one may take any arbitrary bit of reality, abstract it both from its organic connections with other things and from its own essential tendencies to develop, and not only treat it as something having an 'identity' but even assert that its identity is something which does not concern the constitution of anything else or any processes of change in which the chosen bit of reality may be involved. But this (as Hegel sees it) is a wanton perversion of the notion of identity. The identity of a thing is that which makes it the thing it is, which determines its real nature. In order to arrive at the logician's abstract notion of identity, we must either '*leave out* a part of the concrete manifold present' in the thing, or else 'neglect its differences, *pull together* its manifold determinations into one'.[33] In either case, we falsify the only conception of identity which has any application to reality. If, on the other hand, we substitute in the formal logician's principle a correct conception of identity, then what the principle says is that each thing in its real nature is static, dependent only on itself, not essentially constituted by its dependence on other things or by its own tendencies to development. This proposition, though false, is importantly false, and (unlike the formal logical principle as originally *meant*) worth the philosopher's attention.

Hegel has similar objections to the logician's abstract conceptions of difference, negation or contradiction. For Hegel, the opposite of something is some other definite thing which stands in a relation of complementarity or opposition to it in the context of some organic system. The negation or contradictory of a thing is some other definite thing which conflicts or struggles with it, as the heat of a fire does with the coolness of a pot of water, or as the mature form of a plant does with the seed from which it develops. But here again the formal logician abandons the real world for a set of artificial abstractions. The 'negation' or 'contradictory' of a property is not something definite which stands in any real relation to it, but merely the 'abstract negative', the mere lack or absence of the property, which may refer to almost anything. 'In the doctrine of contradictory concepts, the one concept is, e.g., *blue* . . . and the other *not-blue*, so that this other would not be something affirmative, perhaps *yellow*, but would be held fast as the abstract negative.'[34] This conception saves the correctness of the principles of contradiction and excluded middle, but only at the cost of childish triviality. In these principles 'the opposite signifies a mere lack, or rather *indeterminateness*; the proposition is so insignificant it is not worth the trouble to state it.'[35] The notion of abstract negation is wholly artificial; nowhere does it enter into the real constitution of things or explain their processes: 'In fact there is nowhere, neither in heaven nor on earth, neither in the spiritual nor the natural world, an abstract "either/or" of the sort asserted by the understanding.'[36]

If, once again, we state the principle of contradiction using less vacuous notions, then it says something philosophically more significant. It says that no entity is composed of parts, processes, tendencies or stages which really oppose or conflict with one another. It expresses a vision of the world as composed of lifeless, static atoms, whose interactions are merely external and accidental, devoid of organic interconnections, manifesting no essential principles or developmental tendencies. This vision of reality is philosophically significant, because it is just the vision Hegel's philosophy is concerned to deny.

As I read Hegel, then, his real complaint against formal logic (as it is *meant* by formal logicians) is not that its principles are false, but that it is philosophically sterile. It is probably true that the techniques of formal reasoning, either as Hegel knew them or as they have been developed since his time, have no special role to play in expounding his metaphysical vision. But it does not necessarily follow that they are of no philosophical value. Perhaps at the time Marx and Engels wrote it was still possible for an informed and open-minded person to share Hegel's view that formal logic is an arid and scholastic discipline, with little philosophical interest or promise. But present day Hegelians and Marxists betray only ignorance and dogmatism when they repeat Hegel's nineteenth century polemics against formal logic. Our hindsight shows that Hegel badly underestimated the potential philosophical importance of a logic based on 'abstract' conceptions of identity, negation and so on. If the elementary laws of formal logic are (as Hegel thought) trivialities, it has been amply demonstrated that they are not 'insignificant' ones and that they do not 'lead nowhere'. On the contrary, in the foundations of mathematics and semantics, twentieth century formal logic has yielded some very interesting, often counter-intuitive and even revolutionary results. On the other hand, these developments were not even on the horizon when Hegel wrote, and he can hardly be charged with ignorance or philosophical blindness for not anticipating them. The only unfortunate thing about his views on formal logic is that they have led to misunderstandings, needlessly prejudicing Hegelians against modern formal logic and formal logicians against Hegelian philosophy.

XIV

The Marxian Dialectic

1 The 'rational kernel' in the 'mystical shell'

What is unmistakably clear about Marx's attitude toward the Hegelian dialectic is that he accepts some of it, but not all. Marx acknowledges that Hegel's philosophy (especially his system of logic) is of great service to him in constructing the economic theory of *Capital*. He even describes Hegel's dialectic as 'the last word of all philosophy'.[1] Yet when Marx praises Hegel in such ways, he never fails to attack the 'mysticism' of Hegel's method or to emphasize that the Hegelian dialectic is not satisfactory as it is. Marx never fulfilled his intention to 'make accessible to the ordinary human understanding, in two or three printer's sheets, what is *rational* in the method which Hegel discovered and at the same time mystified'.[2] Instead, he left us with two images or metaphors for what he intended to do. Hegel's dialectic is, on the one hand, enclosed or shrouded in 'mysticism'. It must be 'stripped of' this false form, 'to discover the rational kernel in the mystical shell'. On the other hand, with Hegel the dialectic is 'standing on its head'. It must be 'inverted' or 'turned upside down' before it can assume a rational shape.[3] These two images are vivid, but by themselves they are of little use to us in deciding what the 'rational kernel' of Hegel's philosophy is, in determining which Hegelian doctrines Marx accepts and which he rejects.

In Hegel's philosophy we can distinguish two things: first, a vision of the way reality is structured, and consequently a program for the kind of theory which adequately captures that structure; and second, a metaphysics which purports to explain why reality is structured this way, and which implies (in Hegel's view) a certain epistemic status for the theories which capture the structure of reality. Hegel sees reality as structured organically and developmentally. Things display their essential natures when they are seen as organized wholes or systems, and as elements of larger wholes or systems. These systems are characterized by tendencies not only to self-harmony and self-maintenance, but also to development, both temporally and hierarchically. Things which exist through time have essential tendencies to develop, to unfold their natures by continually changing or revolutionizing their organic structures. Organic structures themselves display a hierarchy, developing or unfolding a certain abstract essence or basic principle toward its full concreteness. A theory which captures the structure of reality must conceive things as organized totalities. It must attend to their essential tendencies to temporal development, and it must analyze their organic structure through a hierarchy of concepts of or viewpoints on a whole which reveal all the levels or stages belonging to its nature.

Hegel is sure reality has this structure on purely metaphysical grounds. Hegel believes that absolute reality is self-positing spirit. The marks of thought and its creative self-expression are organic interconnection and development. Consequently, whatever appears or is actual must be an expression or manifestation of spirit, and must display the marks of its spiritual origin. Further, the creative activity of thought is simultaneously the activity of God's original creation; the activity of human thought which apprehends the inherent structure of thinking thus brings God's thoughts to self-consciousness. Since the dialectical structure of thinking is apprehended not by the senses but by reason, our key to the structure of reality is not casual sense observations but the necessary movement of thought, which philosophers can produce out of their own minds. The task of philosophy is to penetrate these observations and 'give to their contents the essential shape of thought's *freedom* (the *a priori*)'.[4]

As I read Marx, he accepts Hegel's vision of reality but rejects the Hegelian metaphysical underpinnings of this vision, together with the epistemological conclusions which are supposed to follow from them. For Marx the world is a system of organically interconnected processes characterized by inherent tendencies to development, and subject periodically to radical changes in organic structure. Because Marx thinks the world is structured in this way, he also believes that the best way to mirror this structure is a dialectical theory, one which views its subject matter organically, traces the hierarchical structure of this subject matter through the stages of its concreteness and explains the systematic changes in this structure by the developmental tendencies inherent in it. Because Hegel was the first to champion this vision of reality and to work out the theoretical program which is capable of understanding things in terms of it, Marx credits him with being 'the first to present [the dialectic's] general forms of movement in a comprehensive and conscious way'.[5]

For Marx, however, the dialectical structure of the world is a complex empirical fact about the nature of material reality. It is not a vestige of God's creative essence, and it is not to be explained or understood by means of *a priori* speculative principles. In particular, it is not the case that the structure of things is dialectical because there is any special relation between phenomena of organization and development and the nature of thought-processes. On the contrary, dialectical thinking only reflects the dialectical structure of the world which is thought about. If people think best when they think dialectically, that is because they think best when their thought mirrors the real world. If they think in terms of universal concepts, that is because it is the nature of thinking to abstract from particulars, and grasp their common properties. And if human thought itself is dialectical, that is because through time (perhaps through natural selection) human faculties have come to harmonize with the real world which is independent of thought. According to Marx, it is this difference from Hegel which makes the Marxian dialectic different from the Hegelian, even its 'direct opposite':

> For Hegel the thought-process (which under the name 'idea' he even transforms into an independent subject) is the demiurge of the actual, which forms only its external appearance. With me, on the contrary, the ideal is nothing other than the material transposed and translated in the human head.

As Engels puts it: 'Marx comprehends (*zusammenfasst*) the common content lying in things and relations in its most universal expression in thought. His abstraction thus only gives back in the form of thought the content already lying in the things.'[6]

The 'rational kernel' of Hegel's dialectic, then, is his vision of reality as structured organically and characterized by inherent tendencies to development. The 'mystical shell' is Hegel's logical pantheistic metaphysics, which represents the dialectical structure of reality as a consequence of thinking spirit's creative activity. Marx's 'inversion' of Hegel consists in viewing the dialectical structure of thought not as a cause or explanation for the dialectical structure of reality, but merely as a consequence of the fact that it is thought's function to mirror a dialectically structured world.

209

Hegel and Marx agree that reality is dialectically structured, that the world consists of organic totalities with inherent developmental tendencies. But we may perhaps wonder what this thesis says about the world, or even whether it says anything at all. Concepts like 'organic whole' and 'developmental tendency' are rather vague ones. Philosophical treatments of teleology have had notoriously little success analyzing the notions of 'organism' and 'goal-directed system'. We may doubt that this is merely a case of the general failure of philosophers to produce counter-example free analyses of philosophically interesting concepts. An organic whole qualifies as such because it possesses a certain inner intelligibility, and not because it shares any determinate properties with other organic wholes. Thus Kant thinks that the discovery of teleological organization requires a creative act of the mind, akin to artistic genius, 'the talent for producing something for which no determining rule can be given'.[7] The attempt to specify a property all organic wholes have in common will probably succeed only to the degree that it manages to be uninformative.

Even the extension of this concept is vague, perhaps essentially so. Organization is something which admits of degrees. A vertebrate exhibits more of it than a single-celled organism, and any living thing exhibits more than a simple humanmade device involving one or two feedback mechanisms. How primitive does organization have to be before we deny it is present at all? I doubt that there is any determinate answer to this question. The truth seems to be rather that towards the lower end of the scale it is not so much a question whether something is an organic whole as how illuminating we find it to treat it as one. Perhaps almost anything can be described as an 'organic whole' with 'developmental tendencies' if we construe these notions generously enough and have a strong enough desire to see them exemplified. Accordingly, we may begin to worry whether the supposedly radical and far-reaching claim that reality is dialectically structured in fact says much of anything at all.

But such worries, I think, are largely misguided. For Hegel, at least, part of the point of saying that reality is dialectically structured is to set up the notions of organic totality and development as paradigms for rational understanding.[8] Even if it is empirically empty to say that reality has some dialectical structure or other, it may be philosophically important to claim that any world having a certain degree of rational intelligibility must exhibit patterns of organization and development.

But we can see that the thesis that reality is structured dialectically is not a truism when we consider its implications for inquiry. To say of social structures, for instance, that they are organic wholes is to recommend that they be studied teleologically. To say that societies change through inherent tendencies to development is to imply that we should try to understand them in terms of such tendencies rather than in terms of causal laws. Whatever these proposals may be, they are not trivial or uncontroversial. In any possible world where it would be advisable to follow them, there would have to be a degree of organization and inner development which is considerably greater than many social theorists have thought there is in the actual world. Looked at in this way, the thesis that reality is structured dialectically, despite its vagueness, undoubtedly has empirical significance.

These considerations may help to account for the fact that Marx describes what is basically a view of the world as a 'method'. Dialectic is not a method in the sense of a set of rules or procedures for inquiry, or a general prolegomenon to science of the Baconian or Cartesian kind, which tries to prescribe the right way to employ our cognitive faculties irrespective of the way the objects of our knowledge may be constituted. But dialectic does involve some recommendations about how science should approach the world, what sort of order to look for in it, what sorts of explanations to employ, even a theoretical program to be followed. In this sense, dialectic is a method, and perhaps the empirical significance of the dialectical vision of reality is most easily seen when dialectic is construed as a set of methodological proposals.

2 'Inverting' Hegel

As I interpret Marx, he accepts Hegel's vision of the way reality is structured, but rejects the metaphysics which motivates this vision in Hegel's philosophy. I think both the negative and the positive sides of this interpretation can be convincingly documented from the Marxian texts. Marx's first critical examination of Hegel was an unpublished critical commentary on § § 261-313 of Hegel's *Philosophy of Right*, prepared in 1842 or 1843. Marx's later writings indicate that he never abandons this critique of Hegel, and even continues to regard it as a valid point of departure for his own dialectical method. Later criticisms of Hegelian philosophy in *The Holy Family* and *The Poverty of Philosophy* in fact add little of substance to the criticisms presented in this early text, though the later writings do grace them with Marx's brilliant satirical wit.[9]

Marx's critique of *The Philosophy of Right* shows clearly that his attack is basically metaphysical, aimed at Hegel's 'logical pantheistic mysticism'.[10] The real topic of Hegel's treatise is the modern state and its political constitution. What is valuable in Hegel's discussion is his insight into the organic interconnections which constitute this constitution. 'It is a great step forward to consider the political state as an organism, to treat the different authorities ... as living and rational distinctions.'[11] Hegel's fatal flaw is that in his treatment the organic connection of empirical facts is expressed 'as the deed of a subjective idea different from the fact itself. ... Empirical actuality is taken up as it is; it is expressed as rational, but it is not rational on account of its own reason, but because the empirical fact has a significance different from its empirical existence.'[12]

Part of what annoys Marx about Hegel's procedure is its apologetic bias. By viewing existing society as 'the idea's deed', Hegel is 'taking up' this society 'as it is', deciding *a priori* that it is rational. But this is only a superficial aspect of Marx's critique of Hegel.[13] Marx does not deny that there is rationality in the modern state, and praises Hegel precisely for bringing it to light. His real criticism is that Hegel mystifies this rationality by misinterpreting its nature and its source.

The origin of Marx's famous metaphor of 'inversion' is his attack on Hegel for 'inverting subject and predicate', that is, turning the rational concept which reflects the dialectical structure of reality into an agent which generates that structure:

> [Hegel's] genuine thought is: the development of the state ... is *organic*. The *actual distinctions* or *different sides* of the *political* constitution are the presupposition, the subject. The predicate is their determination as *organic*. But instead of this the idea is made into the subject and the distinctions in their actuality and development are grasped as its result.[14]

This criticism is closely connected with an attack on Hegel's platonism, which becomes the object of Marx's ridicule in *The Holy Family* and *The Poverty of Philosophy*. Hegel's platonism is his view that the real dialectical agency is the abstract universal concept or idea, which attains to actuality and concreteness by its 'self-moving' and 'self-differentiating' manifestation in the organic development of particulars. For Marx, on the contrary, the concepts employed in dialectical thinking are only abstractions from the real properties of particulars which it is their function to mirror. In *The Poverty of Philosophy*, Marx diagnoses the speculative philosopher's error as one of mistaking

212

the final and most basic abstractions for the ultimate constituents of the reality from which they are drawn.

> When we abstract from a subject all its alleged accidents, . . . we are right in saying that in the last abstraction the only substance left is the logical categories. Thus the metaphysicians, in making abstractions, think they are making analyses; the more they detach themselves from objects, the more they imagine they are approaching and penetrating them.[15]

In his critique of Hegel's *Philosophy of Right*, Marx argues that Hegel's metaphysical error at this point also falsifies what is true in his dialectical method. In dealing with the state as an organism, Hegel's starting point is the 'abstract idea' of an organism, which supposedly differentiates and actualizes itself in the state. Yet merely by saying that the state is an organism, 'I still know nothing about the specific idea of the political constitution; the same proposition can be expressed with the same truth about the *animal* organism as about the *political* organism.'[16] As long as Hegel takes his platonism seriously, his dialectical method must fail to grasp the specific rationality of its subject matter, and must occupy itself only with flimsy abstractions: 'The genuine result he wants is to determine the *organism* as the *political constitution*. But no bridge has been built by which one could pass from the *universal idea* of *organism* to the *determinate idea* of the *state organism* or the *political constitution*, and to all eternity no such bridge can be built.'[17] If we take Hegel at his word, the actual subjects to which he applies his method 'become mere *names*, so that we have only the appearance of actual knowledge. They are and remain uncomprehended, because they are not comprehended in the determinations of their specific essence.'[18] Hegel's method works only insofar as he does not consistently adhere to his own speculative standpoint, but deals with dialectical connections as they show themselves empirically, and treats his theoretical generalizations as abstractions from an empirical subject matter outside them.

For the positive side of my interpretation the evidence cannot be as direct as it would be if Marx had explicitly identified the 'rational kernel' of Hegel's dialectic. But there is evidence, both in Marx's writings and in Engels'. The strongest evidence, I think, is the structure of the self-consciously dialectical theory Marx projected in *Capital*, which we will consider presently. But Marx provides us with unmistakable indications of his adherence to Hegel's dialectical vision throughout his writings.

As we have just seen, in his commentary on *The Philosophy of*

Right, Marx enthusiastically endorses the idea that social structures should be viewed as organisms or organic wholes, and often describes them in this way.[19] He is avowedly concerned with the 'inner interconnections' among social phenomena, with 'tracing their forms of development', and grasping the inherent 'laws' or 'tendencies' which govern their history. He depicts these tendencies as arising from the antagonisms or 'contradictions' which constitute a given social whole. Marx often emphasizes that self-maintenance and transitoriness are mutually necessary aspects of any organism, and that it is the business of dialectic to grasp them in their unity. 'The dialectical method includes in the positive understanding of what subsists also an understanding of its negation, its necessary downfall; and thus grasps every form of becoming in the flux of its movement.'[20]

Marx's historical materialism is a distinctly dialectical theory of society. It views a social order as an organic whole of economic relations, passing through definite stages of historical development and driven by basic tendencies to change. It understands the dynamic of these tendencies as the antagonism between classes arising out of the basic economic relations which constitute the society. Historical materialism is animated by Hegel's philosophical vision, even if there is nothing specifically Hegelian about the explanatory factors it postulates.

Engels is more explicit in endorsing Hegel's dialectical vision of reality, largely because he devotes more attention to a philosophical exposition of dialectic. For Engels, the great thing about Hegel's philosophy is the *task* it proposes, that of 'presenting the whole natural, historical and spiritual world as a process, i.e., as in constant movement, change, transformation and development, and making the attempt to trace out the inner connection in this movement and development'.[21] 'The whole of nature accessible to us forms a system, a connected totality.' Dialectic is the 'science of interconnections' within this system, 'the essentially ordering science', which 'binds natural processes into one great whole', 'comprehending things in their essential connection, concatenation, movement, arising and perishing'.[22] We saw in Chapter XI that Engels, like Schelling and Hegel, views nature as a teleological hierarchy of processes or 'forms of motion'. There are also strong indications that Engels, like Schelling, regards efficient causality as founded on a more basic, organic reciprocity between events, so that final causation or teleology is a more basic category of explanation than efficient cause.[23] Engels' three famous 'dialectical laws' (the unity of opposites, the transition of quantity into quality and the negation of the negation)

214

are all taken more or less directly from Hegel, and are best seen as vehicles for expounding his vision of the world as organically and developmentally structured.

Some writers claim that Marx does not follow Engels in applying dialectical categories to nature. Like other attempts to drive a significant philosophical wedge between Marx and Engels, this thesis was first popularized by Lukács' *History and Class Consciousness*, is usually supported by an essentially idealistic reading of Marx, and has no basis whatever in Marx's texts. It is true that Marx does not often indulge in Engels' *naturphilosophische* speculations and concerns himself almost exclusively with the application of dialectical thinking to social theory. But Marx more than once explicitly asserts that dialectical principles are 'verified equally in history and natural science'.[24] Nowhere does he say or imply the reverse. Marx does endorse Giambattista Vico's idea that 'human history is distinguished from natural history by the fact that we have made the former but not the latter', and in this context criticizes 'the abstract materialism of natural science, which excludes the historical process'.[25] But this is an attack precisely on that materialism which excludes the dialectical category of organic development from nature. It is in no sense an agreement with Lukács' idealistic notion that only conscious human practice confers a dialectical structure on things. As we have seen, Marx parts company with Hegel precisely because Hegel makes the dialectical nature of thought the basis for the dialectical structure of reality, where Marx holds that just the reverse is the case.

Of course Engels also has his own way of distinguishing the Marxian dialectic from the Hegelian. He says that Marx accepts Hegel's 'method' but rejects his 'system'.[26] This is not necessarily wrong, but it is superficial and possibly misleading. On the one hand, it emphasizes (what is obvious) that Marx does not accept Hegel's whole philosophy (in whose details, as Engels says, 'much turns out to be patchy, artificial, forced, in short wrongheaded').[27] But it may also suggest (what is false) that the dialectical 'method' can be clearly separated from Hegel's vision of the way the world is. In distinguishing 'system' from 'method', Engels is concerned to emphasize Marxism's denial of any 'absolute truth'; or, to put it less misleadingly, Marxism's denial that our scientific knowledge will ever be final and complete, its insistence that science is always at best an approximate reflection of reality, subject to constant development and to periodic theoretical revolutions. Whether Hegel really holds views at odds with this is a difficult question to answer, but it is simplistic to think that a systematic thinker is always committed to regarding his own system as forever immune to obsolescence or revision. Marx never feels this way about the system he is building in *Capital*.

3 *Reproducing the concrete in thought*

Probably the commonest cause for misunderstandings of *Capital* is that its readers fail to grasp the theoretical project proposed in the book, and interpret some of Marx's basic theses (such as his law of value and theory of surplus value) as answers to questions different from those he is asking. These misunderstandings are sometimes willful, as when our primary purpose in opening Marx's book is to find reasons for dismissing his dangerous ideas. But not always. In *Capital* Marx is too busy developing his theory to alert his readers to its general aims and structure. To discern them, it may (as Marx warns us) require sympathetic readers, 'who want to learn something new, and thus also want to think for themselves'.[28]

Marx's chief methodological reflections in *Capital* are found in his Afterword to the second edition. They are occasioned by the remarks of a Russian reviewer, who found Marx's 'method of research strictly realistic, but the method of presentation (*Darstellung*) unfortunately German-dialectical'. Marx agrees that his method is dialectical, and he insists that the 'mode of presentation must be distinguished formally from the mode of research'. As Marx describes them, both the 'mode of presentation' and the 'mode of research' used in *Capital* are recognizably dialectical. The task of research is to 'appropriate the material in detail, to analyze its different forms of development and trace their inner bond'. This supposes that the material is structured dialectically, that the economic structure of capitalism is a hierarchy of 'forms of development' connected organically by an 'inner bond'. Once research has traced out this structure, Marx says, 'the corresponding actual movement can be presented (*dargestellt*). If this succeeds and the life of the material is reflected back ideally, then it may appear as if we were dealing with an *a priori* construction.'[29]

A more detailed description of the 'construction' Marx has in mind is found in the *Grundrisse*, in the introduction drafted for (but not published with) the *Critique of Political Economy*. The economic system sketched in this text differs somewhat in its details from the system eventually presented in *Capital*, but in form the general theoretical program is the same. Marx says it is natural in economics to begin by considering 'the real and concrete',

216

to examine the population of a country, its distribution among different branches of production, its imports and exports, its annual production and consumption, its system of relative commodity prices. Most political economists, he says, begin this way. But as they set out to understand the workings of a concrete society, they are compelled to 'proceed analytically to simpler and simpler concepts', to 'thinner and thinner abstractions', until they arrive at a handful of basic, abstract economic notions. According to Marx, it is really only when they have done this that they can begin to develop a genuine economic theory, retracing their journey back to the concrete by ascending from simple abstractions (such as labor, division of labor, value and exchange) back up to the concrete economy with which they began. Thus Marx believes that the economists' 'first path', starting from the concrete and the immediately observable is a theoretically false approach. The 'scientifically correct method' is rather the 'second path', which begins with carefully chosen abstractions and shows how what is observable arises out of the basic economic structures they represent.

> The concrete is concrete because it is a combination of many
> determinations, a unity of the manifold. Thus in thought
> it appears as a process of combination, a result, not as a point
> of departure, even though it is the actual point of departure
> and thus the point of departure for observation and representation. On the first path, the full representation is evaporated
> into abstract determinations. On the second, the abstract
> determinations lead to the reproduction of the concrete on
> the path of thought.[30]

This seems to be a description of the 'method of presentation' as distinct from the 'method of research'.[31] There is no reason to suppose that Marx objects to beginning with concrete empirical observation in our investigation of an economic system. What he eschews is taking the directly observable as a starting point for his theoretical presentation. For Marx as for Hegel, the task of science is to penetrate empirical observations, grasp them in 'concepts' and 'reproduce the concrete in thought'. Marx often criticizes 'vulgar economists' for 'holding fast to appearance', 'reflecting in their brains only the *immediate* form of *appearance* of relations, and not their inner connection'. 'Science', he says, 'would be superfluous if the apparent form of things immediately coincided with their essence.'[32] Marx differs from Hegel only in regarding the thought process not as 'generating the [known reality] out of the concept', but as reflecting the inner connections

217

in an independent reality given to us empirically.[33]

For Marx, a properly constructed economic theory is a 'system of categories', ascending from the simplest, most abstract and most basic to the society, toward those which display a fuller, more concrete conception of the social whole, and reflect 'forms of development' which are more accessible to immediate observation. Marx emphasizes that the 'forms of development' here are not temporal, that the order of categories in the theory is not to be the order in which the corresponding social forms appear historically or become historically decisive. The ultimate aim of Marx's theory, of course, is to reveal the tendencies to change inherent in bourgeois society. But the immediate purpose of his system of categories is to understand the inner structure of society and not to trace its history: 'It is not a question of the relation which economic relations assume historically in the series of different social forms, . . . but of the articulation of these relations within modern bourgeois society.'[34]

Quite plainly (as Marx explicitly acknowledges) the model for such an economic theory is the hierarchical dialectic found in Hegel's system of logic or his *Philosophy of Right*. Of course it is only the general conception of such a system that Marx imitates, and not its details. (It is silly of Engels to look for parallels between the transition in Marx from commodity to capital and the transition from being to essence in Hegel's logic.)[35] Because Marx rejects Hegel's idealistic metaphysics, the transitions in his dialectical theory also have a different meaning: they represent factual or causal necessities, through which a number of inter-related factors and tendencies produce a result, rather than conceptual necessities knowable *a priori*. Nevertheless, the Hegelianism of *Capital* is in the basic conception and structure of the theory; it is not merely a matter of jargon, as some writers would like to believe.

XV

Dialectic in *Capital*

1 *The structure of 'Capital'*

The dialectical structure of Marx's economic theory is perhaps best viewed as a hierarchy of theoretical models, ascending by successive approximation from very abstract models representing the basic social forms present in modern bourgeois society up to fuller, more detailed models of this society.[1] The idea is to use the more abstract models to explain some things we can directly observe, and to show how their workings generate the complicating features which, when we integrate them into our theory, permit us to construct richer models which approximate more closely to other aspects of observable reality. The more abstract models, however, are not for this reason less realistic; in a sense they are for Marx more realistic, because closer to the essence which lies behind outward appearances. Marx's theory works toward a model which mirrors the empirical facts in their concrete detail, but he does not view economic theories or theoretical models merely as devices for summarizing and predicting observations. The task of Marx's theory is to reproduce the structure of the concrete in thought. The function of more abstract models is to penetrate complex appearances, to get at the basic social forms from whose inner tendencies the observable phenomena result.

No dialectical theory can be properly understood or evaluated except in terms of the way it deals with the connections and tendencies inherent in its specific subject matter. Marx's dialectical method of presentation in *Capital* cannot be understood apart from the details of his economic analysis, which lie beyond the scope of this book. But in order to give some specificity to what I have said about Marx's method, I will try to present a thumbnail sketch of Marx's theory, emphasizing Marx's law of value, his theory of surplus value, and his approach to relative price theory. The widespread misunderstanding of these Marxian doctrines by orthodox academic economists is a striking example of the way in which ignorance of Marx's dialectical method can lead to misreadings and unfounded criticisms of his economic theory.

Capital begins with the analysis of a commodity. In Marx's sense, a 'commodity' is any object which satisfies human wants and is produced by human labor with a view to exchange.[2] Following Adam Smith, Marx distinguishes between a commodity's 'use value' (its natural capacity to satisfy human wants of a determinate kind) and its 'exchange value' (its social capacity to be exchangeable for other commodities in certain ratios).[3] For reasons we will be examining in section 3, Marx's most basic model of capitalist production postulates that the exchange value of a commodity is proportional to what Marx calls its 'value', that is, the total quantity of labor time which is socially necessary for producing use values of its determinate kind. This postulate is what Marx calls the 'law of value'.[4]

This model is very abstract. In effect, it is a model of commodity production based on private property, assuming perfect competition and perfect sensitivity of production to labor costs, but deliberately ignoring the effect of all production costs besides labor and treating all commodities as freely reproducible.[5] Marx's eventual aim is to explain most important systematic deviations from this model found in actual capitalism by using the model itself to explain the factors which produce them. The law of value is *not* meant as a general theory of relative prices which is capable of accounting for all the surface complexities of capitalist society. As Marx says explicitly, his dialectical method *requires* him not to attempt such a theory at this point: 'If one wanted to "explain" from the start all the phenomena which apparently contradict the law [of value], one would have to supply the science *before* the science.' 'If I were to *cut short* all these considerations beforehand, I would ruin the whole dialectical method of development.'[6]

Using his simple model, Marx next provides a lengthy account of the 'form of value', whose purpose is to show how in a society which fits the model a need would naturally arise for a 'universal measure of value', and hence to 'trace the genesis of the money form' and dispel the 'riddle of money'.[7] After introducing exchange in terms of money into his model, Marx sets himself the

220

task of explaining how money becomes capital, that is, how money is thrown into the circulation process in such a way as to expand in value.

Capitalists exchange money basically for two things: (1) means of production and (2) the labor power of the workers they employ. The capitalist production process is simply the process by which capitalists get use value out of the things they have bought.[8] The peculiarity of this use value is that it involves an increase in the exchange value of the capitalist's commodities, and hence (according to the law of value) in the value or labor time embodied in them. How does this happen? The value of means of production is the labor time already expended in them. It does not increase in the labor process, but is merely transferred to the product. The value of labor power is the labor time necessary to provide workers with the means of life they can purchase for the wages they are paid. The use value of labor power, however, is labor time itself, which is incorporated into the product and adds to the value present in the means of production consumed during labor. On Marx's theory, capital expands in value because the labor time added by the workers exceeds the labor time represented by their wages. In other words, capital expands because the workers spend only part of each day reproducing the value of their labor power (performing what Marx calls 'necessary labor') and spend the rest of the day performing (unpaid) 'surplus labor'.[9]

Capital can extract surplus labor from workers because of the social-historical fact that in bourgeois society the means of production are largely the property of one class, which thus enjoys a decisive bargaining advantage over a much more numerous class which can acquire the opportunity to work (hence the opportunity to live) only by selling their labor power for a wage whose value is less than that created by their labor.[10] In turn, Marx explains this historical fact materialistically, by showing how the productive forces of society at a certain stage of their development can be efficiently employed, and developed further, only if they are concentrated in the hands of a few.[11] Because capital spent on means of production does not increase in value during the labor process, while capital spent on labor power does, Marx calls the former 'constant capital' (or c) and the latter 'variable capital' (or v).[12] The value created by surplus labor Marx calls 'surplus value' (or s).[13] The capitalist labor process thus expands the value of capital from $v + c$ to $v + c + s$.[14]

On the basis of his first, abstract model, Marx has now shown how value expresses itself in money and how money becomes capital through a determinate historical variant of simple commodity production. By integrating into his model the factors he has explained by means of it, Marx now has a less abstract model, which more closely resembles the observable realities of bourgeois society and permits more of these realities to be explained. According to Marx, capital uses its advantage over labor to increase as far as possible the 'rate of surplus value' (s/v).[15] It does this basically in two ways: by prolonging the working day (producing what Marx calls 'absolute surplus value') and by curtailing necessary labor time by reducing the labor cost of wages (producing what Marx calls 'relative surplus value').[16] Through capital's tendency to produce absolute surplus value, Marx explains the inhuman lengths to which capital has pushed the working day, and discusses the political struggle to limit it by law.[17] Through the tendency to produce relative surplus value, Marx explains capital's extension of the division of labor and its introduction of mechanized labor.[18] According to Marx, capital also tends to accumulate, to concentrate social power in the hands of the propertied classes. Marx documents this tendency, and discusses its observable effects on population growth and unemployment.[19]

So far, Marx has been concerned only with capital's *production* of value and surplus value. In Volume 2 of *Capital*, he turns to the 'circulation' of capital, the complementary process by which capital 'realizes' surplus value through the sale of commodities and 'reproduces' itself through reinvesting the proceeds. Marx uses the 'divergence' between the conditions of producing surplus value and the conditions of realizing it to attempt an explanation of the trade cycle and the periodic crises which plague capitalism.[20]

In Volume 3 of *Capital*, Marx brings together his models of the production and realization of surplus value into a model of the more 'concrete forms growing out of capitalist production as a whole' which is a 'unity of the production and circulation process'.[21] He shows how surplus value appears as profit on capital, discusses the division of profit into interest and 'profit of enterprise', and shows how a portion of surplus value is transformed into ground rent. Marx's discussion of profit includes his famous (though often misunderstood) 'law of the tendency of the rate of profit to fall'.[22] It also includes his discussion of the relation between the values of commodities and their 'production prices', permitting Marx to construct a more complex theory of relative prices than is represented by the 'law of value' in his first model.[23]

222

2 *Values and production prices*

According to Marx's theory, the expansion of a capitalist's money through production depends on the quantity of variable capital (v) with which labor is set in motion and the rate of surplus value (s/v) pertaining to the enterprise. No capitalist is directly interested in these quantities, however. For one thing, capitalists are interested in the surplus value they realize, not in what they produce. Even ignoring this, they are concerned not with the ratio of surplus value to the wages expended in producing it, but in the ratio of surplus value to what Marx calls the commodity's 'cost price', the total capital invested ($v + c$).[24] This ratio ($s/[v + c]$) Marx calls the 'rate of profit'. In *Capital*, Volume 3, Part II, Marx notes that even assuming that s/v is the same for all industries, the rate of profit will differ in different industries because different production techniques will require different ratios of constant to variable capital (c/v, which Marx calls the 'organic composition of capital').[25] Because surplus value depends on variable capital rather than on cost price, an industry with lower c/v will (other things being equal) enjoy a higher rate of profit than one with a higher c/v.[26]

This difference in rates of profit can hold, however, only if we assume that capitalists have no way of shifting investment between industries, that is, if we assume that competition exists between capitalists only within each industry and not between different industries. In Volume 3, Marx develops his model of capitalism further by dropping this unrealistic assumption.[27] On account of competition, he argues, the rates of profit capitalists can *realize* from the sale of their products differs systematically from the rates of profit they *produce*. If in a competitive situation we imagine low c/v industries trying to realize all the surplus value they produce, we see that their higher rate of profit would attract investment away from high c/v industries, resulting in an oversupply of low c/v commodities (which would sell below their values) and an undersupply of high c/v commodities (which would sell above their values): competition would distribute the surplus value evenly throughout all industries.

On Marx's developed model in Volume 3, this is in effect what happens: 'The rates of profit prevailing in different branches of production, [which] are originally very different, [are] evened out by competition to a general rate of profit which is the average of all the different rates of profit.'[28] This of course has a systematic effect on the relative equilibrium prices of commodities. On the Volume 3 model, high c/v commodities 'are sold above their value in the same proportions as [low c/v commodities] are sold below their value'. Prices of commodities thus correspond not to their values (to cost price plus surplus value produced) but to cost price plus profit at the average rate: 'The prices which arise from adding the average of the rates of profit drawn from the different spheres of production to the cost prices of the different spheres are the *production prices*.'[29]

Ignoring Marx's Volume 1 warning that 'average prices do not directly coincide with the magnitude of value in commodities', a long tradition of neoclassical critics (beginning with Eugen von Böhm-Bawerk in 1896) view the Volume 3 theory either as introducing a basic incoherence into the Marxian system or else as amounting to a basic revision of it by Marx between Volume 1 and Volume 3. The suggestion of a revision or change of mind on Marx's part is conclusively (and massively) refuted by his texts. Not only is the Volume 3 theory hinted at in Volume 1, but it is already developed in detail in Marx's correspondence some five years earlier. There are numerous references to the average rate of profit and production prices in the *Theories of Surplus Value*, and even in the *Grundrisse* (which antedates Volume 1 by nearly a decade).[30]

The charge of incoherence only makes sense if we ignore the dialectical structure of Marx's theory and mistake the law of value for a full-blown theory of relative prices. Volume 1 and Volume 3 do not give us incompatible theories of prices, but only different models of commodity exchange, one more basic and abstract, the other more complex and closer to surface phenomena. Marx does insist that production prices are 'dependent on' and 'regulated', even 'determined' by values, and that the deviation of production prices from values only 'apparently' contradicts the law of value.[31] By this he means that prices can be 'developed' out of values, that a dialectical theory beginning with the law of value can explain the factors which give rise to the deviation of prices from values in actual capitalism.[32] An economist who is preoccupied with relative price theory to the exclusion of Marx's other concerns may find his approach to price theory cumbersome or circuitous. But to charge Marx with inconsistency is simply to misunderstand what he is saying.

A more pertinent charge to bring against Marx is that his Volume 3 theory itself is defective. Marx plainly intends to 'convert' or 'transform' the values of commodities into prices, and exhibits awareness of some of the difficulties involved in doing this.[33] But Marx does not actually solve the 'transformation problem'. Subsequent attempts indicate that an adequate solution would entail abandoning some of Marx's actual doctrines. In *Capital* Marx appears to hold both that the total values of commodities in an economy are equal to total prices, and that total surplus value is equal to total profit.[34] Ludwig von Bortkiewicz, the first to produce a solution to the 'transformation problem', shows that one cannot accept both theses simultaneously. Informed opinion seems to agree that Marx's Volume 3 theory is defective as it stands, but also that the revisions necessary to complete it do not strictly require abandoning the value analysis of Volume 1. Opinions differ, however, over how far these revisions would render the value analysis pointless, and thus make it advisable to abandon it. But here it is impossible to separate 'transformation' considerations from other questions about the merits and defects of Marx's value approach.[35]

3 *The law of value*

Marx's treatment of value in Volume 1 of *Capital* starts from two main ideas. First, there is Marx's 'definition of value': the *value* of a commodity is the quantity of labor time socially necessary to produce commodities of that kind.[36] Second, there is the Marxian 'law of value': the exchange value of a commodity is determined by labor time (by its value).[37] These ideas have been widely misunderstood. To begin with, they are not in any sense normative or 'evaluative' ideas. Marx does not believe that labor is the only thing 'valuable'.[38] His law of value is not a theory of 'just price'. Marx does not hold that people have a *right* to the value of their commodities (as measured by labor time) or that commodities *ought* to be exchanged according to their values.[39] He does not think that commodities will be exchanged according to their values in future society, nor does he propose that they should be.[40] The law of value is a proposition of economic science, employed to explain what actually happens in capitalism. But as we have seen, it is not intended as a theory of relative prices for capitalism, but only as a postulate for the basic and extremely abstract model of commodity exchange with which Marx's dialectical theory begins.[41]

We can dismiss most of the traditional objections to Marx's so-called 'labor theory of value' as soon as we understand the meaning and theoretical role of his basic claims about value.[42] One class of objections is the alleged 'counter-examples' to the law of value, that is, examples of exchangeables whose relative price is manifestly not proportional to their labor cost.[43] Some of the examples seem to depend on confusing socially necessary labor with actual labor expenditure (Böhm-Bawerk's heartwarming example of knitting and needlework done lovingly but inefficiently at home). Others are examples of exchangeables which either do not count as 'commodities' at all in Marx's sense (e.g., unimproved land and other 'gifts of nature') or else which are not freely reproducible (e.g., statues, paintings, other 'rare goods') as Marx's simple model supposes all commodities to be.[44] Neoclassical critics often press these examples even when they know that Marx's law of value is not meant to cover them. I think they do so because neoclassical orthodoxy has always prided itself on the generality of its price theory, and its adherents want to call attention to this advantage even if their examples do not really 'refute' Marx's law of value.[45] Marx restricts his initial model to freely reproducible commodities because he regards the production of such commodities as the dominant economic form in bourgeois society, and hence views the laws of commodity exchange as basic to understanding the social forms in which land, rare goods and so on also become objects of exchange. Marx thus deliberately eschews the generality of neoclassical theories because a theory with this generality could not focus sharply on the specific social forms which are basic to capitalism.

Another class of criticisms charges that Marxian value is not a useful notion because the values of commodities are constantly changing with changes in productivity of labor, because value cannot be precisely measured in practice, and because even in principle it cannot be determined independently of demand.[46] The first two criticisms misconstrue the function of value in Marx's theory, and in effect attack him merely for having methods and priorities different from those of academic economists. The place of value for Marx is in a basic, abstract model of commodity production, and not in the empirical measurement of factors determining relative prices on the surface. Following the classical tradition, Marx does in effect assume that changes in demand will not by themselves bring about changes in equilibrium prices of commodities, and his initial model takes it for granted that labor allocations always exactly satisfy aggregate demand.[47] But this does not mean that Marx's law of value depends on any specific assumptions about demand. One of the eventual aims of Marx's theory is to understand the patterns of income distribution which govern effective demand in capitalist society.[48]

The question remains why we should accept the Marxian law of value. In *Capital*, Marx expounds this law by presenting what his critics call his 'proof' (or 'dialectical proof') of it.[49] Marx's exposition does look like a deductive argument, which can be summarized in the following list of quotations:

(1) '[Commodities] form the material bearers of exchange value.'

(2) 'The exchange relation of [two commodities] can always be presented as an equation.'

(3) [This equation tells us] that in these different things there exists something common in equal quantities. . . . [that] both are equal to a third thing, and insofar as they are exchange values, reducible to this third thing.'

(4) [Therefore] , 'The valid exchange values express something equal, [and] exchange value can be only the mode of expression or "form of appearance" of a content distinguishable from it.'

(5) '[Hence] the exchange values of commodities are reducible to something common of which they present more or less.'

(6) 'This common something cannot be any . . . natural property of commodities, since such properties only come into consideration insofar as they are use values.'

(7) 'If we disregard the use value of commodities, there remains in them only one property, being products of labor, [yet not a] concrete form of labor, [but rather] abstract human labor.'

(8) 'If we consider [commodities] as crystals of this social substance which is common to them, they are values.'

(9) '[Hence] the common something which presents itself in the exchange value of commodities is their value.'[50]

(1)-(5) aim at establishing that the exchange values of commodities are reducible to some identifiable thing which any two commodities exchangeable for each other must possess in equal quantities. (6) eliminates a wide range of candidates for this something, and (7) identifies it as 'abstract human labor'. I take (8) as a statement of Marx's 'definition' of value as socially necessary labor time. By equating 'abstract labor' with 'value' in this sense, (9) in effect concludes to Marx's law of value, claiming that the exchange values of commodities are measured by labor time (or value).[51]

If we attend only to this argument, I think we must find it difficult to blame Marx's critics for misunderstanding both the meaning of his law of value and his reasons for putting it forward. The argument does not remind us of the restricted scope of the law, or of the fact that 'exchange values' as measured by value (or labor time) are not supposed to be directly identical with the

227

equilibrium prices of commodities. The argument looks like an attempt to deduce a universal theory of prices *a priori* from a few abstract theses about the general nature of commodity exchange.

Not surprisingly, the argument contains several questionable steps. (6) appears to move from the premise that the concept of use value is different from the concept of exchange value to the conclusion that exchange value cannot be based on use value or on any 'natural' properties relevant to it. Utility theorists are bound to question the conclusion, which in any case clearly does not follow from the premise. (7) is not self-evident. Besides being products of abstract human labor, commodities might have many other 'nonnatural' properties (unless all properties except being products of labor are supposed to be excluded by definition). But surely the most conspicuously dubious premise is (3). Why should we suppose that commodities exchangeable for each other are 'equal' in any respect (except perhaps in the amount of money someone might be willing to pay for them)? Of course (3) is roughly parallel to (if incompatible with) the idea of early marginal utility theorists (such as Jevons and Edgeworth) that when a given person's preferences are indifferent between two objects, it follows that they possess for that person an equal quantity of some psychic stuff ('pleasure', 'value' or 'utility'). But Marx's premise gains little plausibility from its resemblance to this wretched superstition.[52]

Despite its prominent place in *Capital*, Marx's 'proof' of the law of value is not taken seriously as such by its author. I think it is best regarded as an expository device, part of Marx's avowed attempt to 'popularize' his discussion of value of *Capital*.[53] In an important letter to Ludwig Kugelmann, Marx emphasizes that his argument is not a 'proof' of the law of value, and that this law stands in no need of such a proof: 'The prattle about the necessity of proving the concept of value rests only on complete ignorance both of the subject in question and of the method of science.' At the same time, Marx gives us the real rationale which stands behind the law: On the one hand, he insists that 'even if there were no chapter about "value" in my book, the analysis of real relations I give would contain the proof and confirmation of the actual value relation.' On the other hand, he outlines the very abstract considerations which persuade him that the prices of commodities must fundamentally approximate to their values. It is self-evident, he says, 'that the masses of products corresponding to different social needs demand different and quantitatively determined masses of collective social labor'. This 'necessity of dividing social labor in determinate proportions', he insists, is a 'natural law', which 'cannot be done away with by any determinate form of social production, but can only alter its mode of appearance': in a society where the social character of labor expresses itself through the private exchange of products, the form in which this law asserts itself is the exchange value of these products. Science, concludes Marx, 'consists only in developing *how* the law of value asserts itself'.[54]

The justification of Marx's law of value can be viewed in terms of two tasks: first, justifying an assumption or postulate about relative prices for a certain abstract model of commodity production; and second, justifying this model as the starting point for a dialectical theory of capitalist production. The model Marx uses is a system of simple commodity production in which all commodities are freely reproducible, and labor is distributed by the exchange of products in such a way that effective demand is exactly met. In such a system, commodities must exchange in proportion to the total labor time embodied in them. If they did not, then labor would be attracted away from the lower-than-value commodities and toward the higher-than-value commodities; effective demand ('social need') would not be exactly met.[55]

The justification of this model as a starting point, Marx suggests, is to be found in 'the analysis of real relations' carried out on its basis. This means using the simple model to 'develop' or explain the factors and tendencies which on the surface produce a deviation of prices from values. But even before this is done, Marx gives us a reason for thinking that value (socially necessary labor time) is the *basic* determinant of price in *any* society where commodity production is the dominant economic form. The distribution of labor according to social need is a basic 'natural law', valid for all societies. The law of value is only the specific 'form of appearance' through which this law asserts itself in commodity production.

The 'natural law' here is really a historical materialist law. The exchange relation between commodities is in fact only the hidden form of a social relation between producers. Thus the determination of exchange value by socially necessary labor is really a case of a social relation of production which exists because it contributes to the proportional division of social labor, that is, to a set of material work relations between producers. The law of value, therefore, is a special case of the determination of social relations of production by the material work relations corresponding to society's productive powers.

We can see now the Marxian reply to a critic like Benedetto

Croce. Croce admits that the determination of exchange value of labor is 'a fact, but a fact which exists in the midst of other facts; i.e., a fact that appears to us empirically as opposed, limited, distorted by other facts, almost like a force amongst other forces. . . . It is not a completely dominant fact.' Hence Croce argues that we need in addition to Marx's theory 'a general economic science, which may determine a concept of value, deducing it from quite different and more comprehensive principles than the special ones of Marx'.[56] Croce is right that the determination of relative prices by labor time is 'a fact in the midst of other facts'. But it is a basic and even 'dominant' fact both in that it expresses a fundamental truth of historical materialism and in that (if Marx's project in *Capital* is successful) a theory built on this fact can account for the most important of the other 'facts' which enter into the determination of relative prices, apparently 'opposing, limiting and distorting' their determination by labor time. A more 'general' economic theory is desirable only if it does not obscure the basic significance of the 'fact' emphasized by Marx's theory.

Marx's law of value is closely related to his famous idea of the 'fetishism of commodities'. We should not forget that in the first edition of *Capital* the discussion of commodity fetishism closely followed the section of value, because Marx hesitated to interpolate his lengthy 'development of the value form' in between.[57] In fact, the section on commodity fetishism develops the same line of reasoning present in the letter to Kugelmann, indicating that one of the primary considerations behind the law of value is the way in which it reveals the real social relations of commodity production which hide behind the commodity form:

> In all states of society the labor time it costs to produce the means of life must interest men, though not equally in all stages of development. . . . In the accidental and ever varying exchange relations between products, the labor time socially necessary for their production forcibly asserts itself as a ruling law of nature. . . . The determination of value by labor time is therefore a mystery hidden beneath the apparent variations in the relative values of commodities. . . . What is mysterious in the commodity form is that in it the social character of men's labor appears to them as an objective character of its products. . . . It is only the determinate social relation of men themselves, which here assumes for them the fantastic form of a relation between things. . . . For them their own social movement takes the form of a movement of things which control

230

them instead of being controlled by them. . . . This I call the 'fetishism' clinging to products of labor as soon as they are produced as commodities, and which is therefore inseparable from commodity production.[58]

One important function of Marx's law of value is to call attention to this fetishism, to penetrate the social illusions it imposes on us and motivate us to free ourselves from the domination of social relations by abolishing the commodity form of what we produce. This aspect of the law of value is what Paul Sweezy has called Marx's 'qualitative analysis' of exchange, which exists side by side with his 'quantitative' theory of values and prices in *Capital*.[59]

4 *Value and exploitation*

Marx is obviously convinced that the concept of value as socially necessary labor time is indispensable to any adequate theory of capitalist production. Some recent writers moderately sympathetic to Marx claim that both the 'qualitative' and 'quantitative' tasks of Marx's theory can be performed as well or better by a theory which deals (in more orthodox fashion) with prices or (following Piero Sraffa's input-output analysis) with physical commodities.[60] For all Marx or his more devoted followers say to the contrary, these writers may be right. On the other hand, what is not defensible is the complacent dogma of neoclassical economics that Marx's value analysis is fundamentally wrongheaded, untenable, ill-motivated as an economic approach. Marx's methods and theoretical goals are not those of neoclassical orthodoxy, but his methods are reasonably well suited to his own goals, and these goals are (I venture to say) worthier ones than those of neoclassical theories.

The more or less open intention behind most neoclassical criticisms of Marx's concept of value (and even behind much of neoclassical value theory) is to undermine Marx's theory of surplus value, and thereby to refute the subversive idea that profit on capital arises from the exploitation of labor. The presupposition behind all these efforts is that Marx's grounds for believing that capital exploits labor depend on his value analysis. This presupposition is simply false. Marx does of course frame his exposition of these grounds in terms of his value analysis. But the main idea behind Marx's thesis that profit arises from capital's exploitation of labor does not depend on his labor concept of value.

Marx never tells us precisely what he means by 'exploitation'.

231

I think it is a mistake to treat the term as merely a technical one in Marx's economics, referring simply to the appropriation of surplus labor by capital. Clearly Marx regards capital's exploitation of labor as an instance of a more general type of social relation, exemplified (for instance) by masters' exploitation of slaves, and feudal nobles' exploitation of serfs. Roughly, Marx's idea is that A exploits B whenever A lives off the fruits of B's labor and is able to do so not because A makes any reciprocal contribution to social production but because the social relations in which A stands to B put A in a position to coerce B to work for A's bene-fit.[61] Marx often lays stress on the coercion involved in exploita-tion.[62] He also attacks the idea that 'capital' and 'profit' are universal categories built into production as a natural process. Part of his motivation is to emphasize that the capitalist's bar-gaining power arises not from nature but from the prevailing social relations. Marx does, however, view capitalist exploitation as a paradigm of exploitation. He does so because (following Rousseau) he believes that all exploitation is rooted in property, that is, in the exploiter's effective control over the means of production. Because the immediate form of capitalist coercion is economic (rather than, say, legal or political), Marx says that capitalist exploitation is not 'veiled' but 'open', 'direct' and 'dry'.[63]

The basic idea behind Marx's thesis that capital exploits labor is very simple. The capitalist class owns the means of production, or commands the purchasing power by which alone (under com-modity production) these means can be supplied to labor. The workers own little besides their labor power, and can live only by selling this commodity to someone who can supply the mater-ial means to produce what they need. In effect, the wage bargain is one in which workers must offer something to induce capitalists to devote purchasing power to these means. Property is thus the lever by which capitalists extract this inducement, their means of coercing workers to earn the capitalists' living for them without the capitalists themselves having to make any contribution to production.[64]

The Marxian law of value is neither necessary nor sufficient to confirm this basic idea. Marx's value analysis of the wage bar-gains says that capitalists pay workers the value equivalent only of part of their working day, appropriating the rest as 'surplus' or 'unpaid' labor. But there would be no cause for regarding this as exploitative if the situation required the capitalists to make some reciprocal contribution to the production process. Apologists typically claim that capitalists do make some such contribution; they therefore use arguments which (if sound) are perfectly compatible with a Marxian value analysis. Apologists claim that capitalists contribute by 'abstinence' or (in Alfred Marshall's more circumspect phrase) 'waiting', or by assuming the 'risks of enterprise' or by performing the 'labor of supervision'. Of course Marx is aware of all these apologetic claims and regards them as obscene falsehoods. The point is that his law of value has no role to play in rebutting them.[65]

If the law of value is not sufficient to make Marx's point, it is not necessary either. His basic idea, sketched above, can just as easily be presented in conjunction with the orthodox 'marginal productivity' theory of profit.[66] Contrary to Marx's value analysis, this theory holds that capital as well as labor is productive of exchange value. (The furor over the 'contradiction' between Volume 1 and Volume 3 is due largely to the fact that the Volume 3 theory makes capital a factor in commodity prices in a higher proportion than its labor-value, thus apparently conceding the point that capital produces exchange value.) The apologetic use of this theory depends on its suggestion that because capital is productive as well as labor, capitalists make a contribution to production by supplying it, and their profit is rightfully due them.

The suggestion is sophistical. *Capital* (i.e., means of production) may be productive (Marx never denies that means of production are essential to the production of use value and hence to the production of exchange value), but *capitalists* are not. As Joan Robinson so succinctly puts it: '*Owning* capital is not a productive activity.'[67] Capitalists acquire profit not because what they own is productive, but because *they own* what is productive. This ownership puts them in a position to extract profit from the production process, that is, to coerce workers into producing commodities for them. Marx of course agrees that, under capitalist social relations, the capitalist is a 'necessary functionary' of the production process.[68] But this function is parasitic, not productive. As we saw in Chapter IX, Marx also does not quarrel with the claim that surplus value is 'due' to capitalists and appropriated by them 'with full right'. What he would quarrel with is the inference that capitalists are not exploiters or that the justice of capitalist exploitation gives the workers any ground for being contented.

Marx's thesis that capital exploits labor is based on the notion of coercion. It is notoriously difficult to say just what coercion is, or how being coerced differs from freely deciding to do something because one prefers the consequences of doing it to those of not doing it. These difficulties may spell trouble for Marx insofar as they leave the way open for apologists to claim that capitalists use their purchasing power not to coerce workers but only to make them offers they are free to refuse. I must confess I would find it intuitively difficult to accept any analysis of coercion which had the consequence that wage bargains between capitalists and propertyless workers count as noncoercive agreements. But even if Marx's thesis that capital exploits labor could be refuted in this way, it is not obvious that his value analysis would deserve any blame for his error.

Concluding Remark

Marx subscribes to a number of ideas which are philosophical and controversial. Both his dialectical method and his concept of humanity are based more or less openly on the Aristotelian notion that things have essences and that the task of science is to understand the properties and behavior of things in terms of these essences. Marx's concept of alienation involves the further Aristotelian notion that a fulfilling life for men and women is one in which they exercise their distinctively human capacities. Marx's historical materialism employs teleological explanations, apparently presupposing that such explanations are legitimate, informative and applicable to social organizations. The dialectical method, by its intention to penetrate beneath the surface appearance of things and mirror their inner developmental structure, pretty clearly commits Marx to some form of scientific realism in opposition to most familiar forms of empiricism, which view scientific theories merely as devices for recording, predicting and organizing observations. Marx apparently holds some controversial views about morality, giving to moral judgments a more restricted scope and less importance for social practice than is usual. Even more open is Marx's stand against such philosophical positions as theism, metaphysical idealism and skepticism about the existence or real natures of material things.

In spite of all this, I doubt that Marx's social theory is vulnerable to any serious philosophical objections. This is not due to any firm belief on my part that Marx is right on all the philosophical issues, while theists, idealists, moralists, skeptics, empiricists and anti-essentialists are all wrong. For one thing, not all Marx's philosophical views are important for his social theory. Atheism, common sense realism, Marx's low opinion of moral categories

235

for social criticism, perhaps even his concept of alienation, are all peripheral or irrelevant to the central tenets of historical materialism and of Marx's economic theory. For another thing, it might be possible to interpret or reformulate Marx's theory so as to rescue its 'empirical content' from the 'mystical shell' of Hegelian organicism, essentialism, scientific realism and naturalism in which Marx encases it. (I leave this project to others, however, because I think it would involve eliminating much that is valuable in Marx's theory, and that it would be on the philosophical level largely a process of replacing Hegelian or Marxist truths with empiricist falsehoods.)

But the main reason I doubt that Marx's social theory is philosophically vulnerable is that (as I have tried to argue above) the main philosophical objections which are raised against it are unsuccessful. They generally rest on misunderstandings of Marx's theory, of the claims it makes or of its aims and methods. Marx, for instance, is not an 'economic determinist'; historical materialism is not necessarily a deterministic view at all. Marx's value analysis is not based on *a priori* Hegelian sophistics. Marx does not employ it merely in order to make capitalism look bad; his reasons for saying that capital exploits labor are quite independent of his concept of value. Marx's adherence to the dialectical method and his belief that certain changes are historically inevitable based on the tendencies of material production do involve ambitious and vague views about the way the world is, but these views are not metaphysical dogmas or based on metaphysical dogmas. The common charges of 'incoherence', whether between the phases of Marx's economic analysis or between Marx's materialist theory of history and his practice as an empirical historian, are groundless. They result from philosophical misunderstandings of Marx's views themselves.

What *is* controversial about Marx's theory is whether it does accurately describe the real world. Historical materialism is coherent, even plausible, but just how far can large scale social change be explained by the factors and tendencies it postulates? The general conception of a dialectical economic theory may be very impressive, but just how far does *Capital* succeed in reproducing the concrete reality of capitalism in thought? Is Marx's value analysis indispensable, or even useful in making sense of capitalist commodity production, the economic forms it involves, its tendencies to change over time? A philosophical study of Marx's thought like the present one can protect us against fundamental misunderstandings of his views, so that we do not ask the wrong questions about them. But the real issue is how far Marx's theories correspond to the real world and how far they can explain what happens in it. This issue may eventually be decided by detailed empirical studies.

Notes

All translations from the German and French are my own. In such cases I have provided citations both to the original text and to an English translation. Where no direct translation is involved, I have normally cited only the English text.

The German edition I have used is the *Marx Engels Werke* published by the Dietz Verlag (Berlin, 1961-66). (This edition will be abbreviated throughout the notes as MEW. Erg. stands for *Ergänzungsheft*.) In a few places, it has been necessary to cite the older *Marx Engels Gesamtausgabe* or other texts; fuller references are provided below.

My source for Marx's writings in French is Maximilien Rubel's *Oeuvres de Karl Marx*, published by Editions Gallimard (Paris, 1963). (Abbreviated as *Oeuvres*.)

Where possible, I have cited English texts from the *Marx Engels Collected Works* published by International Publishers (New York, 1975-). (Abbreviated as CW.) Because this edition is still incomplete, this was not always possible. Where it was not, I have favored other editions published by International Publishers or by the Foreign Languages Publishing House, Moscow (fuller references are provided below). I have made especially frequent use of the International Publishers' *Marx Engels Selected Works in One Volume* (New York, 1968). (Abbreviated as SW.)

For Marx's *Grundrisse*, I have cited the German text from the edition of the *Europäische Verlagsanstalt*, Frankfurt, and the *Europa Verlag*, Vienna, which is a photographic reproduction of the Soviet edition (Moscow, 1939). English citations of the *Grundrisse* are to Martin Nicolaus' translation published by Penguin Books (Harmondsworth, 1973). In citing this work, the German pagination will be indicated by a 'g' and the English pagination by an 'e'. (Thus a citation of p. 12 in the German — which is p. 90 in the English — would read: *Grundrisse* 12g, 90e.)

Marx and Engels, *Selected Correspondence: 1846-1895* (New York, 1965), is abbreviated as *Selected Correspondence*.

CHAPTER 1 THE CONCEPT OF ALIENATION

1 Cf. CW 3:272-75.
2 Cf. CW 3:220, 308, 321.
3 Cf. CW 3:41-2.
4 Cf. CW 3:153-4.
5 Cf. CW 3:175.
6 MEW Erg. 1:511, 518, CW 3:271, 278.
7 Istvan Meszaros, *Marx's Theory of Alienation* (New York, 1972), 93, 96.
8 MEW Erg. 1:514, CW 3:274.
9 There are other passages where Marx apparently subscribes to this metaphysical principle. See CW 4:285.
10 MEW Erg. 1:521, CW 3:281. Later in the Paris manuscripts, Marx appears to say that alienation is an inherently necessary stage in the process whereby the human essence 'generates itself' or 'objectifies' its 'essential powers': 'The actual, active relation (*Verhalten*) of man to himself as a species being, or the confirmation of himself as an actual species being (i.e. a human being) is only possible at first in the form of alienation.' Marx evidently holds this view because he sees some deep metaphysical (or least historical-anthropological) truth in Hegel's depiction (in *The Phenomenology of Spirit*) of self-alienation as a necessary phase through which spirit must pass in the process of actualizing its own nature: 'What is great in Hegel's *Phenomenology* and its end result — the dialectic of negativity as the moving and generating principle — is that Hegel grasps man's self-generation as a process of objectification and de-objectification (*Entgegenständlichung*), as externalization and the supersession of this externalization' (MEW Erg. 1:574, CW 3:332-3). In Marx's mature theory, on the other hand, it is clearly not a metaphysical fact about man or spirit but a contingent historical fact about Western European society that the material prerequisites for a higher, more fully human society could be achieved only through a form of society in which laborers are exploited, dehumanized and alienated. See Marx and Engels, *Selected Correspondence* (New York, 1965), 313. Cf. CW 5:88, where the conception of human development expressed in the Paris writings appears to be repudiated.
11 See J. Seigel, *Marx's Fate* (Princeton, N.J., 1978), 36. Cf. G.W.F. Hegel, *The Philosophy of Mind*, tr. A. V. Miller (Oxford, 1971), 115.
12 MEW 1:379, CW 3:176.
13 This way of describing alienation quite naturally leads to the speculation that the real nature of alienation does not consist in a state of consciousness about oneself and one's life (a sense of meaninglessness or worthlessness) as in the actual state of that life itself, whether one is conscious of it or not. This is essentially correct.

Alienation for Marx is not fundamentally a state of consciousness; in the next chapter, we will be able to replace our provisional notion of alienation as a lack of a sense of meaning and self-worth with one which is closer to Marx's underlying views, because it identifies alienation with the conditions Marx thinks are necessary to sustain and justify such a sense. For the present, however, I think it is best to stay with the provisional notion of alienation. First, it is in terms of this notion that Marx's differences with Hegel and Feuerbach can be made most clear. Second, the more fundamental notion of alienation is not so much an alternative to the provisional one as a more precise specification of it. Finally, it is not inappropriate or unmarxian to give prominence to the fact that self-consciousness, to reflection on or attitudes toward oneself and one's life, when treating of alienation. For as we will see in the next chapter, if alienation for Marx is not a state of consciousness, it is at any rate a state of self-conscious beings, who are capable of understanding themselves and consciously affirming what they are. People are alienated only because they have the potentiality for this understanding and consciousness, but are unable to realize it owing to their conditions of life.

14 MEW 3:67, CW 5:87; MEW Erg. 1:513, CW 3:273; MEW 1:385, CW 3:182.

15 MEW Erg. 1:515, CW 3:275.

16 MEW Erg. 1:516, CW 3:276.

17 G. W. F. Hegel, *Die Phänomenologie des Geistes*, ed. J. Hoffmeister (Hamburg, 1952), 160; *The Phenomenology of Spirit*, tr. A. V. Miller (Oxford, 1977), 127.

18 Ludwig Feuerbach, *Sämtliche Werke*, ed. F. Jodl and W. Bolin (Stuttgart, 1959) 6:32, cf. *The Essence of Christianity*, tr. George Eliot (New York, 1957), 33.

19 Feuerbach, *Sämtliche Werke* 6:32, *Essence of Christianity*, 26.

20 Feuerbach, *Sämtliche Werke* 2:280, *Principles of the Philosophy of the Future*, tr. M. Vogel (Indianapolis, 1966), 37.

21 MEW 1: 378, CW 3:175.

22 MEW 1:379, CW 3:176.

23 MEW 3:7, CW 5:8.

CHAPTER II THE HUMAN ESSENCE

1 MEW 3:6, CW 5:7.

2 G. W. F. Hegel, *Die Phänomenologie des Geistes*, ed. J. Hoffmeister (Hamburg, 1952), 138-9; *The Phenomenology of Spirit*, tr. A. V. Miller (Oxford, 1977), 108-9; G. W. F. Hegel, *Werke* (Frankfurt, 1970) 9:498, *The Philosophy of Nature*, tr. A. V. Miller (Oxford, 1970), 410; Hegel, *Werke* 7:309, *The Philosophy of Right*, tr. T. M. Knox (Oxford, 1967), 111.

3 For example: 'The Christian excludes the *Gattungsleben* from heaven: there the *Gattung* ceases, there dwell only pure, sexless individuals, "spirits". . . . Thus the Christian excludes the *Gattungsleben* from his true life; he rejects the principle of marriage (*Ehe*) as sinful, dispensable' (Ludwig Feuerbach, *Das Wesen des Christentums*, *Sämtliche Werke*, ed. F. Jodl and W. Bolin (Stuttgart, 1959), 6:204, *The Essence of Christianity*, tr. George Eliot (New York, 1957), 168-9). Marx echoes this sentiment in the Paris writings (CW 3:295) but the centrality of sexual love in Feuerbach's humanism is later ridiculed by Engels (SW, 603).

4 See CW 3:17, CW 5:4, *Capital* (New York, 1967) 1:329.

5 MEW Erg. 1:515, CW 3:275.

6 See Feuerbach, *Essence of Christianity*, 2, and CW 3:275, 277.

7 See John Plamenatz, *Karl Marx's Philosophy of Man* (Oxford, 1975), 66-70.

8 MEW 3:26, 30-1, CW 5:36, 44.

9 CW 3:228, 315, MEW Erg. 1:535, CW 5:295-6.

10 *Marx-Engels Gesamtausgabe* (Berlin, 1932) 1/5:31-2, CW 5:58.

11 MEW 1:346, CW 3:144.

12 MEW Erg. 1:462, CW 3:228.

13 'But man has almost constant occasion for the help of his brethren, and it is in vain for him to expect it from their benevolence only. He will be more likely to prevail if he can interest their self-love in his favor, and show them that it is for their own advantage to do for him what he requires of them. Whoever offers another a bargain of any kind proposes to do this. . . . We address ourselves not to others' humanity but to their self-love, and never talk to them of our own necessities but of their advantages' (Adam Smith, *Wealth of Nations*, Books I-III, ed. A. Skinner (Harmondsworth, 1970), 118-9). Smith of course does not hold that people aid others only from self-love, and even insists that society is happier when people aid each other from motives of love, sympathy and benevolence: 'All the members of human society stand in need of each other's assistance. . . . Where the necessary assistance is afforded from love, from gratitude, from friendship and esteem, society flourishes and is happy. All the different members of it are bound together by the agreeable bands of love and affection and are, as it were, drawn to one common centre of mutual good offices. But though the necessary assistance should not be afforded from such generous and disinterested motives, . . . the society, though less happy and agreeable, will not necessarily be dissolved. Society may subsist among different men, as among different merchants, from a sense of its utility without any mutual love or affection' (*Theory of Moral Sentiments*, ed. D. D. Raphael and A. L. MacFie (Oxford, 1976), 85-6). But Smith still does not regard the possession of other-regarding motives such as love and benevolence, and action on them, as a part of our good, or necessary to it. Marx does, however. For him, a society which 'subsists only from a sense of its utility' is not just 'less happy and agreeable' than one where people benefit from each other from other-regarding motives. It is an unhappy, an alienated society, in which human nature essentially lacks fulfillment.

14 MEW Erg. 1:459, CW 3:225, 227.

15 MEW 3:273, CW 5:292, cf. CW 6:96, 353, and the *Manifesto* itself, CW 6:506. See also *Capital* 1:177, 354, 488.

16 Aristotle, *Nicomachean Ethics*, tr. W. D. Ross, *Works of Aristotle* 9 (Oxford, 1915) 1, 7 (1098a20-6).

17 Richard Kraut, 'Two Conceptions of Happiness', *Philosophical Review* 88 (1979). Kraut, however, regards this Aristotelian conception of happiness as mistaken, or at least as at odds with 'our' more 'subjective'

conception of happiness, which consists, on Kraut's account, in the conformity of a person's life to *that person*'s conception of the good life. I think Kraut is correct in regarding happiness as the actual conformity of a person's life to a conception of the good life held by that person. But I think that happiness requires in addition that the person have an accurate self-conception and that the conception of the good life should be founded on a sound sense of the objective human good. Kraut appears to acknowledge these points, but I do not think he appreciates how far doing so involves adoption of an Aristotelian or 'objective' conception of happiness and abandonment of the 'subjective' conception he thinks he is advocating. In the end, his criticism of Aristotle amounts to little more than the insistence that what we know about the objective human good is limited, and our beliefs about it must be to some extent uncertain and fallible. One can admit this, however, and still prefer an 'objective' conception of happiness over a 'subjective' one.

18 Plamenatz, *Karl Marx's Philosophy of Man*, 353.
19 *Ibid.*, 355.
20 *Ibid.*, 354.
21 Walter Kaufmann, ed., *The Portable Nietzsche* (New York, 1954), 129-30.
22 MEW Erg. 1:578, CW 3:336.
23 *Grundrisse*, 12-13g, 90-92e.
24 MEW 3:21, CW 5:31-2; *Grundrisse*, 15g, 94e.
25 *Capital* 3:820; MEW 19:21, SW, 324; MEW Erg. 1:517, CW 3:276.
26 CW 5:41-2.
27 See T. H. Irwin, 'The Metaphysical and Psychological Basis of Aristotle's Ethics', *Essays on Aristotle's Ethics*, ed. A. O. Rorty (Berkeley, Calif., 1980).

CHAPTER III HUMAN PRODUCTION

1 MEW 23:193, *Capital* (New York, 1967) 1:178.
2 Engels, *Dialectics of Nature* (New York, 1940), 291.
3 MEW Erg. 1:517, CW 3:276.
4 MEW 3:26, CW 5:36.
5 MEW 23:194, *Capital* 1:179; cf. *Dialectics of Nature*, 17.
6 MEW Erg. 1:542, CW 3:302, MEW 23:195, *Capital* 1:180.
7 MEW 23:194, *Capital* 1:179. But compare *Capital* 1:326 and *Dialectics of Nature*, 18.
8 MEW 20:323, *Dialectics of Nature*, 18.
9 MEW 23:194, *Capital* 1:179; cf. Matthew 6:27.
10 MEW 23:192, *Capital* 1:177.
11 Marx, *Oeuvres* 1:1439-40, *Selected Correspondence*, 35.
12 MEW Erg. 1:564, CW 3:333.
13 Marx's idea here is clearly indebted to Hegel's discussion of the way in which the 'servant' consciousness 'posits itself', achieving 'freedom' and a 'sense of itself' (*eigener Sinn*) through laboring and shaping objects

(G. W. F. Hegel, *The Phenomenology of Spirit*, tr. A. V. Miller (Oxford, 1977), 118-19). Hegel's view, however, is importantly different, particularly as regards the necessity of the condition of servitude in the self-genesis of free self-consciousness, and the role played in this process by the servant's fear of death at the hands of the master.

14 Adam Smith, *Wealth of Nations*, ed. A. Skinner (Harmondsworth, 1970), 136.

15 *Grundrisse*, 505g, 611e.

16 Ibid.

17 MEW Erg. 1:513-15, CW 3:274-6.

18 See CW 5:51.

19 *Grundrisse*, 505g, 611e; cf. *Capital* 3:820.

20 *Grundrisse*, 505g, 611e. Plamenatz claims to find an alteration in Marx's views between the early writings (including *The German Ideology*) which espouse 'the ideal, not only of a variety of occupations, but also getting rid of the sharp distinction between work and leisure' and the writings of 'Marx's later and wiser years' where 'the distinction between work time and free time, or between work and leisure . . . is fully recognized' (*Karl Marx's Philosophy of Man*, 143-4, 171-2, 377). But what never changed was precisely Marx's belief that truly 'free' time or 'time for the full development of the individual' (*Grundrisse* 599g, 711e) would be time spent *working, producing*. Marx's distinction between the 'realm of necessity' and the 'realm of freedom' is not a distinction between labor and something else (such as leisure or amusement), but between labor directed to the satisfaction of physical needs and labor which (as Marx put it as late as 1875) has itself become 'the first need of life' (MEW 19:21, SW 324).

21 Aristotle, *Nicomachean Ethics*, tr. W. D. Ross, *Works of Aristotle* 9 (Oxford, 1915), 10, 6 (1176b28-1177a2).

22 MEW Erg. 1:512, CW 3:272; cf. CW 3:302, 331, *Capital* 1:180.

23 MEW Erg. 1:463, CW 3:228.

24 *Grundrisse*, 729g, 846e.

25 MEW Erg. 1:517, CW 3:277.

26 MEW Erg. 1:539, CW 3:300.

27 John Locke, *Two Treatises on Government* (New York, 1973), 134; G. W. F. Hegel, *Werke* (Frankfurt, 1970) 7:106, *The Philosophy of Right*, tr. T. M. Knox (Oxford, 1967), 41; Immanuel Kant, *Metaphysical Elements of Justice*, tr. J. Ladd (Indianapolis, 1965), 52-5.

28 MEW Erg. 1:539-40, CW 3:299-300.

29 MEW Erg. 1:540, CW 3:300.

30 *Grundrisse*, 9g, 87e.

31 *Grundrisse*, 391-2g, 491-2e; cf. CW 3:275.

32 *Grundrisse*, 389g, 489e; cf. 400g, 500e.

33 *Grundrisse*, 396-7g, 497-8e.

34 CW 3:273.

35 MEW 23:596, *Capital* 1:570-1; cf. CW 3:279.

36 MEW Erg. 1:463, CW 3:228.

37 *Grundrisse*, 9g, 87e.

38 MEW 23:99, *Capital* 1:84.

CHAPTER IV ALIENATION AND CAPITALISM

1 MEW 4:467, CW 6:489.
2 MEW 23:674, *Capital* (New York, 1967) 1:645.
3 MEW 4:475, CW 6:495; MEW 3:67, CW 5:87.
4 MEW 23:369-70, *Capital* 1:349.
5 MEW 23:370, *Capital* 1:350.
6 MEW 23:383, *Capital* 1:361.
7 MEW 23:511-12, *Capital* 1:487-8; cf. CW 6:190.
8 MEW 3:33, CW 5:47.
9 MEW 25:832, *Capital* 3:824; MEW 25:274, *Capital* 3:264; cf. *Capital* 1:432, *Grundrisse*, 358g, 454e, CW 3:272.
10 MEW 23:649, *Capital* 1:621.
11 MEW 3:77, CW 5:79.
12 MEW 3:33, CW 5:47.
13 MEW Erg. 1:514; CW 3:274.
14 MEW 3:67, CW 5:88; MEW 3:71, CW 5:82.
15 MEW 2:138, CW 4:131.
16 See CW 6:165-6; *Capital* 1:578.
17 MEW 3:76, CW 5:79.
18 MEW 2:138, CW 4:131.
19 CW 3:295. For example, see Marx on freedom of the press: CW 2:109-31, 311-30. In the same vein, note Engels' praise for English law as 'the only one which has preserved through ages, and transmitted to America and the Colonies, the best part of that old Germanic personal freedom, local self-government and independence from all interference but that of the law courts which on the Continent has been lost during the period of absolute monarchy, and has nowhere been as yet fully recovered' (SW 392).
20 MEW 3:70, CW 5:81; MEW 3:75, CW 5:80.
21 MEW 3:74, CW 5:77-8.
22 MEW 23:791, *Capital* 1:763.
23 MEW 1:344, CW 3:142; MEW 3:35, CW 5:49; MEW 17:343, SW, 294-5. In the Paris writings, where Marx's readers usually pretend to find his 'ideal' of nonalienated society, he says: 'Communism is the necessary form and actualizing principle of the immediate future, but communism is not as such the goal of human development' (MEW Erg. 1:546, CW 3:306). See also SW 690, *Grundrisse*, 387g, 488e.
24 MEW 23:25, *Capital* 1:17.

CHAPTER V PRODUCTION AND SOCIETY

1 SW, 374-8.
2 Among others by A. D. Lindsay, *Karl Marx's 'Capital'* (London, 1937), 32.
3 Engels was explicitly aware of this point. See *Selected Correspondence,*

424.

4 MEW 37:463, *Selected Correspondence* 417; MEW 39:206, *Selected Correspondence*, 467; MEW 37:490, *Selected Correspondence*, 421: MEW 37:467, *Selected Correspondence*, 415-17. Cf. MEW 39:96, *Selected Correspondence*, 459.

5 MEW 3:37-8, CW 5:53. If we inflate this simple point with enough hot air, we can speak (with Louis Althusser) of 'overdetermination'.

6 *Oeuvres* 1:1439, *Selected Correspondence*, 35. The French term *commerce* is Marx's explicit equivalent for the German *Verkehr*, and for this reason is translated here as 'intercourse' rather than 'commerce'.

7 That Marx had both in mind is indicated by his own usage in French: usually he speaks of *forces productives*; but he occasionally also uses *pouvoirs productifs* or *facultés productives*.

8 MEW 6:407, SW, 81.

9 *Oeuvres* 1:99, CW 6:183.

10 *Oeuvres* 1:1440, *Selected Correspondence*, 36.

11 CW 6:166; cf. *Grundrisse*, 100e.

12 John Plamenatz, *Man and Society* (London, 1963) 2:279; H. B. Acton, *The Illusion of the Epoch* (London, 1955), 159.

13 For good discussions of this distinction, see G. A. Cohen, *Karl Marx's Theory of History* (Princeton, N. J., 1978), ch. IV, and William H. Shaw, *Marx's Theory of History* (Stanford, Calif., 1978), 27-42.

14 See, for instance, Marx's criticisms of J. S. Mill in *Grundrisse*, 86-8e, 831-3e, and *Capital* (New York, 1967) 1:516-18. Cohen argues (*Karl Marx's Theory of History*, 108-10) that Mill is innocent of the confusion with which Marx charges him. If correct, this shows only that Marx is overzealous in his use of the natural/social distinction, and not that he is unaware of or confused about it.

15 MEW 3:29-30, CW 5:43.

16 MEW 3:22, CW 5:32.

17 *Oeuvres* 1:1440, 1442, *Selected Correspondence*, 35, 37.

18 Marxists often treat this thesis as self-evidently true, while some critics of Marxism seem to think it is self-evidently false. Both judgments strike me as wrong: the thesis seems to me a highly problematic empirical one. See, for instance, Plamenatz (*Man and Society* 2:281): 'Given any one form of production, widely different systems of property are compatible with it. Some, no doubt, are excluded; the property relations of a tribal society are not compatible with industrial production as we know it today. But the variety of systems of property compatible with any one form of production is so great that it makes no sense to speak of forms of production *determining* systems of property.' As I see it, Plamenatz's judgment in this passage is excessively hasty. For one reason why, see n. 22 below.

19 MEW 31:234, *Selected Correspondence*, 180 (emphasis altered); see SW, 182 and CW 6:166.

20 For three prominent examples, see M. M. Bober, *Karl Marx's Interpretation of History* (Cambridge, Mass., 1948), 6-15, Sidney Hook, *Toward the Understanding of Karl Marx* (New York, 1933), 126, and

Angus Walker, *Marx* (London, 1978), 105-7. Of course Marx does say that 'The means of labor are not only the standard of the degree of development of human labor power, but also indicators of the social relations in which labor goes on' (MEW 23:195, *Capital* 1:180). But of course the means and powers of production may be such indicators precisely because they determine or explain the social relations. It is true that Marx does not commit himself to such a view in this particular passage, but that is hardly conclusive evidence that he did not hold it.

21 MEW 3:30, CW 5:43; *Oeuvres* 1:90, MEW 4:140, CW 6:175; cf. *Selected Correspondence*, 449.

22 *Oeuvres* 1:1439, *Selected Correspondence*, 33; MEW 39:205, *Selected Correspondence*, 466. This point may also help to rescue the theory from Plamenatz's objection (*Man and Society* 2:281) that for any given form of production many different systems of property are compatible with it, and hence that it makes no sense to say that the system of property is determined by the mode of production unless one is already conceiving the system of property as part of that mode. It may be that for any given mode of production, one could imagine many different systems of property which in the abstract might be combined with it as easily as the actually prevailing one. But there could be such a great divergence between the imagined systems and the traditional social relations within which the existing form of production matured that these traditions effectively rule out all these systems of property except the one actually prevailing. In that case, changes in productive powers might, in a given historical context, effectively determine the transition from one system of property to another, even though many different systems of property are theoretically compatible with the new form of production. Marx's own actual analyses of historical change always naturally consider such changes against the background of existing social forms, whose constraining effect he quite legitimately takes for granted.

23 MEW 19:108, *Selected Correspondence* 312.

24 *Oeuvres* 1:135, CW 6:211; MEW 3:30, CW 5:43.

25 Cohen, *Karl Marx's Theory of History*, 44; Shaw, *Marx's Theory of History*, 14-15.

26 See *Grundrisse*, 528e, 700e; *Capital* 1:308-17, 340, 344.

27 Cohen, *Karl Marx's Theory of History*, 33, 34.

28 *Oeuvres* 1:1439, *Selected Correspondence*, 35.

29 *Oeuvres* 1:79, CW 6:166.

30 MEW 13:9, SW 182-3.

31 MEW 23:789, *Capital* 1:761.

32 MEW 23:789-90, *Capital* 1:762.

33 See Chapter VII, Section 2, and especially n. 6.

34 *Oeuvres* 1:1440, *Selected Correspondence*, 36.

35 Here Cohen's admirably clear and precise account of the claims made by the *Critique* Preface (*Karl Marx's Theory of History*, 172-4) seems to me to give an exaggerated picture both of what Marx believes and of what

the basic tenets of historical materialism commit him to. The exaggeration, however, is probably in the *Critique*'s statements themselves, and not in Cohen's interpretation of them.

36 See CW 6:487.
37 MEW 4:462, CW 6:482.

CHAPTER VI CLASSES

1 MEW 13:8, SW, 182-3.
2 Marx, at least, does not apply the term 'basis' to both these distinct elements in the same passage. Engels was not above doing so, however. He begins his well-known 1894 letter to W. Borgius by asserting that the 'economic relations which we regard as the determining basis of the history of society' includes not only 'the manner and mode in which men produce and exchange' (including 'the whole technique of production and transport') but also the 'geographic foundations on which they operate and the remnants of earlier stages of economic development which have in fact been handed down by tradition' (MEW 39:205, *Selected Correspondence*, 466). The most charitable reading of this passage, I think, is one which sees Engels as pointing out the way in which the 'economic structure of society' (what in the *Critique of Political Economy* is called the 'real basis') is in turn based on natural, historical and technical conditions of production. But this would require that 'economic relations' should be *distinguished* from the various factors which Engels here lumps together under that name.
3 MEW 3:22, CW 5:32. Similar identifications of social production relations and property relations are to be found at CW 6:489, CW 7:469, CW 8:269 and *Theories of Surplus Value* (Moscow, 1971) 1:408.
4 MEW 13: 9, SW 182.
5 Ralf Dahrendorf, *Class and Class Conflict in Industrial Society* (Stanford, 1959), 21; John Plamenatz, *Man and Society* 2:280-1.
6 MEW 25:628-9, *Capital* (New York, 1967) 3:615-16. See also CW 5:353; CW 6:209; *Capital* 3:777; *Theories of Surplus Value* 1:314, 2:302. For a fuller discussion of Dahrendorf and the distinction between *de jure* and *de facto* property, see Shaw, *Marx's Theory of History*, 39-47. Dahrendorf attributes the 'narrow, legal conception of property' to Marx chiefly because he believes that this conception is required by Marx's view that the abolition of private property will lead to a nonalienated, classless society. Dahrendorf apparently thinks this view rests on the idea that legal ownership of the means of production by the state would *eo ipso* abolish the relations of domination and oppression which characterize class society and make people in class society lead alienated lives. But this could be so, Dahrendorf reasons, only if such relations are taken to consist solely in the prerogatives of legal ownership. 'Perhaps a Marx without the Marxian philosophy of history would have realized that power and authority are not tied to the legal title of property. Marx himself could not realize this, and certainly could not admit it, for had he done so his philosophical conception of a class-

less society would have become impossible both empirically and intellectually' (Dahrendorf, *Class and Class Conflict*, 31). It may be that some propagandists for socialist states have asserted or implied that the abolition of legal private ownership of means of production *eo ipso* brings a nonalienated, classless society into being. But there are no such shabby sophistries in the writings of Marx. Marx is well aware of the possibility that the abolition of private property might mean merely the establishment of 'the community as universal capitalist' (MEW Erg. 1:535, CW 3:295). (Of people living in such a society Marx says that they 'not only haven't gone beyond private property but have not yet even attained to it'.) Marx's view is only that the abolition of private property (and of course the legal rights corresponding to it) is a necessary step toward achieving a classless society and abolishing alienation. This view does not require him to deny the obvious truth that there can be sources of social power other than legal ownership. In support of his interpretation of Marx, Dahrendorf also cites Marx's view that joint stock companies, where capital is legally owned by people who do not participate in managing it, constitute a 'transitional phase', 'the abolition of capital as private property within the framework of a capitalist production itself' (MEW 25:452, *Capital* 3:436). But such remarks seem to me to support the very opposite interpretation, for they show that Marx includes the administrative authority exercised by nonowner managers in his conception of 'capital as private property'.

7 *Oeuvres* 1:118, CW 6:197; MEW 3:280, CW 5:298.
8 *Grundrisse*, 176g, 265e.
9 For a fuller account of the way Marxian social relations can be analyzed in terms of social roles and effective social control, see Cohen, *Karl Marx's Theory of History*, 217-30.
10 CW 6:100.
11 MEW 25:632, *Capital* 3:618.
12 MEW 3:64, CW 5:85.
13 MEW 25:784, *Capital* 3:776.
14 Plamenatz, *Man and Society* 2:280.
15 MEW 21:297-8, SW, 623-4.
16 CW 6:330; CW 3:293-4.
17 MEW 25:893, *Capital* 3-886.
18 Eric Hobsbawm, *Pre-Capitalist Economic Formations* (New York, 1965), 11. If we accept the idea that social production relations can be defined in terms of such things as claims, requirements and effective control over means of production, then Hobsbawm's suggestion amounts to what Cohen proposes under the name of a 'structural definition of class' (*Karl Marx's Theory of History*, 73-7).
19 *Oeuvres* 1:134-5, CW 6:211.
20 See *Capital* 2:36-7 and *Theories of Surplus Value* 3:420.
21 *Grundrisse*, 27g, 107e.
22 MEW 23:15-16, *Capital* 1:10.
23 MEW 8:198, CW 11:187.
24 *Oeuvres* 1:135, CW 6:211. The 'in itself' and 'for itself' terminology

is of course drawn from Hegel. The 'in itself' is the potential, the 'for itself' is the actual, in the Aristotelian sense of those terms. But since for Hegel all reality is fundamentally mind or spirit striving for self-knowledge, the potential represents for him some respect in which spirit has not yet come to explicit self-consciousness, and hence what still exists in an unconscious form. The actual, on the other hand, is spirit's self-awareness or 'being for itself'. Marx's use of this terminology in relation to classes implies that he thinks a group is only *potentially* a class when its members have a common situation and shared interests. It comes to *actuality* as a class only when it has given rise to a social movement which represents these shared interests, and which generates new general interests of its own. This requirement sharply distinguishes Marx's concept of class from similar ones, such as Max Weber's. Weber makes class membership 'dependent on the kind and extent of control or lack of it which the individual has over goods and services and existing possibilities of their exploitation for the attainment of income or receipts within a given economic order' (Max Weber, *The Theory of Social and Economic Organization*, ed. T. Parsons (New York, 1947), 424). Up to a point, this follows Marx's thinking about classes quite closely (Weber seems to have seen clearly, for instance, the points missed by both Dahrendorf and Plamenatz). But Weber is hesitant to see the proletariat as a single class, owing to its 'high degree of qualitative differentiation', despite the existence of movements purporting to represent its interests (*ibid.*, 427). More basically, Weber does not wish to involve notions like solidarity in his definition of class. Weber's departure from Marx at this point seems to be due at least in part to his hostility toward the notion of *general* class interests, owing to his espousal of what has come to be called 'methodological individualism'. For an excellent discussion of methodological individualism, and the differences between Weber and Marx regarding it see Richard Miller, 'Methodological Individualism and Social Explanation', *Philosophy of Science* 45 (1978).

25 MEW 3:53, CW 5:77.
26 MEW 3:227, CW 5:245. For further evidence that Marx regards the struggle of class interests as essentially the struggle of political movements representing the classes see CW 6:211, and SW, 683.
27 MEW 8:139, CW 11:128. Here again we are misled if we take Marx to be ascribing illusions to individuals concerning their own private psychology. Their illusion, rather, is in their lack of awareness of the social functions served by the moral, philosophical and religious convictions which actually do motivate them subjectively. On account of this lack of awareness, they are often inclined to attribute the widespread appeal of the beliefs they hold to the objective grounds they think they have for these beliefs, or at least to the correspondence of these beliefs with people's moral intuitions, spiritual needs, or healthy common sense. This is an illusion because the real explanation lies in the class interests the beliefs serve.
28 MEW 8:141-2, CW 11: 130-1.
29 MEW 2:38, CW 4:37; cf. CW 10:56.

30 MEW 3:228-9, CW 5:246-7.
31 MEW 8:185, CW 11:173.
32 MEW 3:227, CW 5:245.
33 MEW 3:53, CW 5:77.
34 MEW 4:462, CW 6:482.
35 See SW, 376. It is interesting that the *Manifesto* attempts no explanation for the universality of class antagonisms, but just asserts it as a brute historical fact.
36 See *Anti-Dühring* (Moscow, 1962), 251-2, and CW 6:353.
37 See Cohen, *Karl Marx's Theory of History*, 213-5.
38 *Selected Correspondence*, 312-13, 339-40.
39 MEW 4:91-2, *Oeuvres* 1:35-6, CW 6:132.
40 MEW 34:407.
41 MEW 4:338, CW 6:319. Thomas Münzer's peasant revolt, the 'Levellers' in England, and Babeuf's 1794 movement in France are typically instanced by Marx and Engels as cases of such premature movements. (See CW 6:319, 514; CW 10:469-71.) Marx's considered opinion of the Paris Commune of 1871 also places it in this category (see *Selected Correspondence*, 337-8).
42 MEW 4:467-8, CW 6:489-90.
43 MEW 4:468-73, CW 6:490-5.

CHAPTER VII MATERIALIST EXPLANATIONS

1 MEW 13:8, SW, 182; MEW 37:436-7, *Selected Correspondence*, 415-6.
2 If the thesis that history or social science ought to be 'value free' is intended to deny that people's real (as contrasted with their perceived) needs and interests can ever be relevant to the explanation of social facts, then it seems evident that Marx must reject this thesis. Some writers, however, claim that just as Marx has no concept of human nature in general, so he has no concept of human needs or interests in general. In Part One, I have tried to argue against this interpretation of Marx. If more argument is needed, the following passage from *Capital* (well known because it occurs in the course of some caustic remarks about Bentham) should provide it: 'If one wants to know, e.g., what is useful for a dog, one must study the basis of dog-nature. This nature itself cannot be constructed from the "principle of utility". Applying this to men, if one wants to judge all human deeds, movements, relations, etc. according to the principle of utility, one must deal first with human nature in general and then with human nature as historically modified in each epoch' (MEW 23:637, *Capital* (New York, 1967) 1:609). This passage, because of its polemical character and because of the hypothetical form of Marx's statements, does not seem to me to provide good evidence one way or another on the question whether Marx subscribes to utilitarianism in any form. But it does seem clear that Marx believes: (1) that the nature of man as a historical being involves the historical modification of a basic or 'general' human nature and (2) that people's interests (what is 'useful' to them) are determined first by their general

human nature (according to our earlier exposition, as socially productive beings) and second by the historical modification of this nature in each epoch (fundamentally, by the nature of the productive powers at their disposal in that epoch).

3 MEW 4:465, CW 6:487.

4 MEW 37:463-4. *Selected Correspondence*, 417-18; cf. *Selected Correspondence*, 264.

5 A discussion of teleological (or 'functional') explanation in the context of Marx's historical materialism which does contribute to the literature on the subject can be found in Cohen, *Karl Marx's Theory of History*, chs. IX-X.

6 We can now see how it makes perfectly good sense that capitalist social relations which, on the materialist theory, are 'determined' by capitalist productive powers, should have emerged earlier in time than the most characteristically capitalist productive powers, those of modern industrial society. Marx's contention is that at that stage of productive development, feudal and petty-industrial relations, while they may have accommodated the existing productive powers adequately, did not contribute to their further development and even stood in its way. (As Marx puts it, to eternalize such relations would be to 'decree universal mediocrity'.) Capitalist relations replaced petty industrial ones because under the circumstances only capitalist relations made possible the awesome expansion of society's productive powers that was then in the offing.

7 *Oeuvres* 1:1440, *Selected Correspondence*, 35; MEW 3:69, 71, CW 5:88, 91. Here I accept Charles Taylor's observation that Marx's view of history is teleological, but reject the crude form in which he interprets this view: 'Marxism seems to see history as following, as it were, a plan. History has a goal, the classless society, and the various periods in history represent stages to that goal which, incomplete as they are, represent the highest point attainable at the time. But to say that history follows a plan is to posit some subject of history, some directing mind. And yet Marxism excludes any extra-human subject from consideration. The solution to the riddle in Marxist terms seems to be this: the subject of history is the human race as a whole, not just at this moment of time but over history. It is the human species in this general sense of whom one can say that they direct history to its goal' (Charles Taylor, 'Marxism and Empiricism', in B. Williams and A. Montefiore, eds, *British Analytical Philosophy* (London, 1966), 237). In Marx's view, history is teleological, but its basic tendency is *not* to attain some determinate social form, such as the classless society (if this were so, then it would have been much closer to its 'goal' in primitive times than it is now). History's basic tendency is rather the open-ended expansion of society's powers of production. Neither does Marx fallaciously infer from his belief that history has teleological tendencies to the idealist conclusion that history must be 'directed to its goal' by a 'subject' or 'directing mind'. He explicitly denies the young Hegelian claim that 'man' or 'the human species' is the 'subject of history' in this sense.

8 We usually consider it reasonable to ask for causal explanations for

teleological tendencies and the mechanisms through which they operate, but are seldom inclined to ask for teleological explanations for causal laws. Why is this? The reason, I suggest, is that in a teleological explanation, the *explanandum* must be regarded as belonging to a specifiable organic system of some sort, and we do not find it natural to suppose that every efficient cause, much less every causal law, should belong essentially to an organic system. Schelling and Hegel, however, because they view everything whatever as belonging to a single, embracing organic system, do hold that teleological explanations can be given for efficient causes and causal regularities, and they even hold that such teleological explanations have a kind of ontological priority over causal ones. As we shall see later, there is some reason to think that Marx and Engels follow Schelling and Hegel at this point. (See ch. XIV, no. 23.)

9 The natural direction to look for causal explanations for the tendencies grounding Marx's theory would be psychological laws of some sort dealing with the way people are likely to behave. Marx and Engels, however, often criticize bourgeois social thinkers for positing as universal law the behavior patterns typical of their own class and epoch. Some of these criticisms might be taken as denials that there are any relevant universal causal laws to be discovered. (See *Grundrisse*, 156e, 606e; *Capital* 1:18, 632).

10 Ernest Nagel, *The Structure of Science* (London, 1961), 422.

11 Admittedly, some of the terms used by Marx and Engels ('laws', 'determines', 'brings about', 'driving forces') have causal connotations. But then explanatory language will inevitably have them. On the other hand, the term 'tendencies' is often used by Marx and Engels in their expositions of historical materialism. In *Capital*, Marx equates the 'laws' of capitalism's development (which it is the task of that work to unveil) with 'self-executing tendencies' (*sich durchsetzenden Tendenzen*) (MEW 23:12, *Capital* 1:8).

12 MEW 3:45, CW 5:50.

13 MEW 30:578, *Selected Correspondence*, 123.

14 MEW 20:466, 479, *Dialectics of Nature*, (New York, 1940), 187, 227-8; cf. *Anti-Dühring* (Moscow, 1962), 96.

15 For instance, Acton, *Illusion of the Epoch*, 164-5, Plamenatz, *Man and Society* 2:283-90. The same criticism seems to be implicit in Max Weber's repudiation of 'the idea that it is possible to deduce the Reformation, as a historically necessary result, from certain economic changes', on the ground that 'countless historical circumstances, which cannot be reduced to any economic law, and are not susceptible of economic explanation of any sort, especially purely political processes, had to occur in order that the newly created Churches should survive at all' (Max Weber, *The Protestant Ethic and the Spirit of Capitalism*, tr. T. Parsons (New York, 1958), 91-2). Marx might agree that the success of the Reformation depended causally on many factors (such as political ones) which do not have economic facts or laws as their *causal* explanation. But it does not follow from this that the success of the Reformation is 'not susceptible to economic explanation of any sort'.

It may be susceptible of the sort of teleological explanation Marx's theory proposes.

CHAPTER VIII MATERIALISM, AGENCY AND CONSCIOUSNESS

1   MEW 4:472, CW 6:494.
2   MEW 37:464, *Selected Correspondence*, 418.
3   CW 4:129-30.
4   MEW 3:5-6, CW 5:3-4.
5   MEW 20:106, *Anti-Dühring* (Moscow, 1962), 157.
6   M. M. Bober, *Karl Marx's Interpretation of History* (Cambridge, Mass., 1948), 88. See Jean-Paul Sartre, *Search for a Method* (New York, 1963), 43-65.
7   MEW 3:14, CW 5:24.
8   MEW 3:14, CW 5:24. Metaphysical idealism, however, appears to conflict not with historical materialism as such, but instead with other 'materialist' views Marx and Engels hold along with it. A metaphysical idealist could, I think, consistently accept the materialist conception of history but hold that productive forces, production relations and the other elements of a materialist explanation are (like everything else) only ideas in the mind of God or the world spirit. Hegel's idealism is in fact opposed to historical materialism for quite a different reason. Hegel agrees with Marx that history exhibits certain basic tendencies, and the historical movement can be explained in terms of them. But Hegel identifies these tendencies as tendencies of the human mind to acquire scientific or philosophical knowledge rather than the tendencies of social productive powers to expand and of production relations to accommodate them.
9   MEW 3:14, CW 5:24.
10 A historical materialist need not deny (what Marx and Engels themselves affirm) that changes in people's ideas can contribute causally to social progress, and that the best tactics for social progressives under certain circumstances might be to support a 'reform of consciousness'. By the same token, a Hegelian metaphysical idealist need not hold that changing people's ideas is always the only (or even the best) way to bring down outmoded social conditions. Conversely, a person who believes that critical thinking is the royal road to progressive social change need not hold a Hegelian theory of history, or any comparable theory. (Many liberal moralists who are horrified by all comprehensive theories of history nevertheless agree with the young Hegelians that promoting a more enlightened way of thinking is the best way to achieve progressive social change.)
11 MEW 13:8, SW, 172; MEW 3:26, CW 5:36.
12 MEW 21:303, SW 628; MEW 39:97, *Selected Correspondence*, 459.
13 The *Manifesto* does describe as 'bourgeois ideologues' those members of the bourgeoisie who go over to the proletariat because they have 'worked themselves up to a theoretical understanding of the historical movement' (MEW 4:472, CW 6:494). This is presumably a self-description on

the part of Marx and Engels. If it is, then it seems to follow that they regard the content of the *Manifesto* itself as 'ideology' in a corresponding sense.

14 See Bober, *Karl Marx's Interpretation of History*, 33; Plamenatz, *Man and Society* 2:290, and *Karl Marx's Philosophy of Man*, 220.

15 See Cohen, *Karl Marx's Theory of History*, 46.

16 It is true that Marx sometimes uses the term 'science' in a special sense which implies that the task of 'science' is precisely to penetrate the veil of social appearance and get at the reality behind it (see *Selected Correspondence*, 210, and Cohen, *Karl Marx's Theory of History*, 326-44). In this sense of 'science', I suppose, ideological illusion is by definition unscientific. But in a looser and less technical sense of 'science' (which broadens the scope of the term beyond Marxian economics and materialist historical theory, to include such departments of knowledge as physics and biology) this definitional stricture would not apply.

17 MEW 30:249, *Selected Correspondence*, 128. Marx and Engels are enthusiastic supporters of the notion (which they find in Darwin) that in nature (as in society) there is evolution, progressive development from lower to higher. They also accept Darwin's theory of natural selection as providing a naturalistic explanation of organization and teleology in nature. But they view Darwin's Malthusianism as a false ideological encumbrance on his theory (see *Selected Correspondence*, 171-2, 239, 301-4, *Capital* (New York, 1967) 1:372-3). There is some insight in this, since there is no reason in principle why evolution or even natural selection must operate through competition, scarcity and the Malthusian 'struggle for existence'.

CHAPTER IX MARX ON RIGHT AND JUSTICE

1 Moral and nonmoral goods, though different in kind, may not be unrelated. It is arguable that qualities we esteem as morally good (such as benevolence, courage and self-control) are also nonmorally good for us to have. On the other hand, some moral theorists (such as utilitarians) believe that what is morally good is determined by what is conducive to the greatest nonmoral good. Moralists also typically hold that people have rights to nonmoral goods (such as freedom or economic opportunity) and that justice requires a certain distribution of nonmoral goods (such as wealth or social power). But the various interrelations (real or imagined) between moral and nonmoral goods do not erase the distinction between them.

2 At least after 1843. In a well-known essay of that year, Marx says that 'the critique of religion ends with the doctrine that man is the highest being for man, and thus with the categorical imperative to overthrow all relations in which man is a debased, enslaved, forsaken and despicable being' (MEW 1:385, CW 3:182). He also says that 'the essential sentiment of criticisms is indignation' (MEW 1:380, CW 3:177). (Compare Engels' early essay *Outlines of a Critique of Political Economy*, CW 3:418-43, where both the capitalist economic system and Malthus'

theory of population are repeatedly condemned as 'immoral'.) Such remarks seem to me too slight to support the thesis that Marx's critique of capitalism throughout his career is morally based. In general, I see no ground for postulating a fundamental discontinuity (or, in Louis Althusser's pretentious jargon, a *'coupure epistémologique'*) between Marx's early writings and his mature theory (see Althusser, *For Marx* (London, 1977), 32-9, 249). But in a few cases (this is one of them) there does seem to be a definite shift of attitude. If the above passages are expressions of a morally based criticism of capitalism, then the absence of any similar passages in later writings and the consistent disparagement of morally based social criticism provides strong evidence that Marx changed his views on this point.

3   *Selected Correspondence*, 185.
4   CW 6:169, 319; MEW 19-23, SW 325; cf. *Selected Correspondence*, 148, CW 7:75, 81.
5   MEW 19:382.
6   MEW 3:404, CW 5:419; MEW 4:480-1, CW 6:504.
7   Immanuel Kant, *Gesammelte Schriften*, Academy Edition, 5:59-60, *Critique of Practical Reason*, tr. L. W. Beck (New York, 1956), 61-2, J.S. Mill, *Utilitarianism* (Indianapolis, 1957), 10.
8   See Allen W. Wood, 'The Marxian Critique of Justice', *Philosophy and Public Affairs* 1 (1972), 244-82; 'Marx on Right and Justice: A Reply to Husami', *Philosophy and Public Affairs* 8 (1979), 267-95.
9   MEW 20:87, *Anti-Dühring* (Moscow, 1962), 130-1.
10   MEW 25:351-2, *Capital* (New York, 1967) 3:339-40.
11   Marx and Engels, *Kleine ökonomische Schriften* (Berlin, 1955), 412.
12   Engels offers a very similar criticism of those who condemn ancient slavery as unjust. See *Anti-Dühring*, 250.
13   MEW 20:86, *Anti-Dühring*, 130. Cf. *Selected Works* (in two volumes) (Moscow, 1951) 1:564-5.
14   David Ricardo, *Principles of Political Economy and Taxation*, ed. P. Sraffa (Cambridge, 1951) 1:11; cf. MEW 21:76.
15   See CW 6:138-44.
16   *Theories of Surplus Value* (Moscow, 1971) 1:41-3.
17   See *Capital* 1:537.
18   MEW 23:559, *Capital* 1:537.
19   This *is* a postulate, involving a conscious simplification on Marx's part. Marx knows that all commodities (including labor power) often sell at prices above or below their values as measured by socially necessary labor time (see *Capital* 1:166). But even when labor power sells below its value, this involves no injustice to the worker in Marx's view. Socially necessary labor time is nothing like an Aristotelian 'just price' for Marx. If an oversupply of my commodity (whatever that commodity may be) lowers its price below its value, Marx does not think that I have a right to demand that consumers pay a higher price and that they are doing me an injustice if they refuse to pay an equivalent value for it. Hence even if it were always true that labor power is bought below its value, this would not show (in Marx's view) that capital does labor an injustice.

20 For instance, *Capital* 1:176, 611; *Theories of Surplus Value* 3:533.

21 Ziyad I. Husami, 'Marx on Distributive Justice', *Philosophy and Public Affairs* 8 (1978), 53-4, claims that the exchange between labor and capital is unequal for Marx on the ground that 'wages are part of the surplus value filched from the workers'. In support of this, he cites the following passage from *Capital*: 'Wages are part of the tribute annually exacted from the working class by the capitalist class. Though the latter with a portion of the tribute purchases the additional labor power — even at its full price, so that equivalent is exchanged for equivalent, yet the transaction is for all that only the old dodge of every conqueror who buys commodities from the conquered with the money he has robbed them of' (*Capital* 1:182). But this passage, far from supporting the claim that there is no exchange of equivalents, explicitly says just the reverse.

22 MEW 23:208, *Capital* 1:194.

23 John Locke, *Second Treatise on Government* (Indianapolis, 1952), 17.

24 MEW 23:609-10, *Capital* 1:583-4.

25 MEW 23:610, *Capital* 1:584.

26 MEW 19:18, SW, 321-2.

27 MEW 19:382.

28 MEW 19:359.

29 *Capital* 1:162, 582; see n. 21 above.

30 CW 5:84-5.

31 MEW 19:21, SW, 324.

32 MEW 20:88, *Anti-Dühring*, 131-2.

33 When Lenin says that 'to a communist all morality consists in subordinating everything to the proletarian class struggle', this is certainly an extension, and most likely a modification, of the views of Marx and Engels. See Lenin, *Selected Works* (New York, 1971), 614-16.

CHAPTER X MORALITY AS IDEOLOGY

1 MEW 4:472, CW 6:494-5.

2 MEW 4:140, *Oeuvres* 1:89, CW 6:174. Cf. CW 4:201, SW, 617.

3 MEW 21:287, SW 615.

4 Hegel *Vernunft in der Geschichte*, ed. J. Hoffmeister (Hamburg, 1955), 96-7; *Lectures on the Philosophy of World History: Introduction*, tr. H. B. Nisbet (Cambridge, 1975), 82.

5 Hegel, *Vernunft in der Geschichte*, 79, *Lectures*, 69-70.

6 MEW 21:287, SW, 615.

7 MEW 4:464-5, CW 6:487.

8 MEW 19:22, SW, 325.

9 MEW 4:481, SW 6:504.

10 MEW 37:436, *Selected Correspondence*, 415.

11 MEW 4:479, CW 6:503.

12 Marx's main criticism of utilitarianism is his rejection of the 'absurdity' of 'merging all the manifold relations of people in the one relation of

usefulness' (MEW 3:394, CW 5:409). Hegel describes the standpoint of utility as holding that 'everything is for another', 'at the mercy of everything else'; 'wherever a man finds himself he is in the right place; he makes use of others and is himself made use of' (G. W. F. Hegel, *Die Phänomenologie des Geistes*, ed. J. Hoffmeister (Hamburg, 1952), 399, 400, *The Phenomenology of Spirit*, tr. A. V. Miller (Oxford, 1977), 342-3). Following Hegel's account, Marx ascribes to Bentham a 'theory of mutual exploitation' according to which people are for one another only things to be used or exploited. The hidden truth behind this absurd theory or 'verbal masquerade', says Marx, consists in its being 'an expression, deliberate or unconscious', of real social relations of mutual exploitation, where 'the utility relation has quite a definite meaning, namely, that I derive benefit for myself by doing harm to someone else' (MEW 3:395, CW 5:409). In Marx's defense it must be said that the theory of utility as he portrays it is not an inaccurate description of Max Stirner's view, which is Marx's primary target in this passage. But the discussion of Stirner has little applicability to utilitarianism as presented by Bentham or his followers.

13 MEW 23:636, *Capital* (New York, 1967) 1:609. Perhaps Engels comes closer to articulating Marx's objections to utilitarianism when he criticizes Feuerbach's 'happiness morality': 'It is cut for all times, all peoples and all circumstances, and just for this reason it is never and nowhere applicable; it remains powerless over against the actual world just as Kant's categorical imperative is' (MEW 21:289, SW, 617).

14 CW 5:409-11.

15 *Oeuvres* 1:37, CW 6:134. Read in context, however, it is difficult to regard the passage as an endorsement of utilitarianism. Marx is criticizing Proudhon for treating 'constituted value' (the socially necessary labor time embodied in a commodity) as a 'natural price' which ought (morally) to regulate the production of commodities, and in this sense to determine their 'social utility'. Marx is merely insisting, on the contrary, that the usefulness of a commodity is independent of its labor-costs, that in present society 'social utility' is accorded to the production of low-cost commodities (e.g. potatoes over meat) because the ruling classes can exploit the workers to a greater degree when the latter are forced to live on labor-cheap commodities. In future society, Marx is saying, production will not be governed by this pernicious mystification (as Proudhon's thinking still is). The term 'social utility' is drawn from the theory Marx is criticizing, and his use of it intends no particular reference to any brand of utilitarianism.

16 MEW 23:52, *Capital* 1:37-8.

17 MEW 13:15, *Critique of Political Economy*, tr. S. Ryazanskaya (New York, 1972), 27.

18 MEW 18:274.

19 Some of Marx's and Nietzsche's treatments of more particular moral themes are also strikingly similar. This is especially noticeable in Marx's highly critical discussion of Eugène Sue's *Mysteries of Paris* in *The Holy Family*. Nietzsche's assertion that 'the criminal type is the type of the

strong human being under unfavorable circumstances' (Walter Kaufmann, ed., *The Portable Nietzsche* (New York, 1954), 549) agrees closely with Marx's discussion of the character Chourineur from Sue's novel. (Compare Nietzsche's description of moral 'improvement' as 'taming' or 'domesticating', *Portable Nietzsche*, 501-5, with Marx's description of Chourineur's reform at the hands of Sue's hero Rodolphe as 'the transformation of a butcher into a dog', CW 4:163). Nietzsche's attacks on the insidious, unnatural and life-negating effects of Christianity and especially of the Christian virtues of chastity and repentance are prefigured in Marx's account of the 'salvation' of the prostitute Fleur de Marie. Marx sees the 'savior' Rodolphe as replacing Fleur de Marie's 'free and strong nature' with 'religious hypocrisy' and 'hypochondriacal self-torture' (CW 4:169-74).

20   For a few of the countless expressions of moral praise or blame in the correspondence of Marx and Engels alone, see *Selected Correspondence*, 72, 123, 147, 152, 157, 160, 164, 167-8, 170, 174, 185, 188, 269-70, 278, 329, 429-30.

21   MEW 4:493, CW 6:519.

22   MEW 23:16, *Capital* 1:10.

23   MEW 31:542, *Selected Correspondence*, 185.

24   MEW 33:393, *Selected Correspondence*, 278.

25   Of Sergei Nechaev, Engels says: 'He is either a Russian *agent provocateur* or at least acts as if he were one' (MEW 33:392, *Selected Correspondence*, 278).

26   MEW 20:88, *Anti-Dühring* (Moscow, 1962), 132.

CHAPTER XI MATERIALIST NATURALISM

1   MEW 21:274-5, SW, 603-4.

2   MEW 21:272, SW, 602.

3   MEW 21:275, SW, 604.

4   MEW 21:274, SW, 603-4; MEW 21:277-8, SW, 607; SW, 383. These last are direct quotations from a portion of *The Holy Family* written by Marx (CW 4:127-9).

5   SW, 382, 384 (more direct quotations from Marx). In context, the claim is obviously that scholastic nominalism was the first form of materialism to appear in modern Europe. It does not imply that there were no materialists in the ancient world or in non-European cultures before this time. Nor does it imply that Marx himself endorses nominalism. Nominalism is the first modern European form of the general view that Marx holds, but it does not follow that he holds the view in this form.

6   MEW 21:275, SW, 605.

7   MEW 2:133-4, CW 4:128-9.

8   MEW Erg. 1:543, CW 3:303; MEW Erg. 1:587, CW 3:345. Cf. *Anti-Dühring* (Moscow, 1962), 58, 464.

9   MEW 3:27, CW 5:37; MEW 20:14, *Anti-Dühring*, 22; cf. *Dialectics of Nature* (New York, 1940), 113.

10 SW, 182; CW 5:37.
11 MEW 3:21, CW 5:31. See *Grundrisse*, 304e, *Capital* (New York, 1967) 1:177. Cf. Cohen, *Karl Marx's Theory of History*, 98-102.
12 MEW 21:277, SW, 607; MEW 3:30, CW 5:43-4. Cf. *Dialectics of Nature*, 228, CW 3:304 and *Anti-Dühring*, 55.
13 *Dialectics of Nature*, 174-5, 166-7, 228.
14 MEW 20:327, *Dialectics of Nature*, 25; MEW 20:514, *Dialectics of Nature*, 178; MEW 20:325, *Dialectics of Nature*, 21.
15 MEW 20:515, *Dialectics of Nature*, 179. Engels attempts a number of different versions of this hierarchy of natural sciences and their subject matters. A rough composite of them looks like this:

1 Mechanical motion
    a The mechanics of celestial bodies
    b The mechanics of smaller masses on each celestial body
2 Molecular motion
    a In physics:
        i   Heat
        ii   Light
        iii Electricity
        iv Magnetism
    b Chemical motion
3 Organic motion
    a Life
    b Consciousness

This list comes closest to the only published version (*Anti-Dühring*, 95). See also *Dialectics of Nature*, 21, 35, 156, 165-8, 186, 260-1, 267, 269, 320.
16 MEW Erg. 1:575, CW 3:333; MEW Erg. 1:581, CW 3:339.
17 MEW Erg. 1:577-9, CW 3:336-7.
18 MEW Erg. 1:578, CW 3:336-7.
19 MEW Erg. 1:578-9, CW 3:337.
20 G. W. F. Hegel, *Begriff der Religion*, ed. G. Lasson (Leipzig, 1925), 148.
21 MEW Erg. 1:544-5, CW 3:304.
22 J. Maritain, *Approaches to God* (New York, 1954), 4-5; P. Tillich, *Systematic Theology* (Chicago, 1950) 1:209.
23 MEW Erg. 1:545, CW 3:305.
24 'Nature is the cause of everything. It exists by itself. It will always exist. It is its own cause. Its movement is a necessary consequence of its necessary existence' (Baron d'Holbach, *Système de la nature* (Paris, 1821) 2:155). Compare David Hume, *Dialogues Concerning Natural Religion*, ed. H. D. Aiken (New York, 1969), 59.
25 MEW Erg. 1:515-16, CW 3:275-6.
26 MEW Erg. 1:541, CW 3:301.
27 MEW Erg. 1:538, CW 3:298.
28 MEW Erg. 1:517, CW 3:277.
29 MEW Erg. 1:546, CW 3:306.
30 MEW Erg. 1:545, CW 3:305.

31 C. S. Lewis, *Miracles* (New York, 1947), 197-8.

CHAPTER XII MATERIALIST REALISM

1 MEW 3:5, CW 5:3.
2 J. McMurtry, *The Structure of Marx's World-View* (Princeton, N.J., 1978), 70.
3 L. Kolakowski, *Toward a Marxist Humanism*, tr. J. Z. Peel (New York, 1968), 40.
4 *Ibid.*, 42.
5 *Ibid.*, 41.
6 W. James, *Pragmatism* (New York, 1955), 132. This seems to be the best way to construe Marx's pragmatism, if Marx is a pragmatist about truth.
7 SW, 385.
8 SW, 605-6.
9 MEW 3:5, CW 5:3.
10 Ludwig Feuerbach, *Sämtliche Werke*, ed. F. Jodl and W. Bolin (Stuttgart, 1959) 6:223-7, *The Essence of Christianity*, tr. George Eliot (New York, 1957), 185-92.
11 MEW Erg. 1:543, CW 3:303.
12 MEW Erg. 1:517, CW 3:277.
13 MEW 3:5, CW 5:3.
14 MEW 23:50, *Capital* (New York, 1967) 1:36.
15 See SW, 605, *Anti-Dühring* (Moscow, 1962), 56, *Capital* 1:19, *Grundrisse*, 101e.
16 MEW 3:7, CW 5:8.
17 MEW Erg. 1:542, CW 3:302.
18 G. Lukács, *History and Class Consciousness*, tr. R. Livingstone (Cambridge, Mass., 1971), 204.
19 *Ibid.*, xvii.
20 S. Avineri, *The Social and Political Thought of Karl Marx* (Cambridge, 1968), 65, 136; S. Hook, *From Hegel to Marx* (New York, 1936), 275; N. Rotenstreich, *Basic Problems of Marx's Philosophy* (New York, 1965), 48, 52; A. J. Gregor, *A Survey of Marxism* (New York, 1965), 21; J. -Y. Calvez, *La Pensée de Karl Marx* (Paris, 1957), 380.
21 MEW Erg. 1:574, CW 3:333.
22 MEW Erg. 1:587, CW 3:345.
23 MEW Erg. 1:587, CW 3:346.
24 MEW Erg. 1:578, CW 3:336.
25 Kolakowski, *Toward a Marxist Humanism*, 42-9.
26 G. W. F. Hegel, *Werke* (Frankfurt, 1970) 8:80, *Hegel's Logic*, tr. W. Wallace (Oxford, 1975), 35.
27 *Grundrisse*, 22g, 101e.
28 See Kolakowski, *Toward a Marxist Humanism*, 39; Avineri, *Social and Political Thought of Karl Marx*, 67, 86; Rotenstreich, *Basic Problems of Marx's Philosophy*, 47, 68.
29 MEW 23:27, *Capital* 1:19.

CHAPTER XIII THE HEGELIAN DIALECTIC

1 MEW 23:27, *Capital* (New York, 1967) 1:19.
2 G. W. F. Hegel, *Die Phänomenologie des Geistes* ed. J. Hoffmeister (Hamburg, 1952), 20, *The Phenomenology of Spirit*, tr. A. V. Miller (Oxford, 1977), 10.
3 Hegel, *Phänomenologie des Geistes*, 176-7, *Phenomenology of Spirit*, 140-1.
4 Hegel, *Phänomenologie des Geistes*, 101, *Phenomenology of Spirit*, 78.
5 G. W. F. Hegel, *Werke* (Frankfurt, 1970) 8:140, *Hegel's Logic*, tr. W. Wallace (Oxford, 1975), 88.
6 Hegel, *Werke* 6:440-1, Hegel, *The Science of Logic*, tr. A. V. Miller (London, 1969), 736.
7 Immanuel Kant, *Gesammelte Schriften*, Academy Edition, 5:371, *Critique of Judgment*, tr. J. H. Bernard (New York, 1951), 218.
8 Kant, *Gesammelte Schriften* 5:373-4, *Critique of Judgment*, 219-20.
9 Kant, *Gesammelte Schriften* 5:373, 377, *Critique of Judgment*, 220, 223.
10 Kant, *Gesammelte Schriften* 5:373, *Critique of Judgment*, 220.
11 Hegel, *Werke* 10:374, *The Philosophy of Mind*, tr. A. V. Miller, (Oxford, 1971), 298.
12 Hegel, *Werke* 6:470, *Science of Logic*, 761.
13 Hegel, *Werke* 8:374, *Hegel's Logic*, 280.
14 Hegel, *Werke* 8:307, *Hegel's Logic*, 223.
15 Hegel, *Phänomenologie des Geistes*, 69, *Phenomenology of Spirit*, 51.
16 G. W. F. Hegel, *Vernunft in der Geschichte*, ed. J. Hoffmeister (Hamburg, 1955), 177-9, *Lectures on the Philosophy of World History: Introduction*, tr. H. B. Nisbet (Cambridge, 1975), 145-7.
17 *Hegel's Logic*, 77.
18 Hegel, *Werke* 5:17, *Science of Logic*, 28; *Phänomenologie des Geistes*, 17-18, *Phenomenology of Spirit*, 8.
19 See CW 6:164, 172, 194-5.
20 Hegel, *Werke* 8:181, *Hegel's Logic*, 123.
21 *Selected Correspondence*, 100; cf. *Selected Correspondence*, 187.
22 MEW 20:132, *Anti-Dühring* (Moscow, 1962), 195.
23 MEW 23:791, *Capital* 1:763.
24 MEW 20:125, *Anti-Dühring*, 185.
25 Hegel, *Werke* 5:52, *Science of Logic*, 56.
26 Hegel, *Werke* 8:245, *Hegel's Logic*, 173.
27 Hegel, *Werke* 6:77, *Science of Logic*, 441.
28 Hegel, *Werke* 6:40, *Science of Logic*, 412.
29 Hegel, *Werke* 6:41, *Science of Logic*, 413.
30 Hegel, *Werke* 8:244, *Hegel's Logic*, 172; Hegel, *Werke* 6:73, *Science of Logic*, 438.
31 Hegel, *Werke* 6:45, *Science of Logic*, 416.
32 Hegel, *Werke* 6:39, *Science of Logic*, 411.
33 Hegel, *Werke* 8:236, *Hegel's Logic*, 166.

34 Hegel, *Werke* 8:244, *Hegel's Logic*, 172.

35 Hegel, *Werke* 6:73, *Science of Logic*, 438.

36 Hegel, *Werke* 8:174, *Hegel's Logic*, 246.

CHAPTER XIV THE MARXIAN DIALECTIC

1 MEW 29:561.

2 MEW 29:260, *Selected Correspondence*, 100.

3 MEW 32:538, *Selected Correspondence*, 199; MEW 23:27, *Capital* (New York, 1967) 1:20. Compare SW, 619; The metaphor of 'standing on one's head' is, ironically enough, itself derived from Hegel (see Hegel, *The Phenomenology of Spirit*, tr. A. V. Miller (Oxford, 1977), 15).

4 G. W. F. Hegel, *Werke* (Frankfurt, 1970) 8:58, *Hegel's Logic* tr. W. Wallace (Oxford, 1975), 18.

5 MEW 23:27, *Capital* 1:20.

6 MEW 23:27, *Capital* 1:19; MEW 36:209, *Selected Correspondence*, 379.

7 Immanuel Kant, *Gesammelte Schriften*, Academy Edition, 5:307, *Critique of Judgment*, tr. J. H. Bernard (New York, 1951), 150.

8 Engels may be expressing agreement with this when he describes dialectic as 'the art of operating with concepts, [which are] the results in which [scientific] experiences are comprehended' (MEW 20:14, *Anti-Dühring* (Moscow, 1962), 21). To comprehend experiences is to grasp them in concepts. The structure of concepts is dialectical. These claims may be construed as observations about the proper goals of scientific comprehension. Of course, these goals make sense only because the structure of reality, which concepts reflect, is dialectical.

9 SW, 181-2; *Capital* 1:19; CW 4:57-61; CW 6:162-5.

10 MEW 1:206, CW 3:7.

11 MEW 1:210, CW 3:11.

12 MEW 1:207-8, CW 3:9.

13 It is also, I think, an unwarranted criticism. Hegel professes to be dealing with existing states only insofar as they exemplify the rational structure inherent in all modern states, just as Marx's *Capital* deals with England only as the best example of the general type of modern bourgeois economy. Hegel admits that in any existing state the rational form or 'actuality' he is describing will be imperfectly exemplified. See Hegel, *The Philosophy of Right*, tr. T. M. Knox (Oxford, 1970), 279, and *Hegel's Logic*, 9-10.

14 MEW 1:210, CW 3:12.

15 *Oeuvres* 1:76, CW 6:163.

16 MEW 1:210, CW 3:12.

17 MEW 1:212-3, CW 3:14.

18 MEW 1:211, CW 3:12.

19 For a few of the most prominent references to 'organic wholes' and their development, see CW 6:166, *Grundrisse*, 100e, 278e, 483e, and *Capital* 1:8-10, 18-20.

20 MEW 23:28, *Capital* 1:20.

21 MEW 20:22-3, *Anti-Dühring*, 41.

22 MEW 20:355, *Dialectics of Nature* (New York, 1940), 36; MEW 20:348, *Dialectics of Nature*, 27; MEW 21:294, SW, 620-1; MEW 20:21, *Anti-Dühring*, 36.

23 The ultimate structure of nature, according to Engels, is the 'reciprocal action' of material things, their 'being conditioned through one another'. Reciprocal action is thus 'the true *causa finalis* of things. We cannot go back further than to the knowledge of reciprocal action, just because there is nothing behind it to know' (MEW 20:497, *Dialectics of Nature*, 71). The concept of efficient cause arises out of our practical relation to this original reciprocity. 'We find ... that we can produce a determinate motion by setting up its conditions.... Through this, through the activity of men, is founded the idea of causality, the idea that one motion can be the *cause* of another' (MEW 20:499, *Dialectics of Nature*, 173). Compare F. W. J. Schelling's treatment of causality and reciprocity in the *System of Transcendental Idealism*, *Werke*, ed. O. Weiss (Leipzig, 1907), 2:141-65.

24 MEW 31:306, *Selected Correspondence*, 189; see also *Capital* 1:309.

25 MEW 23:393, *Capital* 1:372-3.

26 *Anti-Dühring*, 37-40, SW, 598-602.

27 MEW 20:23, *Anti-Dühring*, 38.

28 MEW 23:12, *Capital* 1:8.

29 MEW 23:27, *Capital* 1:19.

30 *Grundrisse*, 21g, 100e.

31 In correspondence describing the *Grundrisse* theory, Marx calls it 'the system of bourgeois economy critically presented (*dargestellt*)' and as a 'scientific presentation (*Darstellung*)' (MEW 29:550-1, *Selected Correspondence*, 103).

32 MEW 32:553, *Selected Correspondence*, 210; MEW 31:313, *Selected Correspondence*, 191; MEW 25:825, *Capital* 3:817.

33 *Grundrisse*, 22g, 101e; see CW 6:165.

34 *Grundrisse*, 28g, 107-8e.

35 *Selected Correspondence*, 439.

CHAPTER XV DIALECTIC IN *Capital*

1 This interpretation of Marx's method has been suggested by Ronald L. Meek, *Studies in the Labor Theory of Value* (London, 1973), 299-318, and Thomas Sowell, 'Marx's *Capital* after One Hundred Years', in M. C. Howard and J. E. King, eds, *The Economics of Marx* (New York, 1976), 49-75.

2 *Capital* (New York, 1967) 1:35, 39-41.

3 *Ibid.*, 1:35-6.

4 *Ibid.*, 1:38-41; see *Selected Correspondence*, 209 and *Theories of Surplus Value* (Moscow, 1971) 2:57.

5 In some places, Marx makes the free reproducibility requirement more explicit by characterizing value as the quantity of labor necessary to *reproduce* a commodity. See *Grundrisse*, 673e, and *Capital* 3:870.

6 MEW 32:553, *Selected Correspondence*, 209; MEW 31:313, *Selected*

Correspondence, 191.

7 *Capital* 1:47-8.

8 *Ibid*. 1:185.

9 *Ibid*. 1:217.

10 *Ibid*. 1:167-70.

11 *Ibid*. 1:761-3.

12 *Ibid*. 1:209.

13 *Ibid*. 1:195.

14 *Ibid*. 1:213.

15 *Ibid*. 1:216.

16 *Ibid*. 1:315.

17 *Ibid*. 1:213-302.

18 *Ibid*. 1:322-507.

19 *Ibid*. 1:612-712.

20 *Ibid*. 3:244; see *ibid*. 2:76-9, 185-9, 316-22, 396-415, 453-73, 496-500.

21 MEW 25:33, *Capital* 3:25.

22 *Capital* 3:211-66. On this topic, see Meek, 'The Falling Rate of Profit', *Economics of Marx*, 203-18.

23 *Capital* 3:157.

24 *Ibid*. 3:26.

25 *Ibid*. 3:144-45.

26 *Ibid*. 3:154-5.

27 There seems to be an intermediate model in Marx's theory which involves different commodity prices owing to different turnover periods of different capitals (see *Capital* 2:129, *Capital* 3:144, *Grundrisse*, 546-7e). From the standpoint of commodity prices, Marx regards this stage of the theory as 'effaced' by the production price theory of Volume 3, though turnover periods remain significant for the different rates of profit earned by different industries, whose average determines production prices (see *Capital* 3:161).

28 MEW 25:167, *Capital* 3:158. This passage, it seems to me, confirms Meek's opinion that in Marx's less developed model the assumption is that capitals do not compete between industries and not that organic compositions are the same in different industries (*Studies in the Labor Theory of Value*, xvi). For further confirmation, see *Grundrisse*, 760e and *Selected Correspondence*, 206.

29 MEW 25:167, *Capital* 3:157.

30 See *Capital* 1:166, *Selected Correspondence*, 128-31; *Theories of Surplus Value* 1:416, 2:25-30, 206-13, 3:463-4; *Grundrisse*, 434-6e, 546e, 657e.

31 *Capital* 3:188, 862, 870-1; *Theories of Surplus Value* 2:56-7.

32 *Theories of Surplus Value* 3:164.

33 For Marx's awareness of the transformation problem, see Meek, *Studies in the Labor Theory of Value*, 188-94.

34 *Capital* 3:159-60; *Capital* 3:167.

35 Ludwig von Bortkiewicz, 'On the Correction of Marx's Fundamental Theoretical Construction in the Third Volume of *Capital*', Appendix to Paul Sweezy, ed., E. von Böhm-Bawerk, *Karl Marx and the Close of his System*, (New York, 1949) and R. Hilferding, *Böhm-Bawerk's Critique*

264

of Marx (New York, 1949), 205. Bortkiewicz's solution was anticipated by W. K. Dmitrieff in 1904 (see M. Dobb, 'Marx's *Capital* and its Place in Economic Thought', *The Economics of Marx*, 137). For more recent treatments of the transformation problem, see J. Winternitz, 'Values and Prices: a solution of the so-called "transformation problem" ', *Economic Journal* 58 (1948), and F. Seton, 'The Transformation Problem', *The Economics of Marx*, 162-76. For critical discussions of these solutions from an orthodox academic standpoint, see Paul Samuelson, 'Understanding the Marxian Notion of Exploitation: A Summary of the So-Called 'Transformation Problem', *Journal of Economic Literature* 9 (1971). See also Meek, *Studies in the Labor Theory of Value*, xxiii-xxviii, and Ian Steedman, *Marx After Sraffa* (London, 1977), 29-36. Steedman describes the defect in the *Capital* 3 theory as an 'inconsistency', thus prolonging the tradition of Böhm-Bawerk's criticism, though in a revised version. But strictly speaking, this description is incorrect. There is nothing inconsistent in Marx's theory itself, as Marx presents it. What is true is that an adequate solution to the transformation problem, if Marx had supplied one, would have contradicted some of the doctrines he holds. Had Marx completed his theory in this way, he surely would have removed the inconsistency by abandoning either the doctrine that total prices are equal to total values or the doctrine that total profit is equal to total surplus value.

36 Marx calls this a 'definition of value' at MEW 29:315, *Selected Correspondence*, 105. Marx's occasional assertions that 'value is *determined* by labor time' are evidence either that he does not always *define* 'value' in this way or else that he sometimes uses 'value' in the sense of 'exchange value'. I am inclined to read such passages in the latter way. But see n. 51 below.

37 *Capital* 1:38-40; *Critique of Political Economy*, tr. S. Ryazanskaya (New York, 1972), 30-1.

38 Marx repudiates this misunderstanding at length in his notes on Wagner's textbook: MEW 19:357-70.

39 This erroneous interpretation has been put forward by, among others, A. D. Lindsay, *Karl Marx's 'Capital'*, 57-8. Marx is familiar with this use of the Ricardian concept of value by Pierre Proudhon and Karl Rodbertus, and explicitly rejects it. See CW 6:126-32 and MEW 21:175-87.

40 Among those who have held that 'Marx believed that, under socialism the labor theory of value would come into its own' is Joan Robinson, *An Essay on Marxian Economics* (London, 1969), 23. Marx does hold that under socialism production will be consciously regulated with a view to the labor cost of goods (rather than unconsciously regulated by this as in commodity production) (see *Selected Correspondence*, 199, 209, and *Capital* 3:851). He also seems to hold that under the lowest stages of socialism, distribution will be proportional to labor time contributed (after deductions have been made for accumulation, insurance, those unable to work, and so on) (see SW, 321-5). But Marx repudiates the idea (again, put forward by Proudhon and Rodbertus) that under socialism goods will be bought and sold according to their values. It

seems to be his view that even in the lowest stages of socialist distribution, products will no longer be treated as commodities, and distribution will not be based on exchange (hence not on value or any modification of it). See SW, 321-25, and *Capital* 1:78-9, 2:362.

41 Thus Engels describes the law of value as 'an economists' assumption', which is 'correct' only 'in the sphere of abstract theory' (MEW 16:289, *Engels on Capital*, tr. L. Mins (New York, 1965), 14). Compare *Theories of Surplus Value* 3:72-3.

42 Marx never speaks of a 'labor theory of value'. He appears in fact to regard his entire development of the 'value form' in *Capital* as his 'theory of value'. Although Marx speaks of 'reducing' exchange value to labor time (or value), he resists Wagner's suggestion that he 'reduces value to labor' (MEW 19:357-8). Marx is obviously influenced by the 'labor theory of value' in Smith and Ricardo, but he is highly critical of the Ricardian tendency to apply very abstract models of exchange directly to the empirical facts, 'skipping over the mediating terms (*Mittelglieder*) and *immediately* seeking to show the congruity among economic categories'. Marx of course attributes this to Ricardo's (undialectical) *Darstellungsart* (MEW 26.2:161-2, *Theories of Surplus Value* 2:164-5). See *Capital* 1:307.

43 The classic catalog of these 'counterexamples' is found in E. von Böhm-Bawerk, *Capital and Interest* (South Holland, Ill., 1959) 1:298-301.

44 See *Capital* 3:759. The famous example of aging wine whose price increases without expenditure of labor is treated by Marx as a case of different commodities (wines of different ages) having different use values and demanding different production techniques (viz. different periods of delay between labor and sale): 'The question obviously belongs only in the equalization of the rate of profit. . . . It must be denied absolutely, it is just insipid to claim, that a natural circumstance can *increase* a commodity's value' (*Grundrisse*, 561g, 669e).

45 See George Stigler, 'The Development of Utility Theory', in A. N. Page, ed., *Utility Theory* (New York, 1968), 134-5.

46 Joan Robinson, *An Essay on Marxian Economics*, 14-15, 19-20.

47 See *Capital* 1:43-4, 3:192, 635-6.

48 See *ibid.* 3:877-84.

49 See Böhm-Bawerk, *Capital and Interest* 1:284, 286, 291, 297.

50 MEW 23:51-3, *Capital* 1:36-8.

51 Alternatively, we could interpret Marx as (implicitly) defining 'value' as the 'common something' (what ever it turns out to be) which must exist in equal amounts in any two exchanged commodities and read (8) as a conclusion (essentially equivalent to (9)). Nothing of great importance turns on which reading we adopt.

52 (3) continues to exert an influence on those Marxists who believe that any price theory must base itself on 'some quantity which in any particular case can be known independently of any of the other variables in the system' (Maurice Dobb, *Political Economy and Capitalism* (London, 1937), 6; compare Meek, *Studies in the Labor Theory of Value*, 100, 253-6). It is legitimate to insist that economics should deal not only

with the way relative prices emerge from given systems of individual preferences and resources, but also with the way these systems depend on such factors as production costs and social relations. Moreover, this is a telling point against much of neoclassical price theory. But I fail to see how this requires us to believe (3) or to adopt a 'theory of value' which traces market prices back to 'some uniform quantity not itself a[n exchange] value in terms of which the exchange value of commodities could be expressed'. (Dobb, *Political Economy and Capitalism*, 12).

53 *Capital* 1:7. This does not mean that Marx does not accept the argument. In particular, he endorses the crucial (and dubious) premise (3) in other contexts (*Theories of Surplus Value* 2:164, 3:134).

54 MEW 32:552-3, *Selected Correspondence*, 208-9. See also *Selected Correspondence*, 199.

55 In this context, 'social need' always means 'effective demand' and implies nothing about the human needs of producers (see *Capital* 3:181). Some critics (following Böhm-Bawerk) charge that in the case of means of production, allowance must also be made for the 'point in time' at which the labor is performed (see Walker, *Marx*, 126). Of course the cost of accumulating means of production will be reflected somehow in the prices of commodities. But Marx's initial model abstracts from this cost (or treats it as merely part of the labor cost of commodities) because it is the aim of his theory to develop the specific social forms in which this cost manifests itself under capitalism. To suppose that society must pay these costs to determinate agents of production is to commit the error (often condemned by Marx) of identifying means of production directly with their *social* form as capital.

56 Benedetto Croce, *Historical Materialism and the Economics of Karl Marx* (London, 1966), 60-2, 68.

57 See *Capital* 1:12, *Selected Correspondence*, 186-8.

58 MEW 23:85-9, *Capital* 1:71-5.

59 Paul Sweezy, *Theory of Capitalist Development* (New York, 1970), 34.

60 See Joan Robinson, *An Essay on Marxian Economics*, 20; Meek, *Studies in the Labor Theory of Value*, xxiii-xliv; Steedman, *Marx After Sraffa*, 65-7, 205-7.

61 A number of points need to be made about this loose formulation. Here are a few: First, note that exploitation does not imply injustice or a violation of the rights of the exploited. Exploiters may (on Marx's theory they typically do) have the right to coerce their victims and a right to what they get from coercing them. Second, I suppose that exploitation cannot be mutual. In his early writings, Marx sometimes seems inclined to think it can be (see CW 3:226, 307; CW 5:410). Such passages seem to me ill-conceived; they broaden the notion of exploitation so far as to dilute the force of Marx's critique of capitalist exploitation. For this reason, I choose to ignore them. Next, people who live by the charity of others do not exploit because they do not coerce. Similarly, people who live on welfare do not exploit taxpayers, because the taxpayers are coerced by the state, and not by the welfare recipients.

(Welfare recipients would exploit taxpayers if — as some right wing fanatics claim — the state were in the hands of good-for-nothings who used its taxing powers to plunder hardworking citizens — the white middle class.) Finally, exploiters might choose to give back to their victims some part of what they squeeze from them (as philanthropic capitalists sometimes do in various forms). The relation is still exploitative, since the victim's contributions to the exploiter are coerced, but the exploiter's charity is voluntary.

62 *Capital* 1:169, 540, 573-4, 577-8, 3:819, 823; SW, 92.

63 MEW 4:465, CW 6:487.

64 Of course, workers are *legally* free to refuse any given wage bargain, and sometimes a given worker may be really free to refuse the offer of a given capitalist if he has a comparable opportunity to go to work for another one. In this sense, it is not quite true to say that individual capitalists coerce (or, therefore, exploit) the particular workers they employ. But the capitalist system does give the bourgeoisie as a whole a coercive power over each wage laborer, and the benefit of exercising this power in effect belongs to the particular capitalist who employs that laborer. As Marx sometimes notes, a worker is strictly speaking exploited by the capitalist class as a whole. See *Capital* 1:270, 573-4, 577-8; SW, 84.

65 There could be no accumulation of means of production unless society devoted some labor to goods not immediately consumable, and thus practiced 'abstinence' or 'waiting'. But from this point of view, all members of society must equally 'abstain' if accumulation is to occur. A given social class might be singled out as performing the productive function of 'abstinence' or 'waiting' if that class bore some special burden of deprivation or deferred gratification for the sake of accumulation. But this can hardly be said of the capitalist class. The truth is just the opposite: the capitalist class imposes such burdens mainly on others, and reaps the rewards of everyone's abstinence because its control over the means of production puts it in a position to do so. (Marx's discussion of 'abstinence' theory is found at *Capital* 1:191-2, 591-8.) As for 'risk', workers endure the risk of unemployment just as capitalists endure the risk of failure. Capitalists have more to lose, but that is only because they have more to begin with (the drop to starvation is not as far for the worker as for them). Once again, capitalists are represented as bearing the burdens of risk only because they are in a position to benefit from the risks everyone takes. (Marx replies to the risk argument at *Grundrisse*, 891e.) Nowadays when investors seldom have much role in managing the companies they own we are unlikely to hear appeals to the 'labor of supervision'. When Marx hears such appeals, his only reply is to note the smiles on the faces of capital's hired managers and overseers (*Capital* 1:192-3). (The basic point is that profit is a different economic category from wages: it is paid to owners of capital merely as such, whether or not they do any work for the enterprise.)

66 The marginal productivity theory of profit has been under attack in recent years, and is almost certainly in deep trouble. See E. K. Hunt and

J. G. Schwartz, eds, *A Critique of Economic Theory* (Harmondsworth, 1972), 195-291 (articles by J. Robinson, M. Dobb, D. M. Nuti, and P. Garegnani).
67 Robinson, *An Essay on Marxian Economics*, 18.
68 *Theories of Surplus Value* 2:44; MEW 19:359.

Bibliography

Following is a selected bibliography of secondary literature on Marx dealing with topics covered in this book. Entries are limited to writings in English, French and German. Starred entries are especially recommended. Emphasis is on writings produced in the past thirty years or so. For a full bibliography of Marx literature before 1967, see John Lachs, *Marxist Philosophy, a Bibliographical Guide* (Chapel Hill, 1967).

1 *Books*

*Acton, H. B. *The Illusion of the Epoch*. London, 1955.
————. *What Marx Really Said*. London, 1967.
Adam, H. P. *Karl Marx in His Earlier Writings*. London, 1940.
*Althusser, Louis. *For Marx*. London, 1977.
*————, and Etienne Balibar, eds. *Reading Capital*. London, 1970.
Ash, William. *Marxism and Moral Concepts*. New York, 1964.
*Avineri, Shlomo. *The Social and Political Thought of Karl Marx*. Cambridge, 1968.
*Axelos, Kostas. *Alienation, Praxis and Techne in the Thought of Karl Marx*. Austin, Texas, 1976.
Balz, Albert G. *The Value Doctrine of Karl Marx*. New York, 1943.
Barber, William. *A History of Economic Thought*. Harmondsworth, 1967.
Benner, D. *Theorie und Praxis*. Vienna, 1966.
Bober, M. M. *Karl Marx's Interpretation of History*. Cambridge, Mass., 1948.
Böhm-Bawerk, E. *Karl Marx and the Close of His System*. P. Sweezy, ed. New York, 1949.
————. *Capital and Interest*. South Holland, Ill., 1959.
Buber, Martin. *Paths in Utopia*. London, 1949.
Caire, Guy. *L'aliénation dans les oeuvres de jeunesse de Karl Marx*. Aix-en-Provence, 1957.
Calvez, J. -Y. *La Pensée de Karl Marx*. Paris, 1957.
*Cohen, G. A. *Karl Marx's Theory of History*. Princeton, N.J., 1978.

Colletti, Lucio. *From Rousseau to Lenin.* London, 1972.

*_____. *Marxism and Hegel.* London, 1973.

Cornforth, Maurice. *Dialectical Materialism.* New York, 1971.

*Cornu, Auguste. *Karl Marx.* Paris, 1934.

_____. *The Origins of Marxian Thought.* Springfield, Ill., 1957.

Cottier, G. M. *L'athéisme du jeune Marx.* Paris, 1956.

*Croce, Benedetto. *Historical Materialism and the Economics of Karl Marx.* London, 1966.

Dahrendorf, Ralf. *Class and Class Conflict in Industrial Society.* Stanford, Calif., 1959.

_____. *Die Idee des Gerechten im Denken von Karl Marx.* Hanover, 1971.

Dobb, Maurice. *Political Economy and Capitalism.* New York, 1945.

_____. *Studies in the Development of Capitalism.* New York, 1963.

Dupre, Louis. *The Philosophical Foundations of Marxism.* New York, 1966.

Evans, Michael. *Karl Marx.* London, 1975.

Federn, Karl. *The Materialist Conception of History.* New York, 1939.

Fetscher, Iring. *Marx and Marxism.* New York, 1971.

*Friedrich, Manfred. *Philosophie und Ökonomie beim jungen Marx.* Berlin, 1960.

Fromm, Erich. *Marx's Concept of Man.* New York, 1961.

*Garaudy, Roger. *Karl Marx.* Paris, 1972.

_____. *Qu'est-ce que la morale marxiste?* Paris, 1963.

Gould, Carol C. *Marx's Social Ontology.* Cambridge, Mass., 1978.

Gregor, A. James. *A Survey of Marxism.* New York, 1965.

Habermas, Jürgen. *Knowledge and Human Interests.* Boston, Mass., 1971.

_____. Jürgen, *Theory and Practice.* Boston, Mass., 1973.

_____. *Zur Rekonstruktion des historischen Materialismus.* Frankfurt, 1976.

*Hartmann, Klaus. *Die Marxsche Theorie.* Berlin, 1970.

*Hilferding, Rudolf. *Böhm-Bawerk's Criticism of Marx.* P. Sweezy, ed. New York, 1949.

Hillman, G. *Marx und Hegel.* Frankfurt, 1966.

*Hobsbawm, Eric. Introduction to *Pre-Capitalist Economic Formations.* New York, 1965.

Hoffman, John. *Marxism and the Theory of Praxis.* New York. 1975.

Hook, Sidney. *From Hegel to Marx.* New York, 1936.

_____. *Toward the Understanding of Karl Marx.* New York, 1933.

*Horowitz, David, ed. *Marx and Modern Economics.* London, 1968.

Howard, Dick. *Development of the Marxian Dialectic.* Carbondale, Ill., 1972.

Howard, M. C., and J. E. King. *The Political Economy of Marx.* New York, 1975.

_____, eds. *The Economics of Marx.* New York, 1976.

*Hunt, E. K., and Jesse G. Schwartz, eds. *A Critique of Economic Theory.* Harmondsworth, 1972.

Hyppolite, Jean. *The Evolution of Dialectical Materialism.* New York, 1967.

Kaegi, P. *Genesis des historischen Materialismus.* Zurich-Vienna, 1965.

Kamenka, Eugene. *The Ethical Foundations of Marxism.* London, 1962.

_____. *Marxism and Ethics.* London, 1969.

Klages, Helmut. *Technischer Humanismus*. Stuttgart, 1964.

Kolakowski, Leszek. *Toward a Marxist Humanism*. New York, 1968.

*Korsch, Karl. *Marxism and Philosophy*. London, 1970.

———. *Karl Marx*. London, 1938.

Lefebvre, Henri. *The Sociology of Marx*. New York, 1968.

Leff, Gordon. *The Tyranny of Concepts*. London, 1961.

Lewis, John. *The Life and Teaching of Karl Marx*. New York, 1965.

Lindsay, A. D. *Karl Marx's 'Capital'*. London, 1937.

Livergood, N. *Activity in Marx's Philosophy*. The Hague, 1967.

Lobkovicz, Nicholas. *Theory and Practice from Aristotle to Marx*. Notre Dame, Ind., 1967.

*Löwith, Karl. *From Hegel to Nietzsche*. New York, 1964.

*Lukács, Georg. *History and Class Consciousness*. Tr. R. Livingstone. Cambridge, Mass., 1971.

McBride, William. *The Philosophy of Marx*. New York, 1977.

MacIntyre, Alasdair. *Marxism and Christianity*. New York, 1968.

*McLellan, David. *The Young Hegelians and Karl Marx*. London, 1969.

———. *Marx Before Marxism*. London, 1970.

. *Karl Marx*. London, 1973.

McMurtry, John. *The Structure of Marx's World-View*. Princeton, N.J., 1978.

Mandel, Ernest. *Marxist Economic Theory*. London, 1968.

*———. *The Formation of the Economic Thought of Karl Marx*. New York, 1971.

Marcuse, Herbert. *Reason and Revolution*. Boston, Mass., 1960.

*Markovic, Mihailo. *The Contemporary Marx*. London, 1974.

*Meek, Ronald L. *Studies in the Labor Theory of Value*. London, 1973.

*Meszaros, Istvan. *Marx's Theory of Alienation*. New York, 1972.

*Morishima, M. *Marx's Economics*. Cambridge, 1973.

Oiserman, Theodor I. *Die Entfremdung als historische Kategorie*. Berlin, 1965.

Ollman, Bertell. *Alienation*. Cambridge, 1971.

Pappenheim, F. *The Alienation of Modern Man*. New York, 1959.

Petrovic, Gajo. *Marx in the Mid-Twentieth Century*. Garden City, N.Y., 1967.

Plamenatz, John. *Man and Society*. 2 vols. London, 1963.

*———. *Karl Marx's Philosophy of Man*. Oxford, 1975.

———. *Ideology*. London, 1970.

*Plekhanov, George V. *Fundamental Problems of Marxism*. New York, 1969.

———. *The Monist View of History*. New York, 1972.

Popper, Karl. *The Open Society and Its Enemies*. Vol. 2. London, 1961.

*Robinson, Joan. *An Essay on Marxian Economics*. London, 1969.

———. *Economic Philosophy*. Chicago, 1963.

Roll, Sir Eric. *History of Economic Thought*. London, 1961.

*Rosdolsky, Roman. *Zur Entstehungsgeschichte des Marxschen Kapitals*. Frankfurt, 1968.

Rosen, Zvi. *Bruno Bauer and Karl Marx*. The Hague, 1977.

*Rotenstreich, Nathan. *Basic Problems of Marx's Philosophy*. New York, 1965.

*Rubel, Maximilien. *Karl Marx*. Paris, 1957.

Rubin, I. I. *Essays on Marx's Theory of Value*. Detroit, 1972.

Schaff, Adam. *A Philosophy of Man*. New York, 1963.

*Schmidt, Alfred. *The Concept of Nature in Marx*. London, 1971.

Selsam, H. *Socialism and Ethics*. New York, 1949.

*Shaw, William H. *Marx's Theory of History*. Stanford, Calif., 1978.

Somerville, John and Howard L. Parsons, eds. *Dialogues on the Philosophy of Marxism*. London, 1974.

*Steedman, Ian. *Marx After Sraffa*. London, 1979.

*Sweezy, Paul. *The Theory of Capitalist Development*. New York, 1964.

Thier, Erich. *Das Menschenbild des jungen Marx*. Göttingen, 1957.

Touilleux, Paul. *Introduction aux Systèmes de Marx et Hegel*. Paris, 1960.

Tucker, Robert C. *Philosophy and Myth in Karl Marx*. Cambridge, 1961.

———. *The Marxian Revolutionary Idea*. New York, 1969.

Venable, Vernon. *Human Nature: The Marxian View*. New York, 1945.

Walker, Angus. *Marx*. London, 1978.

Walton, Paul, and Andrew Gamble. *From Alienation to Surplus Value*. London, 1972.

Witt-Hansen, J. *Historical Materialism*. Copenhagen, 1960.

Zeleny, J. *Die Wissenschaftslogik bei Marx und 'Das Kapital'*. Berlin, 1968.

2 *Articles*

Addis, Laird. 'Freedom and the Marxist Philosophy of History'. *Philosophy of Science* 33 (1966).

Allen, Derek. 'Is Marxism a Philosophy?' *Journal of Philosophy* 71 (1974).

———. 'The Utilitarianism of Marx and Engels'. *American Philosophical Quarterly* 10 (1973).

*Apel, Karl-Otto. 'Reflexion und materielle Praxis'. *Hegel-Studien* Beiheft 1 (1964).

Arthur, C. J. 'Labour: Marx's Concrete Universal', *Inquiry* 21 (1978).

Braybrooke, D. 'Diagnosis and Remedy in Marx's Doctrine of Alienation'. *Social Research* 25 (1958).

*Brenkert, George G. 'Freedom and Private Property in Marx'. *Philosophy and Public Affairs* 8 (1979).

*———. 'Marxism and Utilitarianism'. *Canadian Journal of Philosophy* 5 (1975).

*Buchanan, Alan. 'Exploitation, Alienation and Injustice'. *Canadian Journal of Philosophy* 9 (1979).

Carver, Terrell. 'Marx's Commodity Fetishism'. *Inquiry* 18 (1975).

*Cohen, G. A. 'Marx's Dialectic of Labor'. *Philosophy and Public Affairs* 3 (1974).

Drucker, H. M. 'Marx's Concept of Ideology'. *Philosophy* 47 (1972).

Dupre, Louis. 'Idealism and Materialism in Marx's Dialectic'. *Review of Metaphysics* 30 (1977).

Gilbert, Alan. 'Marx on Internationalism and War'. *Philosophy of Public Affairs* 7 (1978).

———. 'Social Theory and Revolutionary Activity in Marx'. *American Political Science Review* 73 (1979).

Heller, Agnes. 'Die Stellung der Ethik im Marxismus'. *Praxis* 3 (1967).

Holmstrom, N. 'Exploitation'. *Canadian Journal of Philosophy* 7 (1977).

Horowitz, Irving L. 'On Alienation and the Social Order'. *Philosophy and Phenomenological Research* 27 (1966).

*Husami, Ziyad I. 'Marx on Distributive Justice'. *Philosophy and Public Affairs* 8 (1978).

Itoh, Makoto. 'Marx's Theory of Value'. *Science and Society* 40 (1976).

*Jahn, Wolfgang. 'Der ökonomische Inhalt des Begriffs der Entfremdung der Arbeit in den Früschriften von Karl Marx'. *Wirtschaftswissenschaft* 6 (1957).

Kangrga, Milan. 'Das Problem der Entfremdung in Marx' Werk'. *Praxis* 3 (1967).

Lauer, Quentin. 'The Marxist Conception of Science'. R. S. Cohen and M. W. Wartofsky, eds. *Boston Studies in the Philosophy of Science* 14 (1974).

*LeoGrande, William M. 'An Investigation into the "Young Marx" Controversy'. *Science and Society* 41 (1977).

Lewin, Haskell, and Jacob Morris. 'Marx's Concept of Fetishism'. *Science and Society* 41 (1977).

*Löwith, Karl. 'Man's Self-Alienation in the Early Writings of Marx'. *Social Research* 21 (1954).

————. 'Max Weber und Karl Marx'. *Archiv für Sozialwissenschaft und Sozialpolitik* 67 (1932).

McBride, William. 'The Concept of Justice in Marx, Engels, and Others'. *Ethics* 85 (1975).

Mahowald, Mary B. 'Marx's "Gemeinschaft" '. *Philosophy and Phenomenological Research* 33 (1973).

Markovic, Mihailo. 'Critical Social Theory in Marx'. *Praxis* 7 (1970).

*Miller, Richard. 'The Consistency of Historical Materialism'. *Philosophy and Public Affairs* 4 (1975).

*————. 'Methodological Individualism and Social Explanation'. *Philosophy of Science* 45 (1978).

Mishra, Ramesh. 'Technology and Social Structure in Marx's Theory'. *Science and Society* 43 (1979).

Moore, Stanley. 'Marx and the Origin of Dialectical Materialism'. *Inquiry* 14 (1971).

————. 'Marx and Lenin as Historical Materialists'. *Philosophy and Public Affairs* 4 (1975).

Nasser, Alan G. 'Marx's Ethical Anthropology'. *Philosophy and Phenomenological Research* 35 (1975).

Nicolaus, Martin. 'The Unknown Marx'. *New Left Review* 48 (1968).

Olafson, Frederick A. 'Existentialism, Marxism and Historical Justification'. *Ethics* 65 (1954-5).

O'Malley, J. 'History and Man's "Nature" in Marx'. *Review of Politics* 28 (1966).

Riedel, Manfred. 'Grundzüge einer Theorie des Lebendigen bei Hegel und Marx'. *Zeitschrift für philosophische Forschung* 19 (1965).

Rockmore, T. 'Marxian Man'. *Monist* 61 (1978).

*Runciman, N. G. 'False Consciousness'. *Philosophy* 44 (1969).

*Ryan, Cheyney. 'Socialist Justice and the Right to the Labor Product'. Forthcoming in *Political Theory*.

Samuelson, Paul. 'Understanding the Marxian Notion of Exploitation: A Summary of the So-Called Transformation Problem'. *Journal of Economic Literature* 9 (1971).

Schaff, Adam. 'Marxist Dialectics and the Principle of Contradiction'. *Journal of Philosophy* 57 (1960).

Sichel, Betty A. 'Karl Marx and the Rights of Man'. *Philosophy and Phenomenological Research* 32 (1972).

Sowell, Thomas. 'Karl Marx and the Freedom of the Individual'. *Ethics* 73 (1963).

*_____ 'Marx's *Capital* after One Hundred Years'. M. C. Howard and J. E. King, eds. *The Economics of Marx* (New York, 1976).

Stojanovic, Svetozar. 'The Dialectics of Alienation and the Utopia of De-alienation'. *Praxis* 5 (1969).

Struve, V. 'Comment Marx définissait les premières sociétés de classe'. *Recherches internationales à la lumière du Marxisme* (1957).

*Taylor, Charles. 'Marxism and Empiricism'. B. Williams and A. Montefiore, eds. *British Analytical Philosophy* (London, 1966).

Thomas, Paul. 'Karl Marx and Max Stirner'. *Political Theory* 3 (1975).

Van De Veer, Donald. 'Marx's View of Justice'. *Philosophy and Phenomenological Research* 33 (1972-3).

Vranicki, Pedrag. 'Socialism and the Problem of Alienation'. *Praxis* 2-3 (1965).

*Wood, Allen W. 'The Marxian Critique of Justice'. *Philosophy and Public Affairs* 1 (1972).

*_____. 'Marx on Right and Justice: A Reply to Husami'. *Philosophy and Public Affairs* 8 (1979).

_____. 'Marx's Critical Anthropology'. *Review of Metaphysics* 26 (1972).

*Young, Gary. 'The Fundamental Contradiction of Capitalist Production'. *Philosophy and Public Affairs* 5 (1976).

_____. 'Justice and Capitalist Production: Marx and Bourgeois Ideology'. *Canadian Journal of Philosophy* 8 (1978).

Index

abstinence, 135, 233, 268

Acton, H. B., 245, 252

actuality (*Wirklichkeit*), 13, 22-4, 38, 92, 94, 156, 168, 191-2, 197-8, 239, 248-9, 262; *see also* self-actualization

actualization (*Verwirklichung*), *see* self-actualization

affirmation (*Bejahung*), 21-2, 34-7

Alexander of Macedonia, 142

alienation (*Entfremdung, Entäusserung*), x, xvi-xvii, 1-59, 95-6, 111-12, 165, 179-82, 230, 236, 239-41, 244, 247-8, 254-5; alienated labor as basis of, 4-5; capitalism as cause of, 44-59; and capitalist division of labor, 44-53; as a diagnostic rather than explanatory concept in Marx's mature thought, 7-10; as enslavement to one's own creations, 5-6; and false consciousness, 10-15; as frustrated self-actualization, 22-26, 34-37, 50-51, 55-56; as lack of meaning and self-worth, 8-10, 16-17, 239-240; Marx's early theory of, 3-6; as necessary stage of human history, 7, 239; as opposite of appropriation, 41-42; and private property, 39-41; and religion, 10-15, 59; and social practice, 12-15; and species consciousness, 16-21, 31-34; young Hegelian theory of, 11-12, 14-15; *see also* unhappy consciousness

Althusser, Louis, 245, 255

altruism, 95-6, 126, 156

Annenkov, P. V., 66-8, 70-1, 74

appropriation (*Aneignung, Zueignung*), 37-43; *see also* property

Aristotle, 23-4, 29, 37, 106, 126, 191-2, 196, 235, 241-2, 249, 255

art, 28, 37, 102, 118

atheism, 164-73, 259

Austin, John, 145

autonomy, moral, 51

Avineri, Shlomo, 182-3

Babeuf, François Noël, 250

Bacon, Francis, 162, 211

Bakunin, Michael, xiv, 154-5

basis, economic, 70-1, 82, 89-91, 105, 229, 245, 246, 247, 248, 252-3; *see also* productive powers; production, relations of

Bauer, Bruno, xii-xiii, 117

behaviorism, 163

Bentham, Jeremy, 145, 250, 256-7

Berkeley, George, 191

Bible, 33, 242

Bober, M. M., 245, 254, 257

Böhm-Bawerk, Eugen von, 224-6, 266, 267

Bonaparte, Louis, xiii

Bonaparte, Napoleon, 113, 142

Borgius, W., *see* Starkenburg, H.

Bortkiewicz, Ludwig von, 225, 264-5

bourgeoisie, 77-8, 98-100, 112, 135-6, 221-2, 232-4, 256, 268

Bray, John 132

Büchner, Ludwig, 109

Bultmann, Rudolf, 172

276

Saint-Simon, Claude Henri de Rouvroy, comte de, 93
Samuelson, Paul, 265
Sartre, Jean-Paul, 253
Schelling, Friedrich Wilhelm Joseph, 164, 191, 197, 214, 252, 263
Schiller, Friedrich von, 178
science, 37, 45, 56-7, 159, 162, 164, 177, 259; Marx's concept of, 120-2, 162, 217, 220, 254; and religion, 164
Seigel, Jerrold, 239
self-activity (*Selbstbetätigung, Selbsttätigkeit*), 46, 50-1
self-actualization, 22-30, 46-8, 126
self-conception, 19-21, 194-6, 239-40, 242
self-exercise, *see* self-activity
self-existence (*Durchsichselbstsein*), 165-73
serfs, 41, 82, 84-5, 138, 232
Seton, F., 265
sexism, 59
Shaw, William H., 72-3, 245, 247
Sidgwick, Henry, 145
Sièyes, Emmanuel Joseph, 113
skepticism, 161-2, 174-82, 185
slavery, 41, 131, 138, 232, 255
Smith, Adam, 22, 35, 66, 220, 241, 266
social democracy, German, xiv
social relations, 68-70, 82-7; *see also* production, relations of
sorcerer's apprentice, 99
Sowell, T., 263
species being (*Gattungswesen*), 16-21, 240-1
Spinoza, Benedictus de, 51, 170, 190
spirit (*Geist*), 10-11, 165-7, 169-70, 191-9
Sraffa, Piero, 231
Starkenburg, H., 247
state, political, 4, 5, 66, 97-8, 211-13, 262
Steedman, Ian, 265
Steuart, Sir James, 133
Stigler, George, 266
Stirner, Max, 117, 145, 256-7
Sue, Eugène, 257-258
superstructure, 66, 77, 82, 85-7, 90-1, 105, 148-9
surplus value (*Mehrwert*), 133-40, 221-2, 265; absolute, 222; rate of, 222; realization of, 222; relative, 222
Sweezy, Paul, 231

Taylor, Charles, 251
teleology, 104-10, 192-9, 210-11, 251-3, 259, 262, 263; inner and external 109; *see also* explanation, teleological; organic wholes
tendencies, historical, 30, 74-6, 78-80, 94-5, 96-7, 101-5, 109-10, 112-14, 211, 248-9, 251-3; and historical inevitability, 76, 80-1, 114-16; and teleology, 104-8, 251-2
terrorism, 155, 258
theory: and practice, 20-1, 171-2, 174-82; dialectical, 196-9, 216-22
Thierry, Augustin, 93
Tillich, Paul, 168, 172
tools, 33, 66-7, 242, 245
Tracy, Destutt de, 117
transformation, of values into prices, 224-5, 264-5
truth, 174-176, 186; pragmatic theory of, 175-6

understanding (*Verstand*), 205
unemployment, 10, 222
unhappy consciousness (*unglückliche Bewusstsein*), 10-11
use, value in (*Gebrauchswert*), 146, 220, 228, 233
utilitarianism, 129, 144-9, 250-1, 254, 256-7; Marx's contempt for, 145, 250, 256-7
utility, 146, 220, 228, 250-1, 256-7

value (*Wert*), xviii, 220-34, 236, 263-7; definition of, 220, 225, 263, 266; in exchange, 220, 227, 233, 265; labor theory of, 133-6, 224, 263, 256-67; law of, 220-1, 224, 225-31, 263, 266-7; in use, 146, 220, 228, 233
Vico, Giambattista, 215
virtues, moral, 154-155, 254
vocation (*Bestimmung*), human, 21, 23-4

wage labor (*Lohnarbeit*), 7, 10, 35, 41-2, 46-7, 84-5, 132-8, 255-6, 268; *see also* proletariat
wages, 132-8, 221-2, 232, 255-6, 268
Wagner, Adolph, 127, 136-7, 265, 266
Walker, Angus, 246, 267
Weber, Max, 249, 252-3
Westphalen, Ludwig von, xii
will, determinants of, 88-9, 112
wine, aging, alleged increase in value of, 266